Fulbright of Arkansas

THE PUBLIC POSITIONS
OF A PRIVATE THINKER

Other books by Karl E. Meyer

THE NEW AMERICA

THE CUBAN INVASION
(with Tad Szulc)

Fulbright of Arkansas

THE PUBLIC POSITIONS
OF A PRIVATE THINKER

Edited by
KARL E. MEYER

With a Preface by
WALTER LIPPMANN

LUCE

ROBERT B. LUCE, INC.
Washington, D. C.

Library of Congress Catalog Card Number: 63-9331

MANUFACTURED IN THE UNITED STATES OF AMERICA

VAN REES PRESS   •   NEW YORK

I can conceive of nothing more admirable or more powerful than a great orator debating great questions of state in a democratic assembly.

—Alexis de Tocqueville

PREFACE

By *Walter Lippmann*

Senator Fulbright has just won re-election in Arkansas in a campaign that has been of great interest to the nation as a whole. For an important part of the opposition to the Senator came from outside of Arkansas. It came from the radical right extremists like Senator Goldwater among the Republicans and Senator Thurmond among the Democrats. It is highly significant and interesting indeed that they chose to do battle not with a man of the left but with as genuine a conservative in the great tradition of conservatism as exists in our public life today.

Thus the Arkansas campaign brought a confrontation between traditional American conservatism and a wholly new phenomenon, a radical reaction sailing under the flag of conservatism. This reactionary radicalism has as little relation to conservatism as the so-called people's democracies beyond the Iron Curtain have to democracy.

The true conservatives, of whom the greatest in this century is Churchill, are indissolubly at one with the constitutional sources of the nation's life. For them the nation is a living thing which grows and changes, and they think of themselves as participating in this growth and change. Because they themselves are so secure and certain about what is essential and fundamental, the most intelligent conservatives are liberal in temper and progressive in policy.

Senator Fulbright is that kind of conservative, and so he is a standing challenge to the reactionary radicals who are in revolt against all the main developments of the 20th century.

They are against the consequences of modern science and technology which have brought into being a concentration of masses of people in cities, masses of people uprooted from their ancestral ways of life. These radical reactionaries are against the welfare state which provides these urban masses with some of that personal security which their ancestors in the country made in their communities. And they are against the regulation of this enormously complex economy, though without regulation it would churn itself up into crisis and chaos.

The reactionary radicals, who would like to repeal the 20th century, are, so they tell us, violently opposed to communism. But communism also belongs to the 20th century and these reactionary radicals do not understand it and do not know how to resist it. Thus they do not want the alliances with which we have contained communism in Europe at the armistice lines of World War II. They are against foreign aid which is used to help new countries and weak countries help themselves without succumbing to communism. They despise the United Nations which has so much to do in opening up for the new and inexperienced countries the roads to freedom. They do believe loyally in American military power. But they do not understand it. They do not understand that the United States, though very strong, is not omnipotent, that we cannot set the world in order and achieve total victory over communism by issuing ultimata. Their irresponsibility in foreign affairs is such that if the President did for the country what they say he ought to be doing, there would be going on at one and the same time another Korean War in Southeast Asia, a somewhat smaller Algerian War in Cuba, and a thermonuclear war about Berlin.

Senator Fulbright, with the authority and with the intimate knowledge that comes to him as chairman of the Foreign Relations Committee of the Senate, has stood firmly against such irresponsible nonsense. The nation is greatly in his debt. The role he plays in Washington is an indispensable role. There is no one else who is so powerful, and also so wise and if there were any question of removing him from public life, it would be a national calamity.

Not only has he been the bravest and wisest of advisers. He is also the most farseeing and constructive. It has been said of him that all too often he has been right too soon. That is a great compliment. In our democracy somebody who is listened to must be right before it is popular to be right. Here Senator Fulbright has a distinguished record which goes back to the Second World War when, still an unknown and unnoticed congressman from Arkansas, he brought out the Fulbright Resolution which led the change of American opinion against isolation.

He was, I think, the first American public man who realized that if Western Europe was to coexist with the Soviet Union it would have to unite. And he is the first responsible American statesman to be saying that the necessary counterweight to the development of the Communist power is a much closer political and economic integration of the Western world.

Grateful acknowledgment is hereby made to *Foreign Affairs* for permission to include "For a Concert of Free Nations"; to *University of Chicago Press,* for "The Legislator," © 1947 by The University of Chicago; and to the *New York Herald Tribune Syndicate* for Walter Lippmann's material on Senator Fulbright.

TABLE OF CONTENTS

          xiv

INTRODUCTION

An anniversary prompts this book. As of January, 1963, J. William Fulbright will have spent twenty years in Congress—eighteen of them in the lofty eminence of the United States Senate. During those two decades, Fulbright has spoken wisely, frequently, and bravely on the central problems of a troubled time—and this in an arena where a man's political life can hang on each sentence he utters.

He is a Democrat from Arkansas and as chairman of the Senate Foreign Relations Committee he is, by definition, an Important Personage. But he is also a good deal more than that. In the eyes of his admirers (and they form a multitude in Washington) he is the closest thing to a public philosopher in Congress, a man who ranges beyond the day's petty contentions and tries to place the immediate within the context of the enduring.

Fulbright came to politics from the academic cloister, where it is easier to take a detached and critical view of prevailing shibboleths. But he has managed somehow to retain the poise of a scholar while staying in office—winning, to be precise, five successive elections in a state that is insular, rural, and economically depressed. This is no small part of the Fulbright phenomenon: the juxtaposition of a legislator whose chief (but not sole) concern is foreign affairs with a constituency whose most immediate worry is the price of cotton and rice. Odd or not, the match has been fruitful for both Arkansas and the country.

Surely, in these circumstances, twenty years of sustained excellence in public life warrants more than a casual nod. Yet it is an anomalous fact that Senator Fulbright is among the least celebrated of our major political figures. There are no books by or about him listed in library catalogues; only a scattering of magazine articles portrays the man; many of his best speeches are lost in the back pages of newspapers or in obscure specialized journals. Fulbright has served the country well, but the country has only indifferently reciprocated.

Hence this volume.

*   *   *

President Truman called him "that over-educated Oxford s.o.b." Senator Joe McCarthy referred to him as "Halfbright," and the massed crankdom of the John Birch Society has his name high on the hate list. Yet when you meet the Senator you cannot help but wonder how so seemingly mild and cheerful a man ever set anybody's temper in flames.

At fifty-seven, he looks what he is, a former college teacher whose compact frame belongs in tweeds. Good-looking but not handsome in the collar-ad sense, a deep cleft splices his chin, and his eyeglasses seem about to slide off his nose. He speaks in a soft Ozark drawl, peering with owlish yet amiable intentness over the rim of his glasses.

Another scholar-in-politics, Senator Paul H. Douglas of Illinois, has said of him: "He's a child of the eighteenth century, a throwback to that age of enlightenment, trust in reason, temperate argument, and slightly aristocratic tendencies. That, I think, explains why he seems a little aloof, a little different from the rest."

What also sets Fulbright apart is his relative lack of ambition, vanity, and partisan fire. This has deceived those who confused lack of aggressiveness with lack of backbone; he was among the few members of the Senate whose spine was stiff enough for him to take on Joe McCarthy in public debate. His detachment has irritated fellow Democrats; President Truman took years to forgive him for suggesting in 1946 that Truman should resign. The Republicans had won the congressional elections, and Fulbright was concerned with the problem of divided government. The Senator off-handedly proposed that Truman step down in favor of a Republican successor. "But there was nothing personal about it," the Senator insists today. "Why, I *liked* the President and I still do."

"In fact, all the ruckuses I get into seem to start in a casual, almost accidental way," Fulbright sighs. This was true of the celebrated military memorandum of 1961, which brought upon him a hailstorm of abuse from the radical right. It happened that a "strategy for survival" meeting was held in Fulbright's home district, and an army officer showed up in uniform to join in a collective expression of indignation against the twentieth century. One of those singled out for attack was Congressman James W. Trimble, who holds the seat that Fulbright himself once occupied for a single term. "I didn't care what they said about me," Fulbright (credibly) says, "but that was dirty stuff about my friend Jim Trimble." The Senator asked the aide who had brought the incident to his attention to gather some more material about military participation in extremist revivalist meetings. The result was a memorandum (you will find the text on pp. 219-229) that Fulbright volunteered to Secretary of Defense Robert McNamara.

The sequel was wholly characteristic. Word of the memorandum got around, and one day Senator Strom Thurmond, a Goldwaterite in Carolina clothing, burst into Fulbright's suite and demanded a copy of the document. Fulbright returned to his office and found his administrative assistant, Lee Williams, literally shaking. The next day, the Senator went to the floor and with Arctic sarcasm described his fellow Senator's improper demands for what was a private communication—and then he placed the entire memorandum into the record. (Senator Thurmond's suite in the New Senate Office Building, incidentally, adjoins Fulbright's—but *that* is an incongruity wholly characteristic of the Senate.)

A few weeks later, the Senator himself received a memorandum from Lee Williams that began, "As a result of your Senate speeches, press conferences, television appearances and other public utterances in the past two weeks, you have succeeded in arousing the ire of practically every organized segment of world opinion." The following groups, Williams noted, had sent messages of displeasure:

John Birchers, McCarthyites, Goldwaterites, Thurmondites, Dixiecrats, militarists, isolationists, Zionists, Germans, Catholics, Chinese Nationalists, Koreans, NAACP-ers, ADA-ers, Communists, private powerists, veterans, farmers' cooperativeites.

"Please, Bill," a campaign supporter in Arkansas appealed, "*no* more memorandums and big speeches—not until the election is over." At that time, Fulbright was on the eve of what was supposed to be the warmest contest of his career; Governor Orval Faubus, who swings a sharp pitchfork, was eyeing the Senate seat covetously; a Texas-size battalion of cranky oil millionaires were aching to send a gusher of money into Arkansas to defeat the junior Senator.

Fulbright tried manfully to suppress his controversialist impulses. He returned to Arkansas to make an extended speaking tour, using no prepared texts (his constituents suspect a ghost when a text is used) but simply submitting himself to questions. However, in January the nomination of John McCone as director of the Central Intelligence Agency was before the Senate. Fulbright opposed the appointment; he was wary of McCone's possibly adventurist views in foreign policy and felt that a man of especially sound judgment was needed in a post ranking just below the President in the day-to-day conduct of foreign affairs. The Senator drafted a statement explaining his doubts. He showed it to Carl Marcy, staff director of the Senate Foreign Relations Committee, and asked if there was anything in it that might damage the committee.

"No," replied Marcy, "and what's more, I agree with what you say in the statement. But somebody could be hurt by it—namely you. . . ." Fulbright read the statement into the record; McCone, of course, was confirmed (the vote was 71 to 12). It was the kind of gesture that gained the Senator nothing—nothing, that is, except the respect of those aware of the value of Fulbright's determined independence.

Months passed. Governor Faubus weighed his chances of beating Fulbright and finally concurred with his supporters who insisted that it would be wisest if he ran again for Governor. In the all-important Democratic primary in one-party Arkansas, the Senator was opposed by a single challenger, a rural school board member whose ideas were as extravagant as his hopes. The junior Senator carried the primary by a two-to-one margin (a margin that was repeated in November, 1962, when Fulbright overwhelmed a splenetic right-wing Republican whose star supporter was Barry Goldwater himself). "Senator Fulbright now has received his expected overwhelming vote of confidence by the people of his home state," the *Arkansas Gazette* commented. "Wholly predictable news though it was, it was great news for Arkansas and the country as well."

*   *   *

His roots are in Fayetteville, a pleasant city high in the Ozarks in the northwest corner of Arkansas. The main streets converge in an attractive square, and there is a scrubbed and well-tended look throughout the town of 20,274 (as of 1960). The state university is here, and large signs direct the motorists to the football stadium where the Razorbacks play half their Arkansas games (the rest are played in Little Rock). Architect Edward Durell Stone is a native son, and several of his designs grace a campus literally cupped in the hills.

Some of Fulbright's genial self-assurance springs from his family status in Fayetteville. "The Fulbrights own everything here but the stop signs on the street," a resident explains. This is modest hyperbole; the Fulbright influence *is* pervasive. A women's dormitory at the university and city library of striking modern design both bear the name of Roberta Waugh Fulbright, the Senator's mother. The family owns the local newspaper, the *Northwest Arkansas Times,* which is directed by the Senator's brother-in-law, Hal Douglas. The Fulbright interests include a bank, a Coca-Cola bottling plant and a lumber mill; the Fulbright home has the classic portico and spacious grounds that proclaim a local First Family.

But the Fulbrights are no ancient dynasty. James William was born on a farm in Sumner, Missouri, on April 5, 1905. He was the fourth of six children, and his father, Jay Fulbright, was a corn-hog farmer. When Fulbright was a year old, the family moved to Arkansas, where his father went into business, and prospered. In 1924, at the time of his premature death at fifty-six, Jay Fulbright was the wealthiest man in Fayetteville.

The family's rise is typical in Arkansas, a relatively "new" state without an elaborate caste structure or venerable tidewater gentry. An epitaph on the gravestone of John Patterson (1790-1886) telescopes the state's history in a riddle.

> I was born in a Kingdom,
> Raised in an Empire,
> Attained manhood in a Territory,
> Am now a citizen of a State
> And have never been 100 miles from where I live.

The Kingdom was Spain, the Empire was France, and Arkansas was a Territory before attaining statehood in 1836. In Little Rock, incidentally, the old Territorial capitol has been lovingly restored with the veneration Virginia reserves for Williamsburg.

When Fulbright's father died, his mother took over management of the family enterprises. A Missouri farm girl and one time schoolteacher, Roberta Waugh Fulbright was an imposing woman of strong features, strong views, and a strong will. She was curious about everything, and her interests were reflected in a daily column, "As I See It," that could be tart and heterodox when she was so inclined. In 1952, shortly before her death, her associates compiled a booklet drawn from the two million words she had written (in longhand) for the paper; the word "expediency," a colleague justly remarked in the introduction, "is not in her vocabulary."

His mother's Missouri liberalism left a mark on Fulbright. So did her love of learning. The Senator entered the state university at a precocious sixteen and his marks were good, if not outstanding. He was a varsity halfback for three and one-half years and graduated in 1925, finding time in his senior year to organize and become first president of the student government.

Then, in one of the casual happenstances that attended his rise, a

xxii

professor suggested that Fulbright apply for a Rhodes scholarship. He did, he won, and was soon on his way to Pembroke College, where he spent three years, earned two degrees, and inevitably took part in soccer and lacrosse. A year's grand tour of Europe followed; the time abroad was formative in developing his interest in foreign affairs and made the boy from Arkansas aware that he was a citizen of the Atlantic world.

Back in the United States during the depression 1930's, Fulbright enrolled in George Washington University law school in Washington, D.C. His decision, he acknowledges, was partly prompted by a desire to be within "courtin' distance" of a pretty girl he had met, Betty Williams of Philadelphia. He married in 1932 (they have two grown daughters and a grandchild) and graduated in 1934, placing second in his class of 135.

For two years he remained in Washington, serving in the antitrust division of the Justice Department and teaching law at GWU. In 1936, he returned to Arkansas, where he divided his time between the family businesses and teaching at the state university A chance occurrence again intervened. The president of the university was killed in an automobile accident in 1939, and the trustees, casting about for a successor, decided upon the home-town boy with an Oxford degree. At thirty-four, Fulbright became president and seemed assured of a serene career as an educator.

His mother's outspokenness altered his circumstances. In 1940, Homer Adkins was elected governor, and Mrs. Fulbright in a front page column indignantly sniffed that the victor was a "handshaking, backslapping politician." A state of tension developed between Adkins in Little Rock and the Fulbrights of Fayetteville. Early in 1941, the feud culminated when the university trustees (packed with the Governor's cronies) requested Fulbright's "resignation." The President refused and demanded that he be publicly fired. And so he was, on Commencement morning in 1941, amid shouts of protest from students and alumni.

It is Mr. Adkins' distinction that he fired a college president and made a senator. In 1942, Clyde Ellis, the congressman from the

Fayetteville district, decided to run for the Senate and asked his friend Bill Fulbright to campaign for the House seat that would be vacated. Fulbright won (Ellis, ironically, lost) and was a freshman congressman when he heard, in 1944, that the ineffable Governor Adkins had decided to run for the Senate. The college President that the Governor had fired lunged into the primary and squashed the hapless Adkins by a 32,000 vote margin. Fulbright has been in the Senate ever since, and in three re-elections has lacked formidable opposition.

Retrospectively, the distinguishing mark of the Senator's career has been the absence of deliberate design. His rise is virtually a study in casual advancement; his Rhodes scholarship, his tenure as university president and his first campaign for office arose out of circumstance as much as choice. But it must be swiftly added that Fulbright has shown shrewd resourcefulness in capitalizing on chance.

"He has always believed in the direct methods of doing things," Brooks Hays said in a debate in Congress in 1943, when both he and Fulbright were freshmen in the House. "When he played football at the University of Arkansas, he was distinguished not by his sensational style of playing but by his direct action. If he found a hole in the line, and he seemed very adept at doing that, he went straight through it."

* * *

In Congress, Fulbright has continued to display the same style—not flashy or eye-gouging, but very adept at finding the hole in the line. In wartime Washington, the new Congressman from the Ozarks caught the benevolent eye of Speaker Sam Rayburn. What committee assignment would he prefer? Fulbright requested House Foreign Affairs, a relatively moribund committee and surely an exotic choice for a young legislator from Arkansas. The Speaker, with an incredulous shrug, arranged the assignment.

No sooner was Fulbright on the committee than he introduced, on his own initiative, a five-line resolution that looked beyond World War II and sought to place Congress on record as favoring United

States membership in a world organization with powers adequate to keep the peace (see pp. 10-15). With surprisingly little fuss, the House adopted the "Fulbright Resolution" on September 21, 1943, by a vote of 360 to 29. Senator Tom Connally sponsored a similar resolution that the Senate passed on November 5 by a lopsided 85 to 5 vote. Thus the national legislature helped shape a national consensus that prepared the way for subsequent ratification of the United Nations Charter.

Once in the Senate, Fulbright tried to repeat the same tactic for a related cause. In 1947, he joined with Senator Elbert Thomas of Utah in sponsoring a resolution that would have placed Congress on record as favoring the political unification of Europe (see pp. 155-158). This was before the Marshall Plan, NATO, and the Common Market made the idea seem humdrum. Though the Senate failed to adopt this and successive other resolutions, the campaigns had a palpable result in stripping the curse of novelty from an important change.

In his single term in Congress, Fulbright also explored the possibility of using the floor as a forum for purposeful debate. With more valor than prudence, he took on the dagger-tongued Clare Boothe Luce, then a freshman congresswoman; but in his rebuttal to her "globaloney" speech, Fulbright ran afoul of English usage and exposed his flank to her cutlery (see pp. 6-10). Fulbright was scathed but not chastened, and over the years few Senators have matched his contribution to congressional debate; the evidence is in the pages that follow.

As a lawmaker, Fulbright shares with his brethren the handicap of living in an age of executive predominance. Most major measures emanate from agencies and departments, narrowing the scope for legislative innovation. Yet, interstitially, the member of Congress can contribute valid new measures, as Fulbright did in winning acceptance for his scholarship program. The time was 1945, and the climate was hospitable for some gesture of international fraternity. Drawing on his own experience as a Rhodes scholar, the Senator saw an opportunity for financing a vast program of educational exchange by using the foreign currencies that were piling up as counterpart payments for war relief. He waited until he saw a hole in the line, sprang his amendment on the Senate when a known opponent was off the floor, and saw the measure instantly adopted (see pp. 44-47). The program has been an unimpeachable success; in 1953, Fulbright's former history tutor at Oxford, now Master of Pembroke College, told his former pupil, with pardonable expansiveness: "You are responsible for the largest and most significant movement of scholars across the face of the earth since the fall of Constantinople in 1453."

Few powers are more basic to Congress than its investigative function, but in its exercise, Fulbright has been only intermittently successful. He is not the Hawkshaw type and is at best a reluctant sleuth. But he presided over the inquiry into the Reconstruction Finance Corporation in 1949-50, uncovering the mink coat and deep freeze that were thrown at the Democrats in virtually every Republican speech in 1952—a circumstance that has not sweetened his relations with President Truman. But Fulbright and Senator Douglas both sought to persuade the President to clean up the RFC before the hearings were held. His "study" (as he insistently termed it) of Wall Street in 1955 had typically casual beginnings. When he became chairman of the Senate Banking and Currency Committee that year, he was asked by a reporter if he planned to look into the erratic behavior of the market. Fulbright replied that he "guessed" he would, and so the study was born. A full-scale (and better-planned) inquiry is underway as this is written into the shadowy activities of registered agents lobbying for foreign governments (see pp. 217-220). It promises to be a major contribution to public enlightenment.

The corollary of the investigative power is that Congress impose some standards of restraint on Torquemadas with a gavel. Fulbright used his personal example to salutary effect during the McCarthy era. On February 2, 1954, he shouted the only "No!" on a vote to grant a $214,000 appropriation to Senator McCarthy's Permanent Subcommittee. This was at a time when only tremors of timidity issued from the White House and when McCarthy had bullied most his brethren into silence. Yet by the end of the year, Fulbright's solitary "No!" had become the voice of a majority of the Senate. Mc-Carthy's own follies contributed to the censure vote, but no less important was the determined effort of Senator Fulbright, working closely with Senator Ralph Flanders of Vermont and a handful of others, in forcing the chamber to face up to the undeliberative reck-lessness of one of its members.

What is striking about Fulbright's legislative career, when viewed as a whole, is the consistency of purpose that he has joined to tactical skill. From the beginning, he has seen the congressional arena as a place where a national consensus can be formed, where important matters can be intelligently debated, where innovations can be pro-posed, where facts can be diligently unearthed, and where the legis-lator himself has a chance to set an example of principle when demagoguery darkens the country. Every elective politician has, to some measure, a margin of freedom in which he can venture beyond the consensus of his constituency. Few members of Congress have used this precious margin more fruitfully than the always inde-pendent if sometimes languid junior Senator from Arkansas.

* * *

Yet, over the years, Fulbright has become increasingly concerned with the limitations of the legislature, particularly in the sphere of foreign affairs. This tendency became especially marked after Ful-bright became chairman of the Senate Foreign Relations Committee. The gavel changed hands on January 30, 1959, when Rhode Island's Senator Theodore F. Green voluntarily resigned as chairman. Green was then ninety-one, and age had impaired the hearing and eyesight of the patriarch of Congress. His generous act of abdication made Fulbright the youngest chairman (at fifty-three) in this century. So a Senator who grew up in the afterglow of Lincoln's presidency gave way to the son of a new century when a trip to the moon was on the national agenda.

There is no parallel in any other democratic parliament for the power wielded by the Foreign Relations Committee. The Constitu-tion instructs the Senate to offer its "advice and consent" to the President on the making of treaties and the appointment of ambassadors. This division of authority gives the committee and its chairman a special eminence; thus Fulbright's predecessors comprise a roll of imposing figures: Henry Clay, Thomas Hart Benton, Charles Sumner, John Sherman, Henry Cabot Lodge, William E. Borah, Tom Connally, and Walter F. George.

Under the benign but ineffectual tenure of Senator Green, the committee had slipped from its commanding position. Fulbright served notice that he intended to take a more energetic lead. In his first press conference as chairman, he criticized administration foreign policy as being "too rigid." A few days later, he sent a torrent of questionnaires to the State Department concerning ambassadorial appointments. This led to a contentious and largely unproductive dispute over the qualifications of two appointees, Ogden R. Reid and (once again) the acidulous Mrs. Luce. Fulbright felt that Reid, formerly publisher of the *New York Herald Tribune* and only thirty-three, was callow; but the Senate disagreed and confirmed him anyway, as ambassador to Israel. Mrs. Luce withdrew herself from consideration as ambassador to Brazil following an uninhibited exchange with Senator Wayne Morse of Oregon. (Fulbright had not opposed her appointment but was blamed anyway for the unseemly rumpus.)

Those first months were the Senator's unhappiest; it appeared as if the new chairman were bent on vindictively harassing the State Department and sowing the very discord that he otherwise condemned. In fact, Fulbright was moving toward a wholly different conception of the chairmanship that was more consistent with his over-all record. His considered view is contained in a lecture he delivered at the University of Virginia in 1961 (the text is on pp. 263-273):

It seems clear to me that in foreign affairs, a Senate cannot initiate or force large events, or substitute its judgment of them for that of the President, without seriously jeopardizing the ability of the nation to act consistently, and also without confusing the image and purpose of this country in the eyes of others.

The persistent theme in Fulbright's speeches is a plea for legislative self-restraint in foreign affairs; rather than restrict or instruct, he would have Congress *widen* the discretion of the executive. Hence he has opposed every attempt to shackle the President with legislative directives. He has opposed riders that would prohibit aid to Poland and Yugoslavia, and he has been wholly consistent in opposing comparable attempts (as in 1960) to deprive the United Arab Republic of aid—a stand that earned him the undeserved hostility of some pro-Israeli groups.

His running criticism of the State Department is that it has ventured too little rather than too much. He has spoken permissively about the need for negotiations with the Soviet Union when the louder voices seemed bent on tying the tongue of the voice of America. He tried to persuade an unwilling Eisenhower Administration to accept the idea of long-term foreign aid financing so that the State Department could think and plan ahead more sensibly. Under the Kennedy Administration, the proposal has been partly adopted and long-term foreign aid authorizations are now possible.

In sum, Fulbright is asking the Senate to provide more consent and less advice. The Constitution was framed for an isolationist country remote from the quarrels of Europe. Today the United States is engaged in distant corners of the world in a conflict with a resourceful and relentless adversary. The need, as the Senator sees it, is for maximum executive flexibility. In a democratic country this, in turn, derives from a popular understanding of what needs to be done. "It is in this role that I see the primary obligation of the Senate," Fulbright said in Charlottesville. "That is, constantly to explain and rationalize the burden which the people bear, to help them to that degree of understanding which will compel their agreement."

This is a view of the chairmanship that will surely be Fulbright's distinctive contribution; it comports with the times; judging by his past success in looking ahead, it is a view that may yet compel the agreement of his colleagues.

* * *

"Your representative owes you, not his industry only, but his judgment, and he betrays instead of serving you if he sacrifices it to your opinion." Thus Edmund Burke to the electors of Bristol in 1774. Yet before a legislator can offer the excellence of his judgments, an American politician might ruefully add, he must get elected. In Fulbright's case, the tension between private judgment and constituent opinion has created complex and difficult dilemmas. He has voted the straight Southern line on civil rights—and there is no reason to shy embarrassedly away from a blunt political fact.

Arkansas is a hybrid state "between the South of the piazza and the West of the pony." Its 53,335 square miles (it is the twenty-seventh state in size) contain loamy pasture lands near the Texas border, rugged Ozark hills near the Missouri line, and wet rice fields in eastern Arkansas that gleam like gems set in a flat checkerboard when seen from a plane. It is a rural state. The largest city is Little Rock, which just tips 100,000 in population, and its people, in city and farm, tend to be friendly and unpretentious; and sometimes uninformed and prejudiced.

It is a depressed state, ranking only above Mississippi in most economic indices. Arkansas places forty-ninth among the states in teacher salaries, which average about $3,600 a year. Lack of opportunity is mirrored in population decline; between 1950 and 1960, Arkansas dropped from 1,909,511 to 1,786,272, a loss of 6.5 per cent. Only West Virginia recorded a larger percentage drain in population.

And it is a one-party state. In his classic survey *Southern Politics* V. O. Key, Jr., titled the chapter on Arkansas "Pure One-Party Politics." Roberta Fulbright caught the flavor in one of her newspaper columns in 1941: "Our politics remind me of the pies the mountain girl had. She asked the guests: 'Will you have kivered, unkivered or crossbar? All apple.' Now that's what we have: kivered, unkivered and crossbar politics—all Democrats."

As in other one-party states, political competition tends to focus on personality rather than on program. Powerful economic interests (notably the utilities) tend to spread their largesse in a democratic fashion among all contenders who have a chance of winning. Still, the Democrats of Arkansas—kivered, unkivered and crossbar—have managed to produce an uncommonly high proportion of influential figures in Washington. Fulbright's senior colleague is John L. Mc-

Clellan, chairman of the Senate Government Operations Committee. Congressman Wilbur Mills heads the powerful House Ways and Means Committee and Oren Harris is chairman of the House Interstate and Foreign Commerce Committee. Thus one of the least populous states sends a delegation to Congress that controls four of the score or so of major standing committees.

Personal relations between the dominant figures in state politics are a study in detachment. Each has his own following, each makes his own electoral accommodations, and each, like rival princes of the realm, has a keen sense of jurisdictional jealousy. This *laisser faire* leads to the kinds of inconsistencies and ambiguities that baffle outsiders. It is not uncommon to hear voters say they favor Faubus and Fulbright because both are "good men"—and never mind that the two have wholly different national reputations.

In representing Arkansas, Fulbright has been an internationalist in foreign affairs and has stuck close to the center in domestic affairs. He is an eloquent advocate of federal aid to education; he has also voted to override the veto of the Taft-Hartley Act. He supports rural electrification through REA; he also has steadfastly opposed federal regulation of natural gas. He is for help to small businessmen and farmers; he also joined in the "Nays" that killed President Kennedy's Medicare bill.

On civil rights, he has been wholly orthodox from the Southern Democratic view, though he is devoid of any bigotry. His unhappiest moment was during the Little Rock school tempest in 1957. This was a crisis that few expected. The city of Little Rock had a generally tranquil racial tradition when the school board took a modest first step in desegregating local public schools. Governor Faubus had been elected as a moderate; the state's oldest and widely respected paper, the *Arkansas Gazette*, supported the school board. Little Rock's congressman, Brooks Hays, was a Baptist lay leader known for his moderate views on race issues.

The accepted interpretation is that Faubus was in need of an issue for his third term campaign (only one other governor had served more than two terms) and he deliberately intruded himself into the school dispute with demagogic force.

Fulbright was in London when violence in Little Rock swelled into headlines. He remained silent throughout. In the Ozarks, where he had grown up, Negroes are few and racial attitudes generally relaxed. (Most of the state's 390,000 Negroes are bunched in the plantation country of eastern Arkansas.) The University of Arkansas admitted its first Negro student in 1949, and the public schools of Fayetteville had desegregated, without fuss, not long after the Supreme Court school decision in 1954. Yet in the light of inflamed local opinion, Fulbright decided against any public collision with Faubus.

The contrast is with Brooks Hays, who vainly sought to play a mediating role among his constituents. For his efforts, he was defeated in 1958 by Dale Alford, a rabid segregationist who conducted a write-in campaign of inspired scurrility with support from Faubus. Out of defeat, Hays won a lasting victory. His principled position rallied moderate opinion and laid the groundwork for the reopening of the Little Rock schools. By September, 1962, some seventy Negroes were enrolled in once-segregated public schools, and Governor Faubus, with canny elasticity, was accepting in practice what he once denounced as unthinkable in theory.

Fulbright's record, in Northern eyes, is hardly unblemished, but the defeat of Brooks Hays points the moral. Surely the country needs both kinds of men; whatever his concessions to local opinion, Fulbright has never made re-election an end in itself. Nor does he succumb to predictable cant in discussing civil rights. In 1958, he filed a brief of *amicus curiae* with the Supreme Court in which he argued for a delay of school desegregation in Little Rock (the text is on pp. 130-136). The key paragraph follows:

The people of Arkansas endure against a background not without certain pathological aspects. They are marked in some ways by a strange disproportion inherited from the age of Negro slavery. The whites and Negroes of Arkansas are equally prisoners of their environment. No one knows what either of them might have been under other circumstances. Certainly no one of them has ever been free with respect to racial relationship.... Each moves through an intricate ritual of evasions, of make-believe and suppressions. . . . All this is the legacy of an ancient and melancholy history.

So in 1962 both Fulbright and Faubus were elected on the same ticket, with neither referring to the other's candidacy. Each seems to satisfy an electoral need in Arkansas; Faubus reaching the darker corners of the state's mind and Fulbright bringing the state external prestige. Indeed, in a curious way, the bad reputation that Faubus has brought Arkansas may have enhanced the hold of Fulbright. The election of a Rhodes scholar, a former university president and chairman of the Foreign Relations Committee dry-cleans the stains left by Faubus, Little Rock, and the mob of rednecks who besieged Central High.

* * *

Fulbright leads an active life in Washington with a measure of serenity rare in a city where the daily round whirls like a carrousel, usually to as much purpose. He makes a fetish of regular exercise, constantly has a book near his chair, and avoids the ceremonial cocktail parties when he can. He spends as much time as possible in his handsome home in the shadow of the Moslem Mosque that gleams ornamentally on Massachusetts Avenue.

He lives in a political city without being overwhelmed by the political rituals. It is no accident that he most frequently quotes Alexis de Tocqueville, the cool-headed French nobleman whose praise of free government was tempered by distrust of the tyranny of the majority. Fulbright has a comparable distaste for mass-produced opinions, for the phony arts of image projection, and for persuasion by wind-machine.

He believes that the leadership in a democracy has a very special obligation to resist the clamor of conventional opinion. He has sought through twenty years to speak candidly about unswerving realities. He has dealt honestly with the limitations of the United Nations Charter and has discussed the mischief of unlimited sovereignty in a world armed with nuclear warheads. He has warned that the United States must learn to live with a tide of change and accept the fact of radical nationalism in former colonial areas. At the same time, he has dealt laconically with the limitations of a General Assembly where every nation has a single vote and where anti-colonial emotion tramples over reason. He has cautioned against the overcommitment of American power in peripheral struggles. He has urged that the first order of priority is the forming of new political bonds between countries in the North Atlantic Community. But he has also insisted that every effort be made to reach an honorable settlement with the Soviet Union through negotiations in which both sides are prepared for tangible concessions.

Although he has argued for great executive authority in foreign affairs, he has also been highly critical of the tendency of the administration to surrender to the pressures of an ignorant bureaucracy. A classic instance is his opposition to the Cuban invasion. The circumstances that led the Senator to offer a private memorandum to the President are described elsewhere (see p. 194). What is significant is that Fulbright, an outsider, a legislator and a nonspecialist, saw the flaws in a plan that hypnotized the military and intelligence chiefs. His counsel reflected the common-sense reasoning of a legislator whose skepticism served as an antibody to the hallucinatory force of secret reports and newspaper panic. After the debacle, at a White House meeting, President Kennedy said to Fulbright within the earshot of others, "You are the only person here who has a right to say: 'I told you so.' "

Thus Fulbright himself provides an ironic counterargument to his own thesis that the legislator, as an outsider, lacks the detailed knowledge necessary to a rounded and informed judgment on foreign affairs. His very perch at the periphery can give the legislator an angle of vision more discerning than those within the bureaucratic barricade. Hence the Senator's admirers restrained their disappointment when Fulbright was not appointed Secretary of State by President Kennedy, though he was among the final handful considered for the post. By temperament and training, Fulbright is a parliamentarian rather than an administrator, a critic and counselor, not a doer and team-player.

Yet impressive as his contribution has been, as this volume evidences, Fulbright has still to reach his full potential of influence as a legislator. Indeed, the challenge of the chairmanship of Foreign Relations may continue to enlarge the scope of his achievement and assure the Senator membership in the exclusive circle of legislators who have left an enduring stamp on their time.

*   *   *

Finally, a word as to editorial method. The staff of the Senate Foreign Relations Committee has generously made available texts of the chairman's public speeches and has helped the editor in a hundred minor chores. In addition, friends and associates of the Senator in both Washington and Arkansas have responded with patient consideration to requests for biographical data and political lore.

In sifting through two decades of political speeches, I have tried to pick representative examples that catch the flavor of the legislative process and that disclose the evolution of the Senator's thinking. The arrangement is both chronological and topical, and prefatory notes have been kept to what I hope is an unobtrusive minimum. Inevitably, any selection involves a measure of distortion. Fulbright has dealt frequently and fluently with the problems of his state— economic, education and social—but these speeches are among the missing in a volume devoted to national and foreign affairs. A bibliographical note at the end of the book lists some interesting additional speeches and articles.

Needless to add, only the editor bears any responsibility for the commentary in the pages that follow.

Fulbright of Arkansas

THE PUBLIC POSITIONS
OF A PRIVATE THINKER

Chapter One

A WAR FOR WHAT?

————————

1. The Atlantic Highway

What should be his topic for a speech in Oklahoma? There was "no choice," the young President of the University of Arkansas felt—it had to be The War. The time is after the fall of France, during the bleak period of the Nazi-Soviet pact, when Britain was a beleaguered bastion of freedom. The theme was conventional, but the handling unusual. J. William Fulbright, then thirty-five, placed his main stress on the concept of an Atlantic community, a concept that may have seemed strange to his listeners in Oklahoma, but which has surely lost its novelty now.

The War or, as Rauschning calls it, the "Revolution of Nihilism" is the one subject of fundamental, universal, and compelling interest today. It is interesting to all people in this democracy because we know that a German triumph means the loss of that freedom of the spirit by which individuals maintain their self-respect....

Too often today we hear the profound pronouncement by an isolationist senator that this country does not want war. Of course, we do not want war, just as Austria, Czechoslovakia, Poland, Norway, Holland, Belgium, France, and England did not want war. The fact is, the world has war, and the question is what should we do about it? The truth is that we are confronted with much more than a mere war. It is not often than one witnesses the collapse or at least the apparent collapse of a way of life, a civilization by which the world has lived for hundreds of years....

Before the declaration of war in 1917, one of our leading national magazines, the *New Republic,* on February 17, 1917, expressed fairly well the true reasons for our interest in the outcome of that war:

The safety of the Atlantic highway is something for which America should fight. Why? Because on the two shores of the Atlantic Ocean there has grown up a profound web of interest which joins together the western world. Britain, France, Holland, the Scandinavian nations, and Pan-America are, in the main, one community in their deepest needs and their deepest purposes. They have a common interest in the ocean which unites them. They are today more inextricably bound together than most men as yet realize. But if that community were destroyed we should know what we had lost. We should understand then the meaning of the unfortified Canadian frontier, or the common protection given Latin America by the British and American fleets—and now that Germany is seeking to cut the vital highways of our world we can no longer stand by. We cannot betray the Atlantic community by submitting. If not civilization, at least *our* civilization is at stake. A victory on the high seas would be a triumph of that class which aims to make Germany the leader of the East against the West, the leader ultimately of a German-Russian-Japanese coalition against the Atlantic world.

These words are prophetic, in that not only did they describe the situation in 1917, but since the German alliance with Russia and an obvious understanding with Japan, today, they are more true than they were twenty-three years ago.

ADDRESS AT THE UNIVERSITY OF
OKLAHOMA, JULY 30, 1940

2. "We Must Make Plans"

Soon the young scholar was in politics, and in 1942 his nomination in the Democratic primary for Congress assured his election. The nation now was at war, but, in his address to the State Democratic Convention in Little Rock, Fulbright was already looking ahead to the peace. What lends interest to the speech is the spaciousness of design, reflecting Fulbright's tendency to define a current crisis in the largest terms—a tendency that gains in sophistication as his career advances.

Great movements that stir mankind are never clear-cut and simple. It is true, therefore, that material considerations are involved in this struggle, but underlying most of the great wars in history, since the time of Christ, is the principle of human freedom, the fundamental equality of all men as opposed to the principle of master and slave. Hitler saw that our modern Western civilization had grown selfish and cynical, and he believed that the ideal of democracy we talked so much about we were unwilling to live up to or to fight for.

This being the fundamental issue of this war, we may say it is a civil war rather than a national war. In other words, it is not merely a war for the aggrandizement of one nation, but it is to determine whether throughout the world all men shall be fundamentally equal or whether they shall be slaves of certain individuals. Such wars are always savage and destructive. Men often fight more bitterly for an ideal than a material thing. For example, the early Christians were burned, torn limb from limb for their faith. But we know of few instances where men give up their lives purely for money. Our own Revolution was fought for this principle as announced in the Declaration of Independence. Our Civil War in 1860 was fought to reaffirm and to establish throughout the nation this principle. President Lincoln recognized this. He saw that we could not live up to our ideal half free and half slave. The French Revolution was another struggle for this same ideal. Today we are in a world-wide civil war for precisely the same reason. You know

3

that from the point of view of time of travel and time of communication the world is today no larger than was the United States in 1860. Where we had national movements seventy-five years ago, we have world movements today....

We must realize, just as Lincoln did in 1860, that the world can no longer exist half free and half slave. This does not mean we can forget about human freedom the day peace is declared. In fact, then will be the time for some of the most difficult work. We must make plans; we must take a leading part in a world organization for the preservation of world peace and the equality of man.

If the Democratic party expects to retain the direction of this nation's destiny, I believe that the party must perform two great tasks. First, it must, of course, win the war. Second, it must evolve some program for the government of the world that will prevent these recurrent wars....

The movement toward a world organization is underway. The so-called good old days of extreme nationalism are, I believe, gone forever. Either the system of Master and Slave will return to rule the world, as it did in the time of the Roman Empire, or a system based on the equality of man and human freedom will become universal. It is obvious that, if the latter is to take place, the United States must take the leading part. It is also certain, I believe, that if the United States is to take that leading part, the Democratic party must remain in power. The only way I think we can remain in power is to rid ourselves of reactionary, defeatist notions that nothing can be done about the world.We must again catch the spirit of 1918 and 1932 and attack the problems of the world with the same daring and originality that we attacked that peace and that depression. Unless we do show the people of the United States that the Democrats still have the vision and the courage to attack and to solve great problems, not only will we be thrown from power, but we will probably see a repetition of that great debacle after the last war. Again all our sacrifices will have been in vain.

ADDRESS BEFORE THE ARKANSAS
DEMOCRATIC CONVENTION, LITTLE
ROCK, SEPTEMBER 16, 1942

4

3. First Speech in Congress: "Our Honorable Colleague Has Wit"

In his maiden speech, the Hon. J. W. (Bill) Fulbright, as the Con-gressional Record listed his name, took on an opponent of "sparkling beauty and suavity of manner"—Congresswoman Clare Boothe Luce of Connecticut, who a few days earlier had made her celebrated "globaloney" speech. His manner was courtly, his argument cogent, but in the end Mrs. Luce wound up by slyly giving the Rhodes scholar a lesson in English usage; Fulbright had tripped over the familiar problem of distinguishing "imply" from "infer."

Mr. Fulbright: Mr. Chairman, I rise today for the first time in this House, sooner than I had intended. I am fully conscious of my de-ficiencies in experience, and otherwise, for this task, but nevertheless, for all new Members there must be a first time, so I beg the indul-gence of this House for the time at my disposal.

The reason I am speaking sooner than I had intended is simply this: Although I am not unconscious of the sparkling beauty and suavity of manner of the honorable lady from Connecticut, yet I find that I am not as susceptible to her logic and to her persuasion, at least on the floor of this House, as some of my colleagues appear to have been.

I realize that I cannot expect as large and as rapturous a gallery, or as attentive an audience in this House, as the honorable lady had. Neither will I have the sympathetic and universal press. Certainly I cannot expect *Life* magazine to support my views in its editorial policy. Nevertheless, and in spite of these obvious and perhaps fatal disadvantages, I feel constrained to offer a few thoughts for the con-sideration of this House in opposition to those of the honorable member from Connecticut. Further, I might add that, since the hon-orable lady is a new Member of this House, I thought it might not be considered inappropriate for me, likewise a new Member, albeit not a very glamorous one, to take exception to her views on the extremely important and delicate issue that she raised in her address to this House a week ago today.

Some of the reasons and conclusions of my honorable colleague may be summarized rather briefly. She says that specific war and peace aims can never be clarified until we know what goes on in the mind of Joseph Stalin; she says that we should pity Mr. Roosevelt and Mr. Churchill for floundering in a sea of uncertainty, and that the Atlantic Charter is a monumental generality and noble catch-all, and the four freedoms a virtuous platitude—I presume just pieces of paper. She says indeed it will be dangerous for us to propose specific international settlements today which Stalin might dispose of tomorrow.

She brushes aside the isolationists and "the bigger and redder and more royal" international New Dealers. With her inspired, feminine intuition she reveals that we all agree, on both sides of the aisle, that—I quote—"We shall all demand henceforth to be secure from attack."

The key to this noble aspiration, she says, is America's position in the postwar air world. The air policy of all young, air-minded Americans is they want to fly everywhere. This statement would seem to indicate that freedom of the skies throughout the world is the desire of young America.

From this point on, the train of her thought is difficult to follow, so I hope that I may not be held strictly accountable if I should misinterpret certain passages. The argument apparently is that the United States has achieved supremacy in the commercial-aviation field by a policy of sovereignty of the skies over a nation's own territory and the denial of free access to its airports. She is fearful that our government is now negotiating to abandon the sovereignty-of-the-skies policy for a policy of freedom of the skies. It is at this point that I confess I get lost. The argument seems to reduce itself to this: that our policy must be to exclude all foreign aircraft from our skies and airports and at the same time proceed to establish air lines and airports over and in all the other countries of the world.

Mrs. Luce: Mr. Chairman, will the gentleman yield?

Mr. Fulbright: Following your practice, I prefer to finish my statement and then I will yield.

It is inconceivable to me that anyone could seriously urge, in these modern days, except in connection with a plan of imperialistic expansion by force, à la Nazi, that we can adopt an exclusive policy

6

with regard to our own country and a freedom-of-the-skies policy for all other countries. What will our friends of the United Nations think of such a noble and altruistic policy, or should I say sinister policy?

Of a similar nature is her argument that, since freedom of the seas did not prevent World War Number 1 and Number 2, freedom of the air will not prevent World War Number 3. With equal force, it seems to me, one could argue that, since freedom of speech and freedom of religion in this country did not prevent two world wars and will not prevent a third, therefore we should abandon these principles as useless to our nation. It seems superfluous to observe that freedom of the seas was not the culprit; it was merely the innocent bystander and no more caused this war than did Holland, Denmark, or Norway.

Being unable to follow any serious logic in this reasoning, I am compelled to conclude that the point of this passage was to ridicule the Vice-President of the United States. Her witty and scintillating remarks about Mr. Wallace were quite equal to the sophisticated style of Walter Winchell and *Time* magazine. Not only is Mr. Wallace spasmodically sane, but he is full of "globaloney," a wonderful word which convulsed the gallery and will certainly live for many seasons in the folklore of Broadway. There is no denying it, our honorable colleague is a wit. . . .

It seems to me a very unwise and dangerous move for us, at this critical time, to adopt a policy of proceeding now to gobble up all the commercial advantages possible, while we and our allies are desperately fighting to defeat the common enemy. Furthermore, I think it exceedingly unfortunate to assume at this time that nothing whatever can be done about controlling the savage and violent elements of the world; to assume that World War Number 3 is just around the corner. Such an assumption is a most powerful inducement to that very result.

I submit that the only rational policy for this great nation of ours, is to assume, what I believe to be true, that the peoples of this earth have learned something by experience, that they earnestly desire to avoid and to prevent another world war, and that they are willing to make reasonable sacrifices to attain this end. Upon this assumption, our representatives should begin negotiations at once with our allies to formulate a specific and concrete system for collective security of the nations of the world. I, for one, believe that such a system is possible, providing the people of this nation, especially our national representatives, are willing to discard our traditional isolationism, now often disguised under the name of Americanism, and to approach the problem of war and peace with a determination to do everything possible to find a practical solution.

Mr. Chairman, I propose that this Congress, instead of assuming a defeatist policy with regard to war, immediately authorize and direct its Committee on Foreign Affairs to undertake a thorough study of all proposals for postwar international organizations designed to prevent war. That committee should be instructed to make a report of its findings to this House in the near future. It should develop specific recommendations regarding this vital matter for the consideration of the executive branch of this government and the people of this nation.

The time is getting short for the development and consideration of a program for peace. It must be done now, while the minds and hearts of the peoples of this world are concerned with universal and fundamental issues—while danger and sacrifice give us humility and understanding....

The Atlantic Charter, it seems to me, is no more of a monumental generality or virtuous platitude than is the preamble of our own Constitution or our own sacred Declaration of Independence. Noble aspirations, nobly expressed, have served and, I believe, will serve a useful purpose in the progress of mankind. They are introductory to the specific and difficult business of creating a sane and practical machinery for the guidance of a turbulent human race. It may be expected that such platitudes have no place in a policy of shortsighted and adolescent, nationalistic imperialism.

In conclusion, Mr. Chairman, I submit that the only substantial benefit this nation can realize from this war is the assurance of a peaceful world, based upon a world-wide system of collective security. Such a system can be achieved only with the genuine co-operation of our gallant allies.

The narrow, imperialistic policy of grab, advocated by the honorable lady, carries within itself the seeds of its own destruction. An exclusive policy with regard to our own airports obviously will induce the same exclusive policy in all other sovereign nations. But the most evil consequence of that policy is that it will so arouse the suspicion and distrust of our allies as to our purposes that we can never convince them that we have a sincere desire to stop, once and for all, the recurrence of these frightful wars which are so rapidly destroying the vitals of our Christian civilization. I, for one, do not wish to base our policy on the assumption that a third world war is just around the corner. On the contrary, I believe this great nation of ours now has, or shortly will have, the power to turn this ghastly, barren tragedy into a tremendous opportunity, which, with imagination, intelligence, and determination, will enable us, together with our allies, to create the world of the future.

MRS. LUCE: Mr. Chairman, will the gentleman yield?

MR. FULBRIGHT: If my time has not expired.

MR. WOODRUM of Virginia: Mr. Chairman, I yield the gentleman two additional minutes.

MR. FULBRIGHT: I yield.

MRS. LUCE: The young and very able gentleman from Arkansas has spoken rather loosely of what he calls my freedom-of-the-air policy. I would like to ask a very specific question of the gentleman. By his definition of what he calls a proper air policy of the United States, does he intend that this country should control its own skies or airports, or does he intend to relinquish that control?

MR. FULBRIGHT: I cannot imagine that this country can relinquish control of the skies and airports any more than it has relinquished control of its seaports under our traditional policy of freedom of the seas.

MRS. LUCE: I would like to ask the gentleman another question. At several points the gentleman said I had inferred this or that. I inferred nothing. I implied and the gentleman from Arkansas did the inferring. Now, would the gentleman from Arkansas be good enough to give me the precise passage, the precise quote from the text of my speech in which I said that America must control the sovereign skies of any other nation?

9

Mr. Fulbright: No, I do not think I said that. You proposed that America gain control of air bases and air routes.

Mrs. Luce: Will the gentleman be good enough to give me the exact text and quote in which I implied or inferred or stated specifically that this country acquire bases and routes from sovereign nations without free negotiations between those nations and ourselves?

Mr. Fulbright: Would you like me to read your speech again to this audience?

Mrs. Luce: I should like you to read that portion of it which you say says such a thing.

Mr. Fulbright: That is implicit throughout the speech, if I recall correctly.

Mrs. Luce: You are inferring.

The Chairman: The time of the gentleman from Arkansas has expired.

Address in Congress,
February 16, 1943

4. The Fulbright Resolution

Fulbright's first constructive effort in Congress was to introduce a resolution of historic importance. It quickly became known as "the Fulbright Resolution" and it consisted of but five lines:

"Resolved, That the House of Representatives hereby expresses itself as favoring the creation of appropriate international machinery with power adequate to establish and to maintain a just and lasting peace, among the nations of the world, and as favoring participation of the United States therein through its constitutional processes."

The overwhelming passage of the Concurrent Resolution laid the groundwork for the acceptance of the United Nations and helped measurably to avert the political debacle that kept America out of the League of Nations. Here Fulbright explains the reasoning behind his gesture.

10

I think all of us will agree that, if we are to win the peace, if we are to prevent a repetition of the egregious mistake of 1919-20, Congress must act now.

To do nothing, as we did in 1920, will be a decision in favor of international anarchy. All the world is watching us for signs that American willingness to help win a lasting peace will match American determination to win a total victory. All of our experience indicates that it is absolutely necessary that some positive, affirmative action be taken before the fighting is over, if we are to achieve anything of lasting value from this war.

I think that we are also agreed that the only thing of lasting value we can obtain from this war is some assurance of peace in the world of the future. The principal question for us is, therefore, what kind of action, designed to accomplish this purpose, is the Congress most likely to take now.

In view of the historic caution and timidity of our illustrious Senate with regard to foreign affairs, it is important that it be not frightened with an esoteric or complicated proposal. The House of Representatives is presently so grossly overburdened with wartime legislation, in addition to the usual domestic measures, and is so distracted by the struggle for political power in anticipation of 1944, that the members have neither the serenity nor the inclination, carefully, to analyze and to formulate at this time a detailed plan for international co-operation.

As a matter of fact, in the field of foreign relations the proper function of the legislative power is to express the broad fundamental policy of the nation. The executive power is better equipped to, and properly should, develop the details of all agreements within the outlines of the fundamental policy, as expressed by the representatives of the people.

For these reasons I think it is highly desirable that any proposal submitted to the Congress at this time should be reduced to the simplest possible terms.

Of all the resolutions so far introduced, I believe House Resolution 200 is the least controversial and the most likely to be acceptable to the Congress now. It consists of only five lines, which I should like to read to you:

Resolved, That the House of Representatives hereby expresses itself as favoring the creation of appropriate international machinery with power adequate to prevent future aggression and to maintain lasting peace and as favoring participation by the United States therein. (An amended version was finally adopted. See p. 10.)

I submit that this simple statement is a positive disavowal of the isolationist policy and a definite commitment that this nation desires to co-operate with the other nations of the world in an effort to create an organization designed to prevent aggressive warfare.

It has been said that this resolution is so general, so innocent, that no rational person can oppose it, but that it really doesn't mean anything. If, in truth, it is so innocent that it is acceptable to the Congress, then it meets the primary requirement of getting action now.

With regard to its significance, I believe that it clearly contains the indispensable minimum upon which our foreign policy must be based. Our immediate and primary purpose is to declare to the world that henceforth this nation intends to bear its share of the responsibility of bringing order into the hitherto chaotic international arena. In short, that we recognize the impossibility, the futility of withdrawing into an illusory shell of isolationism.

The words "appropriate international machinery" provide for all the commonly accepted governmental institutions—executive, legislative, and judicial—which are essential to the control of force and the maintenance of order.

To attempt to specify the exact composition of these institutions, at this time, would be unwise. There is no such thing as a perfect plan in which laws or constitutions are self-executing. Our ultimate reliance for success must be upon the spirit and intelligence of the people who are responsible for the operation of the institutions of law and order and not upon the mechanical perfection of those institutions. To fill in the details at this time would tend to freeze the pattern and to prevent orderly development in accordance with experience. The initial machinery itself should be organized by the executive, only after prolonged study and discussion with the other nations. Even then it should not be frozen so that orderly evolutionary change and progress is prevented. In a new undertaking such as this will be, and with limited experience to guide us, great flexibility with regard to details is highly desirable.

The words "power adequate to prevent future aggression" not only envisage some kind of world police force, which is so frightening to thirty-two of our senators, but it also includes the power to control the productive capacity of instruments of war. As a matter of fact, the control of the existing personnel and weapons of warfare is not sufficient to prevent the development of powerful armaments. If we boggle over the words "police force," we may well be wasting our time on idle words. The essential element is the supervision, not merely of existing force, but of the productive capacity of heavy armaments, of chemical processes, or of any techniques essential to the production of instruments of aggressive war. It is obvious that the supervision of the latter will be a most difficult task, and I think it is impossible to specify at this time how it can be accomplished. Yet I am convinced that, if the same ingenuity is employed in supervision that was used after the last war in the evasion of restrictions, our end can be accomplished. However difficult these problems may be, this resolution contemplates the control of the sources of aggressive force in all its phases.

If, in spite of the innocent appearance of this resolution, it is objected that it is too broad, too far-reaching, this should not be a serious objection. After all, this is not a grant of power to the executive, it is simply an expression by our people that we intend to participate. If such a resolution is adopted, the executive can then negotiate as to the details of the machinery with the assurance that the people are willing to support any reasonable system of collective security. But, as the various components of the system are agreed upon by the different governments, they still must be approved by legislation in the nature of treaties or by joint resolution of the Senate and House of Representatives. If our executive is unable to develop an organization satisfactory to our legislative body, no damage will

13

have been done and we will have acquired experience of great value in case we have a third opportunity to create a sensible world.

I think that the words "to prevent future aggression and to maintain lasting peace" are restrictive in their meaning. They should be interpreted as a limitation on the purposes of the international machinery, to the control of aggressive force. It is true that dividing lines involving functions and jurisdiction are among the most difficult governmental questions, and it is virtually impossible to anticipate and prejudge all the problems that may arise. In any case, I do not think that this resolution can fairly be said to contemplate, without further authorization from the Congress, any infringement upon this nation's independence or sovereignty (whatever that may be) except insofar as it relates to the control of armed force by the co-operative international organization.

The real significance of the action which we want from the Congress now is the assurance that this country desires to make a genuine and honest effort in co-operation with other nations, to put an end to aggressive warfare. This assurance is absolutely essential before our executive can negotiate effectively with other nations. This is not a final acceptance now of any kind of agreements that may be evolved. Even if nothing acceptable results from these negotiations, nevertheless we will have the satisfaction of having tried and cannot in any respect be any worse off than we will be if we do nothing....

The decisive consideration in favor of the simple but positive resolution is that it is more likely than any other to be adopted now, without undue delay and controversy. Every word and comma in any measure before the Congress presents a point of attack to the opposition. Therefore, the fewer the words the less vulnerable the bill. I believe that House Resolution 200 will definitely reassure the world that our future course is toward genuine co-operation. If we get less than this, we get nothing. If we ask for more specific provisions, we run the risk of complete failure in obtaining any action because of haggling and misunderstandings over insignificant details.

Let us not forget that it was just such haggling and misunderstandings by the Senate in 1920 over reservations and restrictions, many of them of little importance, that led to our renunciation of any responsibility for world order, and in a very real sense prepared the way for the savage total war of today.

ADDRESS BEFORE A "UNITED NATIONS TODAY AND TOMORROW" MEETING IN CONSTITUTION HALL, WASHINGTON, D.C., MAY 10, 1943

5. First Senate Speech: "A Certain Boldness Is Essential"

The war in Europe was almost over and peace in the Pacific only a few months away, when the new Senator from Arkansas addressed the Senate for the first time. His primary concern was to allay fears that the Senate might once again play an obstructionist role in ratifying the treaties that would make victory worthwhile. His view of the Soviet Union, like most Americans' at the time, was to hope that an ally in war could become a friend in peace. His sentiment can be taken as a measure of the wartime good will that existed toward Russia before East and West entered the deep chill of the cold war.

MR. FULBRIGHT: Mr. President, myths are one of the greatest obstacles in the formulation of national policy. A myth of some plausibility is being currently revived at the expense of this Senate. The Senate is being held solely responsible for the failure of the United States to join the League of Nations. This myth is a half-truth, and a very dangerous half-truth. At home it is being used to disparage our system of government. Abroad it is being used to explain any hesitation we may show in joining a system of world security. The Senate of the United States, it is said, cannot be relied upon.

As I see it, the responsibility for the rejection of the League of Nations does not belong solely to the Senate. The American people must share that responsibility. The perfectionists among the liberals,

15

quite as much as the reactionaries, contributed to our failure. One has merely to read again what was said a generation ago by our liberal press. Few people were against a league. But they did not like this league, nor did they like the other fellow's league. All of them seemed to want a league which suited them. The Senate of the United States has, I believe, been unjustly maligned.

The responsibility that I would attach to this body is that, in rejecting the League of Nations, it did not suggest some alternative method of establishing and maintaining order in the world. Negation is not enough for this aggressive and restless world. As the poet says, a world is dying and another world is struggling to be born, and the job of creating that new world belongs as much to the Senate as to any other agency in the entire world. We shall be negative again at our own peril, and we shall invite the same travail and tribulation which has kept mankind in agony for five long and terrible years. In peace, as well as in war, victory will not come to the negative, defensive strategy. A certain boldness, a positive resourcefulness, is essential to win any battle in war or peace. General Patton, General Eisenhower, General Hodges, and Admiral Nimitz are proving that today....

I am sure that some will say that we must rely upon the State Department to formulate our foreign policy. I do not think we can afford to entrust this function exclusively to the State Department. In the first place, it is no longer possible to separate foreign from domestic policy. The two are much too closely intertwined, too interdependent, to be regarded as unrelated and separate problems. I know that the welfare of the cotton farmers in Arkansas is directly, and inevitably, dependent upon the maintenance of a free flow of international commerce. When that flow is interrupted by war, as at present, or by a shortsighted tariff like the Smoot-Hawley measure, then we become involved with huge, unmanageable surpluses and such makeshifts as subsidies and loans to cotton producers. No, I do not think a few polished and cultured gentlemen, in the dark and dignified recesses of the State Department, should be entrusted, exclusively, with the formulation of our foreign policy....

It seems to me most urgent, Mr. President, that this body should proceed, in the near future, to the consideration of the basic principles of our foreign policy. The time is drawing near when the great decisions must be made. Unless some means is found to clarify beforehand many of the issues involved in these decisions, then, necessarily, our representatives will be forced to improvise in the dark and by guesswork.

For example, there is a common belief, perhaps a myth, that our people are anti-British. There are several powerful newspapers in this country which for many years have drilled into the minds of their millions of readers hate and distrust of the British. The same newspapers and other papers have done likewise with regard to the Russians, the Jews, and, for that matter, all "furriners," as one governor of a sovereign state used to put it. I do not believe the majority of our people, or the majority of the Senate, subscribes to these narrow prejudices. However, if these matters were clearly and reasonably discussed, along with other matters of similar importance, I think it would do much to reassure our allies in the United Nations and to strengthen the courage of our own representatives. On the other hand, if it be true, which I cannot believe, that we do hate and distrust our allies, then we and they should know about it. If these powerful influences in our press have so far poisoned the minds of our people that they do not desire to co-operate positively and concretely with our allies, then an entirely different policy from that now proposed should be pursued....

Mr. President, I believe that the American people are profoundly interested, and I know that I am deeply interested, in understanding the what and the why of our foreign policy, if any. Since I have been a Member of this body, relatively little time has been spent upon this subject. In the hope that I may promote discussions and criticisms, out of which better understanding may evolve, I am venturing a few observations.

During the past several years I have heard various people say that we have had no recognizable foreign policy. I am inclined to agree. By policy is meant "a settled or definite course or plan adopted or followed by the government." To be definite and settled is of the essence of policy. To be definite, the men responsible for carrying

17

out a policy must know what they are doing and why they are doing it, or it is not definite. To be settled, this knowledge must flow from a responsible source, in our case the people of this country, or it cannot be settled.

Prior to the First World War, in spite of some wavering from time to time, our policy was that of isolation. It was settled and definite. It was justified by the remoteness of our land from comparable great powers and was in accord with the wishes of our people. Our ancestors had come here with the express purpose of getting away from the oppression and disturbances of the Old World. The First World War unsettled that policy. President Wilson and others sensed the fact that isolation had become in fact impossible, but they were unable to control the government. The habits and prejudices of more than a century were too strong, even for the obvious implications of modern science, as exemplified by the motorcar, the airplane, and the radio. The abortive effort of Wilson to adjust our policy to the new conditions of the world, by means of the League of Nations, left our people divided and unable to agree upon any policy. We knew neither what we were doing nor why. Instead of having a policy, we improvised upon considerations of the moment.

We declined to join the League and use our power and influence collectively, to establish order and peace. On the other hand, we participated in disarmament conferences and proceeded to weaken our armed forces. We had neither force nor collective security to protect us. At the peace conference, we insisted upon further fragmentation of an already chaotic political structure and at the same time refused to erect any responsible authority to protect our handiwork. We insisted upon the collection of war debts and at the same time erected tariff barriers which made such payment impossible. We made pious declarations against war in the Kellogg Pact and yet did nothing concrete when Manchuria and Ethiopia were invaded. Our ambassadors reported preparations for war in Germany and Japan long before 1939, yet we continued to sell materials of war. We passed a neutrality act which was more to the benefit of our enemies than our friends; and so, not long thereafter, we had to transfer fifty destroyers to Great Britain. If there was anything definite or settled about our course of conduct, I am unable to see it.

Our floundering and purposeless conduct during this period was due, I believe, to the fact that, as a nation, we did not understand our proper role in the world and had failed to examine and agree upon certain basic convictions which are essential to any policy. Although we had done more than any other nation to develop the scientific technology which destroyed our isolation, we refused to acknowledge the result. We were unable to disentangle our prejudices and superficial dislikes from considerations of major importance to our welfare. Like any person unsure of his convictions, we were timid and reticent in our approach to problems of foreign relations. In short, we were bewildered, and therefore we improvised from day to day.

It is conceivable that, as the leading industrial nation, we might have embarked upon a career of imperialism designed to control the world by force. Germany in fact attempted this solution. But such a policy is alien to all our history and to all our instincts. This policy is so at variance with our very nature that I do not think it could have been followed with success then, nor do I think it can be followed now. On the other hand, I think a system of collective security is not only the best hope for success, but it is also the only one consistent with our political and moral standards of conduct. The principal question that remains in my mind is whether or not we are sufficiently convinced of the necessity of collective security to be willing to make the necessary economic and psychological adjustments.

Many people have assumed that because the House of Representatives, the Senate, and the President have declared for collective security, the job is done. But the establishing of order and the making of peace does not consist merely of a solemn declaration or a well-drafted constitution. The making of peace is a continuing process that must go on from day to day, from year to year, so long as our civilization shall last. Our participation in this process is not just the signing of a charter with a big red seal. It is a daily task, a positive participation in all the details and decisions which together

19

constitute a living and growing policy. What an empty shell the Dumbarton Oaks proposal will be, even if complete agreement is reached at San Francisco, if at the same time, or in the near future, we are unable to agree upon such things as exchange and monetary matters, aviation, the free flow of information, trade barriers, cartels, armaments, and oil, and, I may add, a simple treaty with Mexico on the division of the waters of the Colorado River. Surely we all know by this time that political solidarity in this suffering world is dependent, in the final analysis, upon economic stability.

I do not mean that all of these problems must be solved immediately, and at once, to the satisfaction of all. I do think it very important that the American people, and all people, recognize that these matters are inherently involved in any system of mutual security, and that adjustments and temporary sacrifices must be made. They should be told that the price of peace is high. How high it is, is difficult to estimate, but I am confident that it will not be nearly as high as the price of war. However, unless we are prepared to make these payments for peace we might as well recognize now the futility of Dumbarton Oaks or San Francisco....

Among the prejudices which we must examine, I need mention only a few to illustrate my point. Foremost among them is the anti-British already referred to. I shall not go further into that except to urge most serious consideration as to whether we desire to see the power and influence of the British people destroyed. Is it not true that, in assisting Britain and the Commonwealth of Nations, we were in fact preserving friends who are, in a very real sense, indispensable to our own welfare and the welfare of democratic, freedom-loving peoples everywhere? In this troubled and violent world is it not true that we would feel quite alone in the world if the British Commonwealth of Nations had been subjugated by the tyranny of the Nazis, and its resources directed against us? If that be true, then whose chestnuts did we pull out of the fire?

Another powerful prejudice which has affected our policy, and is vital to our future, is our fear of Russia and communism. Until the revolution in Russia, we had always been on friendly terms with that nation. We had never fought her. We made one very profitable deal with her when we bought Alaska for $7,200,000, and promptly extracted more than $400,000,000 in gold from its mountains. I should say that even the [Chicago] *Tribune* should approve of that kind of a deal. Yet, after the revolution was established by Lenin, we refused to recognize Russia until 1933, the last of the major nations to do so. Moreover, we sent two armed expeditions against her without provocation. When one recalls the birth of our own nation—that in 1776 our forefathers were regarded as being quite radical, by the rest of the world, as Lenin was in 1920—is it not strange that we should be so harsh toward Russia? Since we have been the most successful revolutionary people in history, why are we so critical of others who follow our example? Surely it cannot be because we approved of tsarist Russia with its illiteracy and abject, grinding poverty. As I read history, the Russian experiment in socialism is scarcely more radical, under modern conditions, than the Declaration of Independence was in the days of George III.

I realize that it is not popular even to compare Russia with ourselves, and yet it is necessary to get our ideas straight. When I hear the unbridled and intemperate attacks upon Russia by some of our own people, I cannot help but be troubled. If these people, who profess such profound love and faith for our American system, are sincere in this faith, then why are they so afraid of Russia? I have a feeling that the real reason for their hate and distrust is their lack of faith in our own system.

I believe firmly in the superiority of our democratic capitalistic system, and I desire to preserve it. But we should remember that capitalism is not divine and inviolable. It was not handed down to us by the Almighty; and to question it, or test it, is neither sacrilegious nor treasonable. We have capitalism, and we can defend it, because it has by all standards of decency provided better conditions for more people than any other system on earth. It is of value to us, and is defensible, only so long as it maintains that record.

The highly emotional attacks upon communism and Russia by some of our public orators is an indication of the weakness of their faith in our system. We must demonstrate the superiority of individual initiative under capitalism by our results, by the provision of a superior way of life, not by the violence of our oratory....

Another myth that confuses our attitude toward the other nations is the oft-repeated statement that "we have always been a Santa Claus to the world." The more selfish among us call us "Uncle Sap." The implication from these statements is that we are soft-headed, starry-eyed idealists who know nothing of the realities of this hard-fisted world. It would take too much time to explore fully this thoroughly false prejudice. Its plausibility and the evil of it arise from the confusion of two different ideas. The idea of charity, in regard to which we have been and should continue to be generous, is confused with the idea that we do not know how to look after our own interests in a business deal. One often hears, when on the floor of the Senate, that Great Britain is too smart for us, that they always out-trade us. If we are so stupid, how is it that we are the richest and most powerful nation in the world? Are we Americans willing to admit that all our success is due solely to luck? I am not ready to admit that our people are inferior in brains or ability to the British or to any other people. This whole line of attack upon our policy of co-operation is so silly that it would not warrant attention, except that it is so constantly repeated that it, like Hitler's lies, has found receptive ears among the uninformed. How ridiculous it would be for the United States to refrain from dealing with other nations because we are too silly and stupid to know what we are about....

In conclusion, Mr. President, I repeat that I think it is most urgent that the people of this nation should give sustained and serious consideration to our long-term relations with the other peoples of the world. If we are to have a definite and settled policy for the guidance of our representatives, the people must understand, and must develop convictions regarding that policy. I believe it is dangerous in the highest degree to continue to improvise from day to day in answer to fleeting and superficial emotions.

Since the Senate shares the responsibility for translating into action our foreign policy, it obviously is our duty to assist the people in determining what that policy shall be. By the greatest good fortune, and enormous sacrifice, we have earned a second opportunity to help save the world and ourselves from self-destruction. Twenty-five years ago, the Senate of the United States did not advise the President or the people, and it rejected the treaty then submitted to it. This time I urgently recommend that we advise them both in preparing a treaty which we can accept, so that this troubled world can live again in peace, free from fear of another world cataclysm arising out of the refusal of those who will win this war to accept the responsibility for the peace. Let us seek peace, and let us insure it with all our talents. A better life may then dawn for all mankind.

SENATE ADDRESS,
MARCH 28, 1945

6. *"This Malady of Mankind Is Not a Recent Affliction"*

By July, 1945, the charter of the United Nations was before the Senate for ratification, and Fulbright joined in the debate to offer a scholarly analysis of the nature of sovereignty, and to express his views on the dangers of too much unanimity. The editor has resisted the inclination to trim because the speech was the only one in the Senate debate to plumb deeply into the problems of sovereignty that were embedded in the charter the United States was about to ratify. His comments at the time form the secure framework for his subsequent evaluation of the promise, and limits, of the U.N.

MR. FULBRIGHT: Mr. President, I rise in support of the charter. I have no hesitation in saying that I think it is the most important document that has come before this body, or any other body, during the last twenty-five years.

In fact, I think it ranks in importance alongside the Declaration of Independence, the Constitution of the United States, the Emancipation Proclamation, and the League of Nations, as one of the most important documents in the history of our country.

Before going further, I wish to pay tribute to the wisdom and foresight with which the distinguished Senator from Texas [Mr.

23

Connally], so ably assisted by the members of his committee, has laid the background for the adoption of this charter. Likewise, I think all of us should remember that President Roosevelt was the inspiration for much of the good work which has been done during the past several years in the promotion of the conditions which are favorable to the adoption of the charter. Especially does he deserve credit for having had the good sense to bring into the service of peace the talents of the Members of the Senate. It was the mark of a truly great statesman that he utilized the Members of this body both at Chapultepec and at San Franciso.

The able and distinguished chairman of the Committee on Foreign Relations and the senior Senator from Michigan [Mr. Vandenberg] have explained the charter so thoroughly and so persuasively that I hesitate to say anything further by way of persuasion. Sometimes I wish that they had not been quite so persuasive. A little more spirited debate, a little more opposition on the floor might serve to sharpen our understanding and our appreciation of the true significance of this agreement. I find myself somewhat suspicious of the unanimity with which the charter is apparently received by this body. Practically no measure of real importance has been accepted with such docility by the opposition. Only a few days ago the Reciprocal Trade Act and the Bretton Woods proposals were vigorously opposed, and yet they are integral parts of the general plan and purpose embodied in this charter. It is somewhat difficult for me to understand how senators who opposed those two acts can now accept the San Francisco charter, unless they misconstrue the significance of the charter.

Mr. Lucas of Illinois: The Senator might include the Food Conference also.

Mr. Fulbright: Yes, and the Food Conference. When we recall the great tension and excitement which prevailed in this chamber only a short time ago when we were considering the nomination of a relatively minor official of the government, it is strange indeed to contemplate the contrast in the interest which is evident upon that sort of thing and the consideration of certainly one of the greatest and most important acts that has ever come before this body.

24

Can it be that the senators do not recognize that, if we are accepting this charter in good faith, it means a complete departure from our traditional policy in international relations? Is this docility attributable to the belief that this charter means nothing, that it is an idle gesture? Is it possible that those who steadfastly and sincerely have believed that America can live apart from the world, have changed their minds, or do they think that the present sentiment is only a passing fancy and that as soon as the horrors of war recede into the past we shall return to the exclusiveness of the twenties and thirties? This unanimity disturbs me because I feel that it may not reflect the true convictions of this body.

I have the feeling, Mr. President, that perhaps the charter has been oversold, both to the public and to the Senate. By this I mean that the obligations and responsibilities we are assuming have been played down and have been presented in a negative manner.

Mr. Fulbright: I yield.

Mr. Hatch [of New Mexico]: The Senator said he was disturbed over whether the unanimity of opinion in the Senate might not truly reflect the sentiments of Members of this body. What does the Senator think about the sentiments of the people of the country?

Mr. Fulbright: I think the sentiments of the people of the country are, as was reported earlier today, twenty to one in favor of the charter. I have no doubt in my mind that that is, practically speaking, unanimity.

Mr. Hatch: The lack of opposition to the charter in the Senate then does truly reflect the sentiment of the people of America?

Mr. Fulbright: But I think in 1919 there was likewise quite the same unanimity among the people of the country, but it did not show up in the Senate. I call the Senator's attention to the opposition to the important measures which I have just mentioned, and I think the sentiment of the American people in regard to them is likewise as strongly in favor of them. I am simply questioning the unanimity in the Senate now. I said I was suspicious of it. When I say it is oversold, I mean that the obligations and responsibilities we are assuming have been played down and have been presented in a negative manner. Some discussions of the charter would lead one to believe that it is a thoroughly innocuous organization. Of course, I do not subscribe to that view, but it is of the utmost importance that we have a true understanding of its powers, of the positive things it proposes, as well as of its limitations, if we are to avoid disillusionment about the charter in the future.

It must be clearly understood that this charter does not *ipso facto* prevent war. This United Nations Organization is only the framework within which nations have an opportunity to solve their problems by mutual agreement rather than by force. It is the machinery by which reason may be applied to the adjustment of conflicting interests among nations, but it does not automatically adjust those conflicts. The making of peace is a process continuing from year to year so long as our civilization shall last. This process cannot be reduced to a simple formula. Peace is not a negative, static concept. It is not a tranquil state of felicity and blessedness. It is a positive method of adjusting the endless conflicts inherent in the nature of restless and energetic men. The institution of law based on justice and adaptable to the ever-changing life of man has been such a method in the history of mankind.

Some machinery is essential for this purpose, but of much greater importance than any particular provision or device in the machinery, is what the governments and the peoples of the powerful nations are likely to do during the years ahead. If the peoples of the Big Five nations, and more particularly of the Big Three, are determined to exercise their power with wisdom and foresight in the cause of peace, then this charter is adequate as a vehicle for the transition to a world of law and order. On the other hand, if these peoples refuse to make the transition, the charter will fail and catastrophe will again overtake us. That will not be because of a defect in the charter itself.

So much has been said, Mr. President, about the virtues of the charter that it seems to me it would serve no purpose to repeat them now. I am quite confident that I could not improve upon the exposition of the senior Senator from Texas and the senior Senator from Michigan in that respect. Therefore, I should like to offer a criticism, not as a reason to oppose its adoption or to disparage its immediate value, but simply as a suggestion for consideration during the process of making it work in the years ahead.

The first principle of the organization contained in Article 2 states:

The Organization and its members, in pursuit of the purposes stated in Article 1, shall act in accordance with the following principles:

1. The Organization is based on the principle of the sovereign equality of all its members.

I think this is a very unfortunate principle to begin with. It is unfortunate because it is not true in fact, and the organization itself denies it in the allocation of power in the Security Council. It is unfortunate because it reaffirms our allegiance to the concept of national sovereignty under which our civilization has so closely approached self-destruction. It is unfortunate because, if the absolute sovereignty of the nation-states is rigidly preserved, then it means a denial to begin with of the only evolutionary goal which might eventually give us a rule of law based on justice, in place of the capricious and ruthless rule of force. Finally, it is unfortunate because it has caused some of the most ardent supporters of the charter to assure this nation and the people that there is absolutely no sacrifice of our sovereignty and none is intended, thereby denying by implication the ultimate objective of the organization itself.

The very word "sovereignty" is uncertain and to me objectionable, and much confusion results from its use. To many people it has some mystical connotation in some way associated with divinity. In days gone by when men were slaves, their masters imposed their will by an appeal to the divine right of kings. "Your sovereign by appointment from the All Highest" was the doctrine. My Funk and Wagnalls dictionary says this about "sovereign":

Exercising or possessing supreme jurisdiction or powers; royal. One who possesses supreme authority, especially a person or a determinate body of persons in whom the supreme power of the state is vested; a monarch.

27

Roget's Thesaurus uses these words:

Ruler, potentate, monarch, suzerain, king.

It seems to me most inappropriate for us at this late date to go back to the Middle Ages to find a concept for the first principle of this organization. More than three hundred years ago, our forefathers started the long, hard struggle to destroy the sovereignty of the kings and rulers who enslaved the people and to substitute the rule of law in their place. Sovereignty, according to our democratic principles, resides in the people or community, not in the governments which they create. Only a totalitarian or fascist state is sovereign. The people may create laws to preserve peace among them, and, in fact, peace with freedom has been and can be preserved only by the rule of law. The people may delegate any powers they wish to their representatives, but they do not delegate their sovereignty to their government.

Ever since men have first banded together to form democratic communities, they have delegated powers to govern to various institutions—tribal, municipal, and national. Today, within these United States the community of citizens has delegated different powers to the townships, the municipalities, the counties, the states, and to the nation. These delegations do not exhaust the powers of the people, as the Constitution expressly recognizes in the reservation to the people of all powers not specifically granted. Hence it is clear that the people of this nation, and of all democratic nations, have not only the power, but also, one may say, the duty to create by additional delegation an institution adequate to preserve their integrity and freedom.

This United Nations charter is an agreement among governments, not peoples. When it states that the first principle is the sovereign equality of its members, it does not state the facts as they exist. Does anyone believe that the states of Nicaragua and Luxembourg, within the charter or without the charter, are equal to Russia or the United States? The people of the countries as individuals may be equal before the law, but there is no established international law, and the agreement does not relate to people. Equality alone has no meaning.

It has meaning only in the sense of equality under the law or before God. The document itself recognizes the inequality of these so-called sovereignties by the unequal allocation of power and responsibility to the Big Five. I do not complain of this. It is a necessary recognition of the world as it is. I complain only of the deception resulting from the first principle as expressed.

The most serious consequence of the use of this unfortunate word is the probability that it fortifies and revitalizes the extreme nationalism which is quite inconsistent with the establishment of rules of conduct for all nations. I do not expect the nations to disavow their nationalism under the circumstances as they exist in the world today. There is entirely too much suspicion and distrust. It is for that reason that I do not complain of the use of the veto power or the organization of the Security Council at this time. But it does seem to me that the ultimate objective of international co-operation and peace necessarily involves the development of rules of conduct universally accepted and enforceable. Any rules or laws universally accepted and enforceable are inconsistent with the absolute sovereignty of present-day nations.

This malady of mankind is not a recent affliction. More than two hundred and fifty years ago, in 1693, William Penn, who gave us the great Commonwealth of Pennsylvania, was deeply concerned over the problem of war. He recognized at that early date that the sovereignty of independent states was one of the principal obstacles to peace. His answer to the objection that such states would never give up their sovereignty is worth our consideration. He said that a state may remain as sovereign as ever at home, which surely is all the unlimited power any state should want to have; for indeed does not a demand for sovereignty abroad simply mean sovereignty over another state that itself wishes to be sovereign? In the course of his exposition, Penn made a statement which might well be quoted:

So that the sovereignties are as they were, for none of them have now any sovereignty over one another. And if this be called a lessening of their power, it must be only because the great fish can no longer eat up the little ones, and that each sovereignty is equally defended from injuries, and disabled from committing them.

If this be true—and I think it is—the only rational excuse for insisting upon absolute sovereignty must be that the big fish has designs upon some little fish. If this nation does not have such designs, it is pure stupidity to encourage the designs of others.

Just one hundred years after Penn, Immanuel Kant, one of the greatest thinkers of all time, had this to say about sovereignty in his "Essay on Perpetual Peace":

There is no intelligible meaning in the idea of the law of nations as giving a right to make war; for that must be a right to decide what is just, not in accordance with universal, external laws limiting the freedom of each individual, but by means of one-sided maxims applied by force. We must then understand by this that men of such ways of thinking are quite justly served when they destroy one another, and thus find perpetual peace in the wide grave which covers all the abominations of acts of violence as well as the authors of such deeds. For states, in their relation to one another, there can be, according to reason, no other way of advancing from that lawless condition which unceasing war implies, than by giving up their savage lawless freedom, just as individual men have done, and yielding to the coercion of public laws. Thus they can form a state of nations, one, too, which will be ever-increasing and would finally embrace all the peoples of the earth.

In 1795, when Kant wrote, war was incomparably less destructive than it is today, yet he recognized its evil potentialities, and he clearly expressed the only principle by which war may be eliminated. That principle is no less valid today than it was a hundred and fifty years ago. The necessity for its application, however, has become infinitely more urgent.

I cannot help but think that the principal reason for the unexpected approval in certain quarters of the charter may have been induced by the assurance which some proponents have made that we sacrifice none of our American sovereignty. This implies that there will be no change in the *status quo,* that we shall have peace without paying anything for it.

There is confusion of thought about this sacrifice of sovereignty. In truth, we would not sacrifice anything by delegating authority to

30

an organization even more powerful than the one herein contemplated.

The question is not one of surrendering or sacrificing national sovereignty. It is not a negative action and does not involve giving up something we already have. The objective is positive; it is the creating of something we do not have. It is the acquisition of a power for the lack of which we and the world have narrowly missed domination by the most ruthless forces the world has ever seen.

The people of the United States created their government under law, for the purpose of promoting tranquillity among themselves and protection against aggressive enemies. They exercised their sovereignty in adopting the Constitution and creating the federal government. For more than a century and a quarter, this was an effective system. Now within twenty-five years they have, much against their will and in spite of all they could do, been involved in two wars. The lesson of this war is, I believe, clear: namely, that as a civilized society of free men we cannot survive another world war. The destructive power of science is simply too great. The conclusion is that our government cannot longer fulfil completely the purpose for which it was created. It can no longer protect our people from the disastrous effects of war, even though victorious in the warfare itself. Therefore, it is entirely appropriate, in fact it is essential, that our people consider the delegation of power to some other and higher organization which is reasonably designed to perform the functions which this government cannot perform. This we shall do by the acceptance of this charter and in the progressive building of the United Nations Organization into an effective system of law and order. In creating a more effective instrumentality to protect the people from war and destruction, how can it possibly be said to be the surrender of sovereignty or of anything else? It is not a surrender. It is the acquisition of a power previously nonexistent. Just as we have acquired new powers through machines, we must acquire new powers through political organization. In truth, our real purpose is the adjustment of our governmental machinery to the consequences of the machine tool, radio, the airplane, the robomb, and the submarine.

Except for these machines there would not be the urgent necessity which now faces us for a United Nations Organizations.

The one error which we must not, above all others, make is to assume that this organization is the final word. On the contrary, it is certain to be merely the first modest and hesitant step, sufficient to point the direction, but utterly inadequate to achieve the goal of lasting peace. Like the confederation of the thirteen colonies, it will serve to point the way, to delineate the problems; but it will not solve them. It will be a fatal error if we do not follow the example of our founding fathers and be prepared and willing to strengthen this organization so that eventually a body of laws may be developed to keep the peace. We are entering a new field. It is a transitional period, and we must be wise and alert to see that the movement toward the goal is sure and certain. The penalty for failure is likely to be the destruction of everything we value as civilized human beings....

In conclusion, Mr. President, I recognize that we are striking out into new and unfamiliar territory. We are assuming great responsibilities, and there will be unforeseen difficulties. There can be no guarantee of success. Our hope lies in the good sense and the understanding of our people as to the nature of the process and of the goal to be achieved. We must not be impatient. It took countless centuries for us to develop rules of conduct first for the families, then for the tribes, villages, cities, provinces, principalities, and nation-states. The destructiveness of modern science has increased the urgency for speeding up the process of extending rules of law throughout the world, but so has our ability to respond been accelerated.

Within the short space of five years this nation has come to recognize the utter futility and absurdity of passive detachment from the affairs of the world. Regardless of the skeptics, who think people never learn from experience, I believe our people now recognize that neutrality and nonintervention constitute a disastrous foreign policy. In the quest for new principles to guide us, I am confident that eventually we shall see that absolute national sovereignty is an obsolete and dangerous principle, and that a system of law and justice is the only method of maintaining peace. The organization we are now creating is the first step in that direction. The court and the executive have been provided. Surely the senseless and tragic sacrifices of this war are sufficient to induce us to create the rules of law.

With the adoption of this charter, together with the measures to which I have previously referred, we have fashioned the tools with which our President, with our continuing help, should be able to create a more decent and a happier world for ourselves, our children, and the suffering and bewildered peoples of the world.

SENATE ADDRESS,
JULY 23, 1945

Chapter Two

THE TRUMAN ERA

---

7. The Bomb: "It Cannot Be Kept a Secret"

The year 1945 brought the end of a war, the death of a President, and the birth, on August 6, of a bomb that burned brighter than a thousand suns. Of all Fulbright's speeches, few are more thoughtful or prescient than his address on the meaning of Hiroshima. In prose as straightforward and unadorned as homespun, the Senator from Arkansas spelled out the hard truths to a country suddenly "exposed at close quarters to the violent forces of a turbulent world." He warned that other nations could develop the bomb in three to five years (the figure turned out to be four) and that lacking effective control, our own cleverness in science would force us to "live underground with the moles." The text of the address that follows is virtually complete; it could be given today with only minor emendations.

Science has so changed the world that the ancient international political order is intolerable. The conflict in a world united by science and separated by outworn political barriers will continue either until science destroys man, or man destroys that archaic political system. In July, after months of preparation and weeks of debate, we adopted the United Nations charter. We thought we had taken quite a large step toward the creation of an effective political system for the maintenance of a stable and peaceful world. Although some of us thought the charter, as adopted, inadequate to maintain a lasting peace, we believed there would be sufficient time to improve it later on. At least, the United States had joined it, and there seemed to be that universal support which was lacking in the creation of the League of Nations. But our satisfaction was short-lived. Within a few days of the adoption of the charter, the atomic bomb not only blasted the Japanese into submission, but also blasted our confidence in the charter. Since then we have felt a profound uneasiness of fear of the unknown. Like primitive man in the darkness of the caves and jungles, we, too, are faced with elemental and infinite forces which we do not understand, forces which threaten to snuff out our lives as one does a candle between the fingers. We are doubtful of our ability to control this terrifying new force. We have lost our bearings and are unsure of our future.

Ten years ago, it was unthinkable that human beings could possibly be as savage and as completely immoral, according to Christian ethics, as the Germans have proved to be. We have had an ugly but powerful demonstration at Belsen, Buchenwald, Dachau, and many other extermination camps, of what lies beneath that thin crust of civilization so laboriously acquired by man through countless centuries of struggle up from the jungle. Although we talk bravely about our prowess, we in the United States are worried in our hearts. Like children who have lost their parents, we have lost, since the airplane and the rocket bomb, the protection of two great oceans. We are now exposed at close quarters to the violent forces of a turbulent world. Our confidence in our own invincibility and our faith in the solicitude of a beneficent providence have been shaken by the atomic bomb.

The incredible scientific progress of the last few decades induced in many people, besides the Germans, a certain arrogance and a feeling of superiority which seemed to make them unconscious of moral obligations to other men. Few people were bothered about the fate of the peoples of other lands. "Let them stew in their own juice" was the common slogan. They were great, they were powerful, they could take care of themselves, and, therefore, they reasoned they

35

must be good. But the cleverness of man has now brought into the world a power of destruction against which there is no defense. We are troubled by a feeling of helplessness. We are beginning to take a greater interest in our fellow human beings. Now we wonder if those people who concerned us so little are good people. We hope that they are and that they will not use the bomb against us first. On every hand, this fear, amounting almost to hysteria, causes otherwise rational men to act in strange ways and to utter the grossest absurdities. Men react in strange and unpredictable ways when afraid.

Even before the affair of Hiroshima, we were unpredictable in our own policy. We declared great principles on occasions, but we faltered in carrying them out. In September, 1943, by an overwhelming vote, the House of Representatives declared that it favored the creation of appropriate international machinery with power adequate to establish and maintain a just and lasting peace, but we have wavered in our path toward this objective. Our principles surely include the support, wherever possible, of liberal democratic governments and the creation of a multilateral organization to preserve peace. What have we done?

We went down the line, with all our strength, for Argentina under Perón, at San Francisco. We insisted upon exclusive jurisdiction over conquered bases in the Pacific, thereby setting the precedent for similar demands from Russia. In the drafting of the charter, we supported the concept of national sovereignty as the first principle, and we defended the veto power in the Council, both inconsistent with the ultimate purpose of the United Nations Organization.

In spite of our professed intention to build an organization with adequate power, we have done little to achieve that end. Instead, we have already fallen to quarreling with Russia, like two big dogs chewing on a bone. While I am sure the alleged stubbornness and bad manners of the Russian diplomats are irritating, it should not be decisive of policy. To be tough, or to be soft, toward a nation is not a policy. Our objectives must be clear and our principles must be adhered to if we are ever to have a policy. Our policy should not be merely to love or to hate Russia or any other people; it should be to obtain their assistance in the creation of a bona fide organization

36

based upon law, and with force and vitality in its system. The control of the atomic bomb, coupled with important strengthening of the organization's powers, could be that vitality.

Inconsistencies between our declared policies and our actions indicate the confusion in our minds. We undertook to play a large role in the occupation and pacification of the conquered nations, but we precipitately withdraw our armed forces and demobilize even before the peace treaties are signed. One may wonder: Are we, or are we not, going to use our influence and play a leading role in world affairs?

On the subject of the disposition of the atomic bomb, there is similar inconsistency and confusion as to the proper course. A few have chosen, apparently, to ignore its significance. They still talk of armies and navies, ships and planes, just as if nothing important had happened. They seek refuge in the old saw that after every discovery of offensive weapons, a defense has been developed. They discount the advice of the physicists who tell us that they are unable even to imagine a defense to the ruthless use of such power....

I cannot imagine how a nation can maintain constantly, and indefinitely, an effective defense against a sudden attack without warning. I do not believe there is a defense against total destruction inflicted instantaneously.

There are others who say that the bomb is a secret and that we must keep it for our own protection and for the peace of the world. We paid for it; we found it; why shouldn't we keep it? And besides we are good people; we should be trusted for the good of mankind. These ideas, which you may think superficial and worthy of little notice, are nevertheless held by many people, some with considerable influence, and cannot be dismissed as being of little consequence. Such views are the natural reactions of unsophisticated people: They are easily understood; they are simple; they are popular; and they are in accord with our traditional isolationism. They require no mental effort and no break with the past. They give one a feeling of security. It is the same basic philosophy that led us to believe that we were so sufficient that we could live apart from the world, that we, all by ourselves, had created a rich, comfortable life and should not be disturbed in our enjoyment of it by concern over the troubles of other peoples in China, Spain, Ethiopia, or Poland.

In opposition to this popular conception, we have the word of the scientists themselves, practically all of them, that there is nothing secret about the bomb except the industrial process of manufacture, and that any one of several industrial nations probably can produce bombs in from three to five years. Further, it is common knowledge that the scientists of many nations, men and women from Italy, Germany, Hungary, Denmark, and England, to mention only a few, contributed to the production of the atomic bomb. This discovery is ours only in a limited sense. Our money would have been fruitless without the brains of others. But even if we had found it by our efforts alone, is it possible that we regard this cosmic discovery as a mere chattel for our personal use? To those good citizens who think the peoples of the world should trust us to use the bomb to protect them, I can only say that I am sure those other peoples disagree. It is already clear that the Russians have some doubts about the stability and security of such a world. More than words will be necessary to convince them. We should ask ourselves: Would we be content to entrust our lives and fortunes to the Russians if they alone had the atomic bomb?

I agree that we have, on the whole, been relatively peaceful and nonaggressive people, but there is no guarantee that we shall remain so. In fact, I have heard of some people who advocate our immediate attack upon potential enemies, and one prominent general recently asserted publicly, in no uncertain terms, that a third war is inevitable. With whom is it inevitable? we may well ask. I do agree that such foolish talk is calculated better than anything I know to induce another war. But, regardless of these considerations, a peaceful and decent society has never been, and is not likely in the near future to be, founded solely upon the assurances of individuals or the good will of peoples. Throughout the long and troubled history of mankind, the only organizations which have been successful in providing security for human beings have been based upon law. It seems clear to me, therefore, that the only possibility for a decent and peaceful

38

world lies in the adoption of laws of universal application and sanctioned by the moral and physical force of the civilized world.

The discovery and use of atomic energy has dramatized in a highly effective manner a fact that many observers had already sensed. That fact is the fundamental disequilibrium that has gradually grown up between the natural sciences and the art of government. Regrettable as the use of the atomic bomb may have been in the opinion of some people, it may well be that without the awful warning of Hiroshima the world might have stumbled along into the atomic age without any realization of its arrival, and therefore without the shock necessary to arouse it to a realization of the danger, and compel action before it is too late. Hiroshima provided that shock, and I do not think it is too late. There is the question of whether or not we have the intelligence and courage to adopt the proper means of control within the short time at our disposal. In other words, can we bring back into balance the art of government and natural science? Can we readjust the disequilibrium which has been growing for approximately one hundred and seventy years?

The last significant advance in the art of government occurred in the era of the American and French Revolutions. Democratic representative government and the federal principle for the association of states were great and momentous political events, bringing to a close in vast areas of the world the oppression and slavery of feudalism. With the release of human beings from bondage, a great surge of energy and inventiveness brought on the industrial revolution and the rise of modern science. Throughout these one hundred and seventy years, with ever-increasing rapidity, we have advanced from one scientific miracle to another: from the wagon to the railway, the automobile, the airplane, and the rocket ship; from sailing vessels to submarines; from smoke signals to radio and radar; from buckeyes to penicillin; from foot power to electricity and atomic energy. The advance has been at a dizzy pace in science, but can any of us recall during that entire period a truly significant advance in the art of government?

It is true that during this period the petty German principalities and the autonomous Italian states were welded into large nations.

Russia exchanged the absolutism of the tsars for the dictatorship of Stalin, but it is scarcely a novel principle of government. Throughout this period, no important step for the control of independent sovereign states was adopted, nor any machinery seriously considered, except the League of Nations. On the contrary, nationalism and the principle of absolute national sovereignty were enormously enhanced in every land. During this period when science was rapidly reducing the world to a small community and making it interdependent economically and socially, nothing whatever occurred politically to compensate for this change. In a very real sense, I think it may be said that both world wars were the logical consequence of this disequilibrium.

It should not require an extended argument to persuade anyone that something is seriously wrong with our world order. Two world wars within a quarter-century should be sufficient proof. Likewise, it should be clear that the trouble is the lack of any law or rules of conduct, agreed upon and binding, as among all nations. This void in the international field must be filled either by reason and agreement or by force, as attempted by the Germans. The alternative to a system of law for the settlement of differences is constantly recurring warfare of rapidly increasing destructiveness. Peace and order have rarely, if ever, been achieved by good will alone. In all ages, rules of conduct accepted by all and superior to all have been the indispensable basis for a decent and peaceful society.

To me, it seems clear that the medieval political status under which the world operates is obsolete, and that it must be discarded just as we discarded the horse and buggy, not overnight, but by stages as we develop the appropriate machinery. We have, in a very limited sense, already begun the process in the creation of the United Nations Organization. But this organization provides us only with a skeleton machinery, without life and vitality. Before it can become an effective instrumentality, it must be given more definite and certain powers. The greatest defect of the charter, which was quite clear at the time of its adoption, is the requirement of unanimity of the five big powers on all matters of importance. This rule of unanimity is but another way of saying that we shall go along and abide by the rules if it suits us in each particular instance. As a practical matter, it is a hopeless principle for any governmental organization. The League of Nations demonstrated its weakness, and more recently the London Conference of Foreign Ministers has shown us what to expect from its operation. I know of no instance in history in which it has been effective. At the time of San Francisco this requirement was apparently indispensable to obtaining agreement.

However, since the atomic bomb, it may well be that all the nations will agree that, at least in the field of armaments and especially the production of atomic weapons, a complete and definite power to inspect and control throughout the world should be given the organization. This power should be carefully limited, but within its proper limits it must be positive and complete, or there can be no confidence in its efficacy. The scientists who are familiar with the theory and techniques of nuclear physics should act as the agents of the organization to maintain a continuous system of inspection and reporting. By an extensive system of exchange of students and of industrial scientists, together with unrestricted access to industrial records of various kinds, it should be possible to know of any serious effort to evade the rules pertaining to atomic weapons.

I feel very strongly that the path of wisdom is not secretiveness and suspicion, but is the widest possible dissemination of scientific knowledge, coupled with an efficient system of control. If many people in all advanced nations know something about nuclear physics, it will be difficult to prepare secretly for an aggressive attack upon an unsuspecting neighbor. The knowledge will spread through many channels. On the other hand, in an atmosphere of suspicion and secrecy each nation naturally and inevitably will suspect every other nation of preparing an attack, and sooner or later someone will no longer endure the suspense of impending annihilation.

I do not pretend to be qualified to describe to you the exact nature of regulations which would be adequate to insure the world against the possibility of a sudden devastating atomic-bomb attack by some future Hitler. The details of such rules are for the scientists themselves. One problem is to reconcile legitimate research and use of atomic energy with the prevention of illegitimate production for aggressive purposes. The greatest difficulty is, I believe, not in the technical problem, but in the problem of authority for the agents of the United Nations to enter and inspect as a matter of right. The great obstacle to this step is the ancient and antiquated concept of sovereignty. The absolute sovereignty of nations is utterly inconsistent with the establishment among nations of any laws with sufficient force to give confidence in their effectiveness to the peoples of the earth. For centuries, treaties and compacts have been made among nations, but whenever a nation believes its vital interests are threatened, it always ignores the treaty. We have pretended that treaties are binding, but at the same time we have refused to recognize any power superior to the independent sovereign state. There is an inconsistency in the position which has never been solved. The only solution that I can conceive of is the recognition, by all nations, that at last the time has arrived for all of us to delegate certain and definite powers over armaments to the United Nations Organization. Safeguards and limitations should be carefully worked out and agreed upon. Disputes of any kind relating to the subject should be under the compulsory jurisdiction of the international court, and every nation, and every individual in every nation, must be subject to the verdict of the court. If a nation, or individuals within a nation, should prove to be recalcitrant, then the full power of the organization collectively and severally should be pledged to the enforcement of the judgment.

To those who object that this is setting up a world government, I can only reply that, call it what you will, there is no other principle with the slightest chance of success in the control of the atomic bomb. All other methods of controlling armaments and preventing wars have been tried. It is entirely vain to say that we shall renounce the use of the bomb or that we shall outlaw it by treaty. The very words "to outlaw" as between sovereign nations are a fraud. There is no law in the real sense between sovereign nations, and it is fallacious to speak of outlawing any practice they may believe to be to their advantage to use. It is just barely possible that atomic power is so deadly that all people will be afraid to use it, but this is a very faint hope upon which to erect a decent and peaceful world. If it

42

is so deadly, why should we object to a strict regulation of it by the United Nations Organization?

To those Americans who find so much satisfaction in the thought that we alone have the bomb and at least for three to five years no other will have it, I repeat that the scientists are unanimous in the opinion that the principles are not secret and that the industrial know-how cannot be kept a secret for long. In addition, they should ponder the physical organization of our industry and the location of our population. Our great cities, which contain a third of our population and a much greater percentage of our industry, are perfect targets for atomic bombs. The twenty largest metropolitan areas contain forty million people. In one night of carefully planned attack without warning we would be paralyzed. Compared to the dispersion of Russian industry and population, we are infinitely more vulnerable. It is not so much the ability to make great quantities of the bombs above an essential minimum that would count in an atomic war; rather is it the ruthlessness and the will to attack first, without provocation, that would be decisive. Does anyone believe that America, with its history of reluctance to make war, with its aversion to militarism, will be the first to attack? The very qualities which inspire our devotion to this country are the ones which make it the most vulnerable in a war of atomic bombs.

One of the most desirable and attractive qualities of these United States, before this war, was the freedom and openhandedness, the easy hospitality of the people, both socially and commercially. Having been permitted to grow to maturity without outside interference, and with no hereditary enemies, we were not a suspicious people. I, for one, would dislike to see this quality destroyed. Not only does it make life agreeable, but, if it can be preserved without danger to our security, I believe it will induce, in time, a reciprocal trust and friendliness in others. If we are suspicious and distrustful of others, we must expect the same in return, and that road leads to trouble. I recognize that it is difficult for us to forsake any ancient political custom or practice, because we associate those practices with happier days. Two characteristics of our people have been the alacrity with which we adopt and apply, for the comfort and happiness of our citizens, the new discoveries of science, and at the same time the stubborn reluctance with which we entertain new ideas in politics.

I, for one, would rather adopt a new idea in politics than risk vaporization by an atom bomb or, as some have suggested, spend the remainder of my days in the subterranean recesses of the earth. What a curious picture it is to find man, *homo sapiens,* of divine origin, we are told, seriously considering going underground to escape the consequences of his own folly. With a little wisdom and foresight, surely it is not yet necessary to forsake life in the fresh air and in the warmth of the sunlight. What a paradox if our own cleverness in science should force us to live underground with the moles!

The hope for America, and for the world, does not lie along the road of secret methods of destruction or more and bigger armaments. I do not suggest disarmament in the world as it is now constituted. The only hope lies in the application to all men of the principles of law, which are the only principles that have ever brought peace to mankind....

A great poet, many years ago, described our present opportunity in these fitting words:

> There is a tide in the affairs of men,
> Which, taken at the flood, leads on to fortune;
>
> .   .   .   .
>
> On such a full sea are we now afloat;
> And we must take the current when it serves,
> Or lose our venture.

ADDRESS BEFORE THE FOREIGN POLICY ASSOCIATION IN NEW YORK CITY, OCTOBER 20, 1945

8. *The Fulbright Scholarships*

The few phrases that follow launched a thousand scholarships— about forty-five thousand as of 1962—and represent one of Fulbright's most felicitous contributions as a legislator. The idea of the

44

student-exchange was born of the Senator's own experience as a Rhodes scholar and came to fruition through his skill as a parliamentarian. Fulbright sensed in 1945 that there was a desire to do something concrete to achieve international amity and also that Congress was reluctant to draw on treasury funds. His idea was to finance a student-exchange program through foreign credits frozen abroad as a result of sales of military surplus—thus combining virtue and thrift in a single package. By adroit maneuver, he obtained Senate approval by bringing the bill up as a routine measure when he knew that the chief opponent of the idea, the late Kenneth McKellar of Tennessee, was off the floor. The strategy worked, and learning has profited since. Fulbright maintained his interest in the program, and quietly aided its expansion until some forty countries became partners in an international campus that graduates about four thousand five hundred new alumni each year.

Mr. FULBRIGHT: Mr. President, I ask unanimous consent to introduce a bill, for reference to the Committee on Military Affairs, authorizing the use of credits established abroad for the promotion of international good will through the exchange of students in the fields of education, culture, and science.

Mr. President, the enactment of this bill will assure that at least a part of the returns from the sale of our surplus materials to foreign countries will accrue to the interest of America. Most of the nations desiring to purchase our trucks, railroad equipment, and so forth, abroad, do not have American dollars or even the goods to pay, and it will, therefore, be necessary for our government to establish credits for this purpose. These debts may never be paid in full and might, like the war debts after World War I, become a source of irritation between nations and prevent the orderly re-establishment of trade and commerce and the strengthening of our political relations with other countries.

I do not mean that other countries have any plans to try to cheat our country. It is merely a recognition of the facts as they exist today with regard to the international exchange and ability to make settlements as between nations.

If this bill is approved, the funds will be utilized to exchange students, create a better understanding of our mutual problems, and promote friendly relations, while avoiding possible ill feeling between nations resulting from inability to meet obligations set up in accordance with traditional methods.

The Surplus Property Administrator has recently indicated that the disposal of surplus property abroad would be placed under the jurisdiction of the Secretary of State, to assure conformity to American foreign policies. The disposition of such funds as may be allocated for this educational fund as proposed in this bill will be in accord with such regulations as may be prescribed by the Secretary of State.

This bill also provides that expenditures shall be made in accordance with the program to be initiated under the Social and Economic Council of the United Nations, under which the proposed educational and cultural organization of the United Nations will be established under the United Nations charter, so as to co-ordinate all educational activities in the international field.

A precedent for this program may be found in our action with regard to the indemnity paid this country as a result of the Boxer Rebellion in China in July, 1900. By the protocol of September 7, 1901, an indemnity of $333,000,000 was imposed upon China, payable to those countries who were involved in the Boxer Rebellion in the preceding year. Of this amount the United States had claimed $25,000,000. This proved more than adequate to indemnify the claims of nationals of the United States, and in 1908 approximately ten million dollars was returned to the Chinese government. The Chinese government placed the money in a trust fund for the education of Chinese youth in China and in the United States. The balance of the amount due, slightly over $6,000,000, was remitted by the United States in 1924. These remunerations were made by Senate Joint Resolution 23, May 25, 1908, and House Joint Resolution 248, May 1, 1924.

This act of friendship has had a very great influence in the promotion of the good will and friendly relations that have prevailed between the people of America and the Chinese. I do not think that one can deny that the exchange of students has been one of the most successful of our international policies. The foresight of our government, nearly fifty years ago, has paid great dividends in our relations with the people of Asia. The good will and understanding created by the exchange of students has been our greatest bulwark against unfriendly criticism of our policies in the Far East. Many students of the Chinese and other Asiatic peoples agree that our enlightened attitude toward China was our greatest defense to the propaganda of the Japanese in recent years and is to a great extent accountable for the loyalty of these people during the recent war. I think it is reasonable to assume that, if a similar program can be intelligently administered among the several nations contemplated by this bill, a great contribution will have been made to the future peace of the world.

THE PRESIDENT *pro tempore:* Without objection, the bill introduced by the Senator from Arkansas will be received and referred as requested.

SENATE ADDRESS
SEPTEMBER 27, 1945

9. *The Cold War Begins: "Is It the Purpose of Russia to Dominate the World?"*

The Second World War was scarcely over before the first tentative warnings of a new kind of conflict dissolved the hopes for cooperation with the Soviet Union. The expansionist thrust of Stalinist Russia was evident in Eastern Europe and in Iran and Greece. Sooner than most, Fulbright saw the outlines of the cold war; this, his first speech on the postwar Soviet threat, came at a time when many Americans still cherished the wishful illusion that East and West could remain warm allies. Some, like Henry A. Wallace, then Truman's Secretary of Commerce, blamed the West for the discord. (Wallace's differences with Truman led to his resignation in September, 1946.) But Fulbright took the view that he has maintained

47

since in his sober appeal to resist appeasement while remaining ready to negotiate.

I realize that it is extremely difficult to be objective and judicious in one's analysis of the motives and actions of a great power like Russia. There is ever present the danger that one's ignorance of the facts or prejudices will distort one's judgment. We all know that Russia was badly treated after the First World War and had some justification for resentment toward the Western democracies. We also know that without these same democracies she could not have saved herself from the domination of the Nazis. That old score, it seems to me, has been washed out with blood and treasure and is no longer a valid reason for suspicion or antagonism.

During the past several months the question which haunts us most persistently is: Is it the purpose of Russia to dominate the world through a subtle combination of infiltration and force, or is she only seeking security? She persuaded us that in the dismemberment of Poland she sought only security. But can we believe that her security requires the domination of Trieste, Iran, Tripoli, and Manchuria? Since 1939, according to a recent article by Mr. William Henry Chamberlin, Russia has annexed 273,947 square miles of territory containing more than twenty-four million people. In addition, he lists twelve other nations and areas with a population of one hundred and sixty-five million which she controls. These are facts, not theories, and are persuasive as to the purposes which inspire her policy. Her recent actions in Iran, in which for the first time in a matter of major importance she positively violated a definite, unequivocal agreement, are indicative of her increasing boldness and determination in challenging the United Nations and her former allies. While the Security Council had its say, it is also evident that Russia did not retire from Iran without compensation.

As I said before, it is not that any particular act of Russia has affected our confidence in her purposes; it is the cumulative effect of many acts: her ruthless stripping of Manchuria; her extravagant demands of reparations from Italy and for bases in Tripoli and the Dardanelles; the annexation of the Baltic states and Polish territory;

48

the violation of her pledges to establish free governments in the Balkans; and, last but not least, her refusal to permit official representatives or citizens of her former allies to enter any of these territories under her control, except under the most stringent restrictions. By imposing communism by force upon such countries as Yugoslavia and Romania, she has gone far beyond her agreement with her allies.

These overt actions of Russia, coupled with the speeches of her leaders, in which they do not deign even to mention the contributions of her former allies, are scarcely designed to inspire confidence in her self-restraint. The recent rejection of Secretary Byrnes's proposal for a twenty-five-year alliance is not consistent with a policy of security only. I recognize that, since I have no inside information about the long range plans of Stalin or the Politburo, my views are necessarily speculative. I am sure that these conclusions based upon rapidly changing events are necessarily tentative in nature. With the qualifications understood, I may venture the opinion that Russia's policy seems to partake of both opportunism and fanaticism. Her traditional and, to a considerable degree, her legitimate desire for warm-water ports may be said to be the objective of her opportunists. They are simply taking advantage of the universal confusion and Anglo-American indecision to advance these ancient interests.

On the other hand, there are leaders in Russia who apparently believe that they have a sacred mission to save the world from what they assert is the decadence of the capitalist democracies. The opportunists, as such, are not so dangerous, but every success they achieve enhances the fanaticism of the zealots and fortifies their conviction that only communism can bring peace and prosperity to the world. It is characteristic of all authoritarian systems that they identify their regimes with God and the highest moral precepts. The Nazis and the Japanese pursued this course successfully with their own people. Crusading communism appears now to be on the march. As one sage so aptly put it, "The world has suffered more from the errors of the good than from the crimes of the wicked." No wars have been more marked by passionate hatred than the wars between Christian sects,

49

both sides alike proclaiming a mission of righteousness and mercy and proclaiming it, moreover, with deep sincerity. It is the religion of the state, of the party, the pagan principle that the individual is nothing and the party everything, that is the real danger to our Western Christian civilization. If, as some assert, Russia is interested simply in a higher standard of living and security for her people, there is little cause for alarm, but if she is intent upon saving our souls, there can be no limit to her aggression or to her ruthlessness.

The crucial question for all of us who have some responsibility in these matters is: What should we do to keep the bounds of reason and safety for ourselves and Christendom? That, I submit, is not an easy query to answer. Before venturing an opinion on that question, may I first suggest that we have made some mistakes and neglected some of our responsibilities to the end that, in a negative way, we have contributed to the aggressive forces within Russia....

The one bright spot in our actions in recent months is the Lilienthal Committee report on the control of atomic energy. This report exemplifies what I believe to be the proper approach for an effective foreign policy. It is well reasoned, clear, and, above all, it presents a positive and definite proposal for action. If the report is accepted by Russia, it will be the most important step forward since the end of the war. On the other hand, a rejection of the proposal by Russia will provide a very significant clue as to her future policy, and we should shape our own policy accordingly.

It is my own feeling that until the appearance of this report our policy was inclined to be negative and indecisive. I would suggest to our government that after a thorough study we attempt to formulate equally concrete proposals with regard to the infiltration and expansion of Russia in Europe, the Middle East, and the Far East. We, of course, must be just in our position. I think certainly that we should give recognition to her need for adequate warm-water ports and a fair and equitable share in such essential commodities as the oil of the Middle East. It would be far more sensible if we should, in co-operation with the other nations concerned, make positive and, I might say, generous proposals to Russia than to have her continue to gnaw away at the *status quo* in defiance of the principles of the United Nations.

For example, I think we should lend our influence to the procurement of complete freedom for Russia in the use of the Dardanelles, but that we should oppose exclusive military domination by Russia of that waterway. It seems to me that the United Nations might well be used in this and other instances to guarantee free and equal use by all nations. The process of subjecting other strategic areas should be in accord with the development of confidence in the power of the organization. Like disarmament, it cannot effectively be brought about haphazardly, but only in accord with a well-planned agreement and after the United Nations Organization has warranted the respect of the world.

I need not go into all the specific problems which may be treated in a manner similar to atomic energy, of which I think there are several. The principal point I wish to emphasize is the positive, affirmative character of the proposal. Our government has so often apparently had no positive program and has been in the position of quibbling and quarreling with, but finally giving in to, the demands of Russia. It does not necessarily mean that we should never compromise our views in any specific instance, but it does mean that we should be contributing direction and leadership, rather than merely going along or obstructing.

There is one further observation that I should like to make regarding a common misconception as to our policy. There grew up after the last war the belief that our policy is peace at any price. I think Hitler believed this to be our policy and relied upon it when he undertook to overrun all of Europe. Our present reluctance to maintain an army and navy, together with the determined and articulate band of irreconcilable isolationists in our midst, may revive this belief. I do not think this country really believes in such a policy, and it is highly important that all the world know that, while we do not seek war, yet we are willing and able to fight whenever we believe any power threatens the right and opportunity of men to live as free individuals under a government of their own choice.

This does not mean that we intend to concern ourselves with every local quarrel in every part of the world. There is, and can be, no automatic rule of thumb that can tell us when the point is reached where our security and the security of all free peoples is endangered by the persistent expansion of any power. Nevertheless, we know that such a point has been reached in the past, and it can be reached in the future, and, if and when that time arrives, this nation must and will resist with all its power. In any case of difference of opinion as to rights, whether it be in domestic or foreign affairs, if one party to the controversy is committed in advance to the principle of surrender rather than resistance in case of a deadlock, there is little chance of an equitable settlement. I think, therefore, that a basic principle of our foreign policy must be that there is a point beyond which we cannot, in justice to ourselves and to the civilization of which we are the heir, permit any nation to expand without offering resistance by force.

ADDRESS BEFORE A JOINT MEETING OF THE
AMERICAN ACADEMY OF ARTS AND LETTERS
AND THE NATIONAL INSTITUTE OF ARTS IN
NEW YORK CITY, MAY 17, 1946

10. Should Mr. Truman Resign?

Though he was born in Sumner, Missouri, Fulbright's relations with Mr. Truman developed, at least on the President's part, into sniffish coexistence. Fulbright speaks regretfully about a feud he never sought, and ascribes much of the misunderstanding to a celebrated controversy in 1946. The November elections of that year gave the Republicans control of Congress, and it was the Senator's conviction—based, perhaps, on his bias toward the parliamentary procedures of Britain—that the President should resign in favor of a Republican successor. Fulbright disclosed his view to a wire-service reporter during a chance meeting in the Senate cafeteria. In obligingly offering the reporter a story, Fulbright created a minor uproar. Some major newspapers, including the Chicago Sun, *endorsed the idea— which simply made Harry Truman madder. "I'm afraid," says*

Fulbright, "that Mr. Truman still doesn't understand that there was nothing personal about it." Indeed, on July 18, 1954, the Senator, with bipartisan scrupulousness, also suggested that President Eisenhower resign if the Democrats won control of Congress. The Democrats did; Ike didn't—but the Senator's notable lack of converts has not lessened his concern about the evils of divided government, which he elaborates in this 1946 statement.

Clear Republican majorities have been elected in both the Senate and the House of Representatives. We have a Democratic President. Under these conditions, neither party will have complete responsibility for or the authority to govern, and each party will place the blame for the inevitable stalemate on the other party. These times are too perilous for this nation to bicker and to drift for two years without a responsible government.

I have suggested as a possible solution to this difficulty that the President, after consulting the Republican members of the new Congress, appoint a Republican Secretary of State, and then resign. This would simply mean that we are turning over the full responsibility for our government to the party which won a decisive victory in the election.

Probably the first question to arise is whether or not the proposal is in accord with the Constitution. There is no question as to the constitutionality of the proposal. The language of Article II, Section I, clearly contemplates the occurrence of the resignation of the President when it says:

In case of the Removal of the President from office, or of his Death, *Resignation,* or inability to discharge the powers and duties of the said office, etc.

Following this provision of the Constitution, the Congress in March, 1792, enacted the provision contained in Title 3 U.S. Code, Section 23, which provides for the method of resigning. This statute states that any President or Vice-President who wishes to resign can do so simply by delivering "an instrument in writing declaring same" to the Secretary of State.

53

In view of these clear provisions it is needless to labor the point of constitutionality.

The further point has been raised that a Democratic President should not have the power or, if he has it under the Constitution, he should not exercise the power to appoint his successor, especially from the opposite party. Under my proposal the President would consult the Republican leadership in the Congress and would accept as his successor their recommendation. It seems to me that under the circumstances that prevail today, with so much talk of war on the one hand and depression on the other, there can be no serious objection to having the recently elected representatives of the people, in strict accord with the Constitution, designate the man who is to execute the laws to meet these problems which they will enact during the next two years. The men chosen by a clear majority of the people in hotly contested campaigns are more likely genuinely to represent the will of the people than the delegates to a national party convention, who are chosen in a much more perfunctory manner.

From an examination of the Constitutional Convention in 1787, it is clear that the selection of the President by the Congress was not then considered to be so alien to the spirit of our democracy as some prominent figures of today seem to think. During the convention, the delegates debated at length the various methods proposed for choosing the President. Some favored direct election of the President by the people; others favored selection by the national legislature or by one of the two houses....

If the proposal suggested is proper under the letter and spirit of the Constitution, as I believe it to be, the decisive question then becomes its wisdom. Its wisdom should be considered primarily from the point of view of the national welfare, and then, because it is the party initiating the decision, it should be considered from the point of view of the Democratic party.

As for the welfare of the nation, I am quite unable to see why it is not highly desirable to have at all times, but especially in a time of tense international relations and confusion at home, a government capable of functioning in a definite, positive manner. Practically

54

every responsible commentator on national affairs has agreed that, as a result of the divided responsibility in our government, we are faced with a stalemate for the next two years....

From the point of view of the Democratic party, the results of the election should leave little doubt as to the opinion of the people regarding the present administration. No one can ever prove why people vote as they do, but we know *how* they have voted. Without any reflection upon the individuals in the administration, we must accept the fact that, as now constituted, it is unacceptable to the American people. This being so, is it not only a contribution to the national well-being, but also wise as political strategy, to accede to the wishes of the people as of this time? Then we might proceed as rapidly as possible with a thorough review of our policies and a close examination of our organization, in order that from the ranks new blood and more vigorous leadership may be brought to the top....

In urging this proposal there was no intention to reflect in any way upon the character or capacity of President Truman. The circumstances which gave rise to the suggestion have occurred before, and, unless an appropriate amendment to the Constitution is adopted, will undoubtedly occur again. The condition which confronts us is not because of any malfeasance on the part of the President; it results from a serious defect in our electoral system, from which we suffered under President Wilson, a Democrat, and President Hoover, a Republican. It is quite unwarranted for anyone to assume that this proposal was motivated either by a desire to embarrass President Truman or any of the Republican aspirants for the White House....

Regardless of whether the suggestion is followed, I hope that it may have induced far wiser heads than mine to give serious consideration to the problem of making our government more responsive to the desires and needs of our people.

PRESS STATEMENT,
NOVEMBER 10, 1946

11. The RFC Scandals:
Law Alone Is Not Enough

Fulbright's relations with President Truman were not improved by the Senator's vigorous role as an investigator. In the spring of 1950, Fulbright detected an unsavory aroma rising from the Reconstruction Finance Corporation, a federal loan agency established by Herbert Hoover. In the company of Senator Paul H. Douglas of Illinois, Fulbright paid a visit to the White House and proposed that a single administrator be appointed to clean up the RFC, which had fallen into lax ways under an indifferent Board of Directors. Ultimately, Stuart Symington, later Senator from Missouri, was named as RFC administrator, but not until after a senatorial investigation brought to light serious conflict-of-interest abuses implicating Donald Dawson, a White House aide, and involving the celebrated mink coat and deep freeze. In March, 1951, Fulbright reflected on the meaning of his findings and wondered whether "we have come to accept the totalitarian concept that the end justifies the means." His address came at a time when the country was aroused by an exposé of bribery in college basketball and by the use of faked pictures to defeat Senator Tydings of Maryland. Fulbright's proposal for a national commission to study the problem of ethical standards was, regrettably, not adopted.

MR. FULBRIGHT: Mr. President, when the Subcommittee on the Reconstruction Finance Corporation undertook its study, more than a year ago, I anticipated the development of little more than the usual issues which grow out of an investigation of the executive branch of the government. I expected just another case study of an agency, with a finding of facts to be made and an orthodox legislative remedy recommended.

Before we had proceeded very far, however, it became evident that we were dealing not simply with a legal or legislative problem but with a moral problem. The first case to which my attention was called was one involving the employment by a borrower of an RFC employee who had recommended the granting of the loan. The Board of Directors of the RFC thought this practice quite proper. I thought it improper. So from the beginning we were confronted with a difference in ethical standards. It presents a very difficult problem. It is difficult because the evils to be dealt with are so seldom amenable to the processes of law. When confronted with an evil, we Americans are prone to say, "There ought to be a law." But the law does not and cannot apply effectively over wide fields of men's activities. It cannot reach those evils which are subtle and impalpable. Generally speaking, it reaches only the overt and the blatant acts of the wicked.

Much of the evil of the world is beyond the reach of the law. The law cannot prevent gossip. It cannot restrain men from avarice and gluttony. It cannot restrain a man from betraying his friends. In short, it cannot prevent much of the evil to which men are, unfortunately, too prone. The law being inadequate, men long ago supplemented the law courts with courts of equity, where the spirit of the law, rather than its letter, is paramount. Underlying the law are the codes of ethics promulgated by the great religions and recognized by all civilized men as being essential to a humane and enlightened existence.

As our study of the RFC progressed, we were confronted more and more with problems of ethical conduct. What should be done about men who do not directly and blatantly sell the favors of their offices for money and so place themselves within the penalties of the law? How do we deal with those who, under the guise of friendship, accept favors which offend the spirit of the law but do not violate its letter?

What of the men outside government who suborn those inside it? They are careful to see that they not do anything that can be construed as illegal. They operate through lawyers—men who are known as clever lawyers, a cleverness which is like the instinct of the rat that knows how to get the bait without getting caught. Many businessmen, ostensibly reputable businessmen, employ these knavish lawyers to circumvent the law and enrich themselves at government expense. Too often the law cannot touch them.

Who is more at fault, the bribed or the bribers? The bribed have been false to their oaths and betrayers of their trust. But they are often relatively simple men—men of small fortune or no fortune at all—and they weaken before the temptations held out to them by the unscrupulous.

Who are the bribers? They are often men who walk the earth lordly and secure, members of good families, respected figures in their communities, graduates of universities. They are, in short, of the privileged minority, and I submit that it is not unreasonable to ask of them that high standard of conduct which their training ought to have engendered. Is it too much to ask of them, the favored few of our country, that they behave with simple honesty, with that honesty which looks, not to the letter of the law, but to its spirit?

Mr. President, the essence of what we have been studying in our committee is but a reflection of what may be seen in many other phases of our national life. The government and its activities are, in a very real sense, a mirror of our national life. The inquiry into the RFC has revealed conditions which unfortunately may be found in other activities of our people.

Let us consider what has developed in our colleges, where the characters of our young men and women are being molded. Our colleges, under extreme pressure from the alumni, have become so intent upon winning football and basketball games that they use any means to gain their ends. They hire players who are not bona fide students and thus make a mockery, a farce, of the whole concept of amateur sport for the health and entertainment of our young men. They corrupt not only the hired players, but also the entire student body, who learn from their elders the cynical, immoral doctrine that one must win at all costs.

A by-product of this doctrine, this necessity for big money, led naturally to betting and to the shocking episode of the widespread bribery of basketball players in New York. I find it difficult to blame the players. They are but following a logical sequence of influences, beginning with the corruption of the sport at its source by pressure from the alumni.

This question of the moral strength of our people is not just an internal domestic matter. It has grave implications in our international relations. Without confidence in their government, the people will not make the sacrifices necessary to oppose Russia successfully. Professor Toynbee, in his well-known historical study, demonstrated clearly how the vast majority of great civilizations have been destroyed, not as a result of external aggression, but as a consequence of domestic corruption. A democracy can recover quickly from physical or economic disaster, but when its moral convictions weaken it becomes easy prey for the demagogue and the charlatan. Tyranny and oppression then become the order of the day.

I wonder whether in recent years we have unwittingly come to accept the totalitarian concept that the end justifies the means, a concept which is fundamentally and completely antagonistic to a true democratic society. Democracy is, I believe, more likely to be destroyed by the perversion of, or abandonment of, its true moral principles than by armed attack from Russia. The evil and insidious materialism of the Communists is a greater danger to us than their guns.

One of the most disturbing aspects of this problem of moral conduct is the revelation that, among so many influential people, morality has become identical with legality. We are certainly in a tragic plight if the accepted standard by which we measure the integrity of a man in public life is that he keep within the letter of the law.

Mr. President, the growing size and complexity of our government, as much as we may deplore it, only emphasizes the need for a clarification, a restatement of the moral standards of governmental conduct. When our government was small, when it took only ten per cent of our earnings in taxes, we could afford a certain amount of official boodling. Today, it has become too important. We simply can no longer afford moral obtuseness in our public officials.

Scandals in our government are not new phenomena in our history. What seems to be new about these scandals is the moral blindness or callousness which allows those in responsible positions to accept the practices which the facts reveal. It is bad enough for us to have corruption in our midst, but it is worse if it is to be condoned and accepted as inevitable.

Mr. President, is there anything we can do here in Washington to help our country reaffirm or re-establish a higher concept of public conduct? Some weeks ago, I suggested, informally, that it would be beneficial to have a commission of eminent citizens designated by the Congress, to consider the problem of ethical standards of conduct in public affairs. I renew that suggestion now, and I have a resolution which will be ready for presentation to the Senate tomorrow. Such a commission should be composed of private citizens of outstanding achievement and character, whose integrity is beyond question. As examples of the type of men who should serve, I suggest the following: former Justice Owen Roberts, of Pennsylvania; former Senator La Follette, of Wisconsin; Judge Learned Hand, of New York; Mr. Walter Reuther, of Detroit; Mr. Paul Hoffman, of the Ford Foundation; Dr. Reinhold Niebuhr, of the Union Theological Seminary; Dr. Theodore Greene, of Yale; Dr. Hutchins, of Chicago; President Clinchy, of the Conference of Christians and Jews; Father Parsons, of Catholic University. Such a list could be extended indefinitely, but I think I have adequately indicated the type of person I have in mind.

Such a commission, as I conceive of it, would be a catalytic agent, stimulated by public indignation, to draw forth meaning from the mass of data revealed by the several current investigations. The commission would evaluate the conditions which have been exposed, and, drawing upon its combined wisdom, would restate again, or formulate anew, principles which, it is hoped, would strengthen the faith of all decent men in our democratic society.

Too many people in our nation do not believe anything with conviction. They question the precepts of God or of man, indiscriminately. The values of life which were clear to the Pilgrims and the founding fathers have become dim and fuzzy in outline. False propaganda and the "big lie" of demagogues have created doubts in the minds of men. Professional political hucksters, imported from afar, without local responsibility or restraint, corrupt our free elections and poison democracy at its source. The principal objective of the study I suggest is the restoration of the faith of our people in the validity of the traditional precepts of our democratic society. It is not a job for politicians; it is not a job for the inexperienced; it is a job for the wisest of our citizens under a mandate from the nation.

Mr. President, in making this suggestion I am quite prepared to be dubbed naïve. It will not be the first time. As I look back upon our history or upon my own experience, nearly every progressive or fruitful move, especially if it was novel, has been considered naïve. To expect or even hope for an improvement in the moral climate of Washington is, in the eyes of the boys who know, I am sure, thoroughly utopian.

I confess that I do not know what should be done. If I knew, I would not call upon the wisest men of our country. I would suggest it myself. But, Mr. President, I am not willing to accept the view that nothing can be done, that the moral deterioration, which is so evident to all, must continue to its logical conclusion, which is the destruction of our free democratic system.

SENATE ADDRESS,
MARCH 27, 1951

12. General MacArthur's Dismissal: The Risks of Recklessness

On April 11, 1951, the country gasped at the news that President Truman had fired General Douglas MacArthur, commander-in-chief of the United Nations forces fighting in Korea. "I have just left him," Major General Courtney Whitney confided. "He received the word of the President's dismissal magnificently. He never turned a hair.... This has been his finest hour." Whitney's breathless adulation was widely shared in the United States, and MacArthur's subsequent speech to Congress on April 19 prompted an outpouring of attacks on Mr. Truman.

Seven days later, Fulbright rose to the defense of a President who had spoken only scornfully of the Arkansas Democrat. Fulbright's speech came before a joint Senate committee investigation did much to puncture the legend of MacArthur; it took some spunk for a politician to speak out for Truman—indeed, the Senator was repeatedly needled by exultant right-wing Republicans.

Throughout the Truman era, Fulbright was a sympathetic but critical ally of the administration in foreign affairs; lending his voice in support of every major innovation. His most significant contribution was his continued advocacy of a European political union; his speeches on this theme are included in a subsequent chapter, "From Coalition to Community." Fulbright's closing words in the following selection may properly stand as his valedictory to the Truman years.

It is rare in history that a major question of governmental policy is presented so forcibly, so dramatically to a nation as in the present case. General MacArthur has drawn the issue. It is now for the people and the Congress to make the decision....

Now let us consider as objectively as we can the issues in the Truman-MacArthur controversy. No one, I think, seriously questions President Truman's authority to dismiss General MacArthur as commander of our Far East forces. The subordination of the military to the civilian authority in our political system was long ago decided in terms of the maxim that "when two ride a horse, one must go in front." Our founding fathers decided that the President is the front rider as commander-in-chief of our armed forces. If the nation is not now content with this solution of the question by the founding fathers, it may change the President's place on the horse by amending the Constitution. But until it does so he remains the front rider. One may approve or disapprove of his action in the given case. But no one may reasonably doubt his authority.

Beyond this, there are many military, political, and politico-military questions involved in the present controversy. In our complicated world it is often impossible to say what is a strictly military question, since it is also so often bound up with the political, and what may be meat to the military may be poison to the political. Winning a battle, we may lose a war. I am painfully aware, in this discussion, of my lack of competence as a military expert. My distinguished colleague Senator Taft, however, would place more emphasis upon our navy and air force than upon our ground forces, and he does this with great assurance because he has perhaps a greater military knowledge than I have. But I, less assured in my ignorance, am willing, on strictly military matters, to be guided by the advice of our Joint Chiefs and the Secretary of Defense, all of whom are military experts tried in the crucible of war. They may be wrong, and if they are we shall grievously suffer, but they are our military advisers and, while their word is not law until the Congress enacts it into law, it is highly persuasive—certainly to one who, like myself, is not a military expert.

General MacArthur's views on the bombing of Red China, whether or not it bombs our bases in Korea and Japan, are opposed not only by his own government, but also by the governments of the free world, on military and political grounds. Joining this group is *L'Osservatore Romano,* the newspaper published in the Vatican, which indicated that it did not think MacArthur's way was the way to peace. I do not know how much this article reflects the views of the pope, and it would be a little wide of the mark to say that its newspaper is a Communist organ. It may be, of course, that General MacArthur is right and the whole world is wrong. But, considering the gravity of the possible consequences if we should follow him, I shall go along with the majority in this case until there is a presentation of overwhelming evidence to the contrary.

There is no man in this nation who does not share General MacArthur's desire to end the Korean war honorably, end our casualties there, and end the Chinese menace to our forces in the East. The quarrel is about the method. The General believes that the method is to bomb the enemy's supply bases in Manchuria, to blockade the Chinese coast, use Chiang Kai-shek's troops on the mainland, and send large American reinforcements to Korea. This method raises certain questions in my mind.

Boldness and bravery are one thing; recklessness and headlong dispatch are another. History teaches us that the fortunes of war are unpredictable, that war once begun, no man can tell how far it will spread and in what directions. Hence, I ask:

Is China our primary enemy, or is Russia our primary enemy?

If knocking out China should involve us in large losses of men and material, would not this weaken us relative to Russia, which up to date has not expended a single man in the wars since the end of the last world war?

Who is prepared to say how much the conquest of China might cost us?

Who can tell us how effective bombing may be against a primitive economy such as China's, where there are few large factories and thousands of small, scattered handicraft industries?

We can perhaps learn something by re-examining the experience of Japan during twelve years of bombing China. If, however, you conclude that we could knock China out of the war with little loss to ourselves, you would then merely go on to the next question, which is even more difficult to answer.

In war, as in life generally, prudent men want to pay a price commensurate with the gain, to weigh the benefits against the risks. General MacArthur seems to believe that, if we use his method against China, Russia will not intervene.

How does he know this? With what accuracy can he read the minds of the men who direct the destinies of Russia? If we should attack China proper, to what extent would Russia feel obliged to intervene under the terms of the Sino-Russia treaty? Does General MacArthur know what the secret agreements may be between the two countries? How far would Russian prestige in the Orient be dissipated if she should stand idly by and see knocked to pieces her Chinese ally? And if Russia intervened, would we not then, while precipitating the third world war, doom our Far Eastern forces to destruction, lose Japan, and lay all of Southeast Asia open to easy invasion?

If, I ask, we have had to struggle hard to meet even the limited requirements of the Korean war, are we now prepared for the unlimited requirements of the third world war? Have we sufficient planes? Have we enough guns and ammunition? How far along is our guided-missiles project? What is the state of our merchant marine and navy, especially with respect to antisubmarine devices and submarine-killer ships? What is the state of our civilian defense against Russian A-bomb attacks? What right have we to assume that the Russian bombers will not get through to us when our own

64

air force people tell us point-blank that many of them will get through to us, just as many of our bombers will get through to the Russians? Where are the meager four divisions that we have promised to send Europe? Are they ready? Are they equipped? Going beyond this, are our allies ready? Are they equipped? Winston Churchill has it that, if you must fight a war, you ought to fight it, if possible, at the most favorable moment. Let us ask ourselves: Is today or tomorrow the most favorable moment for the United States and its allies? Does the risk in this case equal the possible gains?

I was deeply disturbed—to come to another question—by an extraordinary omission in General MacArthur's speech. The United States is one of the founders of the United Nations and its most powerful member, while the General himself was the first commander in history of a United Nations force. Yet never once did he mention the United Nations or the brave men, few though they may be, who are now fighting alongside our troops in Korea. Is this organization dead? If it is not dead, shall we make over-all strategy, involving the life or death of millions of people, without consulting our allies? Shall we commit them to a world war without their consent? Do we prefer to face Russia alone? Shall we make a war with Russia an all-American war?

Shall we, by our impetuousness, cause our allies to fall away from us, until, disheartened and hopeless, they make the best deal they can with Russia and become our active or passive enemies?

We all know how difficult it is to hold together a coalition composed as it is of nations with differing interests and points of view. Do we believe that we can cement this shaky structure of the United Nations by cavalierly disregarding the opinions of those who compose it outside ourselves? Shall we gain Chiang Kai-shek and lose Britain, France, Italy, the Low Countries, Scandinavia, Greece, and Turkey? General MacArthur desires that the United States maintain a global policy. Shall we maintain it through that rather small part of the globe that the United States covers? If we are to have a global policy, how shall we conduct it effectively without the invaluable air bases of France, Britain, North Africa, and other places around the globe that we neither own nor control? How shall we protect the sea approaches to the United States without bases in Greenland, Iceland, and the Azores, territories that are not American real estate?

And remember, as you ponder these questions, that every government in the free world is opposed to General MacArthur's views on the solution of the Chinese war. He may be right, but so far he has not convinced our allies, much less a united America, that he is right....

Here let me say a personal word. My paths have never crossed those of General MacArthur. And, as you know, they have seldom crossed those of President Truman. For a long time we have been walking on opposite sides of the street, neither of us nodding to the other. He has often thought me wrong and unspeakable, while I have sometimes thought him wrong and incomprehensible. I retain the right to agree or disagree with him as the case may be. But I do have a real sympathy for him in the awful responsibility which he alone must carry.

I do not know what the verdict of history upon Mr. Truman will be. His contemporaries, such being the frailty of human nature, are more likely to exaggerate his faults than to enumerate his virtues, while he, as most men, has a full quota of both. I am not in his good graces. I have spoken with him on official business only once in several years. This, however, does not blind me to the fact that he has made decisions on a number of occasions that equal in imagination, courage, and effectiveness any ever taken by an American President. Nearly all of these decisions are without precedent in our history. Some of them are:

The dropping of the A-bomb on Japan.

Aid to Greece and Turkey.

The Marshall Plan.

The Berlin airlift.

The North Atlantic Treaty.

The sending of divisions of American troops to Europe in peacetime, troops under the command of General Eisenhower.

The going into Korea, a decision that at the time had the approbation of the nation and of nearly the whole of the free world.

No one can doubt that, in the absence of some of these stupendous decisions, much of the present free world would now be lost to us, and our struggle against Russia would be the more difficult.

These momentous decisions are the President's responsibility, taken though most of them were with the advice and consent of the Congress and the people and the approbation of the military. Mr. Truman remains the President, and in these terrible times I submit that it is necessary for us to keep him in perspective. Let us not permit his occasional lapses of speech or temperament or his misguided loyalty to unworthy friends to endanger a calm and objective judgment on the present controversy.

SENATE ADDRESS,
APRIL 26, 1951

Chapter Three

THE LIGHT OF LIBERTY

~~~~~~

13. McCarthyism: Tyranny Without a Tyrant

Who can forget the year 1954—the implausible time when an entire country was in intense debate over such jejune questions as "Who promoted Peress?" The hopes that the election of President Eisenhower would contain the extravagances of Senator Joseph R. McCarthy proved bootless. Indeed, in January, 1954, a Gallup poll indicated that fifty per cent of the American people had a generally "favorable opinion" of the junior Senator from Wisconsin. "In the Senate in the early fifties," Richard Rovere has written, "hardly anyone protested against anything McCarthy did. Hardly anyone dared refuse approbation. In February, 1954, there was exactly one man in the Senate, William Fulbright of Arkansas, who found it possible to cast a vote against an appropriation of $214,000 for [McCarthy's] Permanent Subcommittee."

Yet by the end of the year the Senate was in a mood to condemn McCarthy, and the career of the gifted seditionist from Wisconsin went into permanent eclipse. Fulbright was not alone in opposing McCarthy, but no Senator was more forthright in his criticism at a moment when it took an extra ration of courage to speak out. What set Fulbright apart was his ability to see the controversy in broader terms and to place the menace of McCarthyism within the

68

context of America's vulnerability to the tyranny of an unthinking majority. His text throughout was Tocqueville, as is evident in this address of April, 1954, soon after the Army-McCarthy hearings had begun:

A correspondent for the *London Daily Mirror* cabled his paper as follows:

I have been watching a circus so fantastic, so degrading, so puerile, and so recklessly dirty that the disgust one feels is matched only by the alarm over the behavior of our closest ally in the conduct of their domestic affairs.

I have observed not only the present hearings, but have participated in some of the past ones, and I think there is ample basis for this estimate of the proceedings. The whole career of the Senator from Wisconsin—at least, since he has been in the Senate—is incredible. Words cannot describe him, so I shall not burden you with the attempt. He must be seen and heard to be appreciated.

The point to this is that this performance is dangerous to our security and to the preservation of our system of society, governmental and social. If we had not neglected the education of our citizens, I do not believe we would be witnessing this phenomenon today....

Do you believe, if the people of Wisconsin—or even the members of the Senate thoroughly understood the lessons of Hitler, Mussolini, and Stalin, that we would permit the trifling with our basic institutions and our liberties that has been going on for months?

Thoughtful and informed people know that demagogues, who debauch the institutions of representative government, help Moscow. They help Moscow by destroying the faith of people in their own institutions and the confidence of people in their ability to govern themselves.

I doubt that the Senator from Wisconsin can become another Führer, but that is small comfort. As a prominent editor recently expressed it:

The danger to our country is of a tyranny without a tyrant—an ever-mounting, impersonal, thoughtless oppression. The facts are piling up, the habits are being established, and they all point the same way: to a stultifying debasement of national standards. Who can measure how far below the level of our constitutional standards we have sunk since the idea of "security risk" came into our lives— the idea of never-ending investigation, of the never-clear clearances, of the "unevaluated reports" with "derogatory information" ever piling up.

More than a hundred years ago, Alexis de Tocqueville warned us, in one of the greatest books ever written, of the dangers that might be expected from the "tyranny of the majority," as he put it. This is the tyranny that presently is growing in our country. It is the instinct of the human being for security, the shrinking from danger that inheres in nonconformity. The result is sure to be the atrophy of the originality, the initiative, the generosity, and the kindliness which have been the great distinction of this nation. Instead of these qualities, we see the growth of suspicion, of caution, of conformity, and of bitterness, first among the leaders and then among the followers....

I should like to conclude with the thought that the treachery and subversion and disloyalty about which the Senator and his followers have talked so much has been greatly exaggerated. We have a great country. During the last fifteen years, our nation has contributed a major share in the winning of two wars without any serious sabotage of our production or efforts. We have also made a magnificent effort in the rebuilding of a war-torn world, without thought of gain other than the creation of a free and peaceful world, which all people would enjoy. Can any rational person believe that our country could have made this unprecedented effort, have achieved such magnificent results if our State Department, our army, our factories, our schools, and our churches had been permeated with disloyal people?

ADDRESS, UNIVERSITY OF MINNESOTA
APRIL 29, 1954

14. Lessons for the Senate

During 1954, Fulbright in a quiet way used every opportunity to lend a little more candlepower to the light of liberty. In March, 1954, he was not afraid to refuse to see an FBI agent, who was checking on an official's loyalty, when evidence came to light that the bureau's files had been misused and that politicians, McCarthy among them, had obtained access to confidential information. In addition, he acted as a patient tutor to his colleagues by inserting pertinent quotations about the malady that had seized the country. Two samples follow:

MR. FULBRIGHT: Mr. President, recently, in a letter from a learned and wise man, my attention was called to a short passage written by one V.I. Lenin, the leader of the Communist revolution in Russia in 1917. I think we can assume that Lenin had some understanding of communism.

In view of present conditions in our country, I believe this observation of Lenin will be of interest to the Members of this body. I ask unanimous consent that the passage by Lenin be printed in the body of the *Record* at this point in my remarks. . . .

(From the selected works of V.I. Lenin, Vol. 10, pp. 143-147.)

At present, the millionaires of all countries are behaving, on an international scale, in such a manner as to deserve our heartiest thanks. They are hunting down bolshevism with the same zeal as did Kerensky and Co.; they are overdoing it and helping us quite as much as did Kerensky. When the French *bourgeoisie* makes bolshevism the central point of the election campaign, abusing the comparatively moderate or vacillating Socialists for being Bolsheviks; when the American *bourgeoisie,* having completely lost its head, seizes thousands and thousands of people on suspicion of bolshevism and creates an atmosphere of panic spreading broadcast alarming stories about Bolshevik plots; when the British *bourgeoisie*—the most solid in the world—in spite of all its wisdom and experience, commits acts of incredible stupidity, founds the most richly endowed societies to combat bolshevism, creates a special literature on bolshevism, and engages for the struggle against it an extra number of scientists, agitators, and priests—we must bow and thank *Messieurs* the capitalists. They are working for us.

SENATE ADDRESS,
FEBRUARY 26, 1954

MR. FULBRIGHT: Mr. President, I ask unanimous consent to have printed in the Appendix of the *Record* a quotation from Jonathan Swift's *Gulliver's Travels,* Book III, Chapter 6.

I told him that in the kingdom of Tribunia, by the natives called Langden, where I had sojourned some time in my travels, the bulk of the people consisted wholly of discoverers, witnesses, informers, accusers, prosecutors, evidences, swearers; together with their several subservient and subaltern instruments; all under the colors and conducts of ministers of state and their deputies. The plots in that kingdom are usually the workmanship of those persons who desire to raise their own characters of profound politicians; to restore new vigor to a crazy administration; to stifle or divert general discontent; to fill their pockets with forfeitures; and raise or sink the opinion of public credit, as either shall best answer their private advantage. It is first agreed and settled among them, what suspected persons shall be accused of a plot; then, effectual care is taken to secure all their letters and papers, and put the owners in chains. These papers are delivered to a set of artists, very dexterous in finding out the mysterious meanings of words, syllables, and letters. For instance, they can decipher a closestool to signify a privy council; a flock of geese, a senate; a lame dog, an invader; the plague, a standing army; a buzzard, a minister; the gout, a high priest; a gibbet, a secretary of state; a chamber pot, a committee of grandees; a sieve, a court lady; a broom, a revolution; a mousetrap, an employment; a bottomless pit, the treasury; a sink, the court; a cap and bells, a favorite; a broken reed, a court of justice; an empty tun, a general; a running sore, the administration.

SENATE ADDRESS,
MAY 13, 1954

72

15. Six Counts of Censure: "Thou Shalt Not Raise a False Report"

The press, it might be said, helped make McCarthy, but television was his undoing. The Army-McCarthy hearings had given the country a firsthand opportunity to judge the purposes and methods of Joe McCarthy. On July 30, Senator Ralph Flanders of Vermont, who had been in consultation with Fulbright, took the major step of offering a resolution of censure based on McCarthy's contempt for the Senate, truth, and people. It was complained that the censure resolution was too vague, and Fulbright sought to remedy the defect. After a flourish of Biblical scholarship—the mark of a true Southern legislator—the Arkansas Senator presented a six-point indictment that he wanted inserted in the resolution. For reasons of space, his discussions of both the precedent for censure and of McCarthy's receiving a $10,000 fee from the Lustron Company, a corporation financed by the government, are omitted.

On August 2, the Senate voted 75 to 12 to create a Select Subcommittee to consider the various charges against Joseph R. McCarthy.

Mr. FULBRIGHT: First, Mr. President, I wish to make one or two observations with regard to the remarks made last night by the distinguished junior Senator from Illinois (Mr. Dirksen). The Senator from Illinois is a very powerful speaker and makes an extremely interesting address. I invite attention to his opening remarks, as found on page 12,119 of the *Record,* in which he said:

Mr. President, if I were to select a text tonight, I think I should dip into the Old Testament and find it in the Book of Exodus. It comes to mind because in the Republican convention of 1952 in Chicago a very eminent rabbi was asked to deliver the invocation on one of the convention days, and in that eloquent invocation he used an expression from the Old Testament which said: "Thou shalt not follow a multitude to do evil."

Mr. President, I regret very much that the Senator from Illinois stopped with that quotation. It would have been extremely appro-

73

priate, I believe, if the Senator had read all of that particular passage. I might even recommend the reading of the preceding two or three paragraphs from chapter twenty-three of the Book of Exodus, which I shall read. Beginning in the paragraph preceding the one read by the Senator from Illinois, I read:

Thou shalt not raise a false report: Put not thine hand with the wicked to be an unrighteous witness.

It seems to me that that passage is peculiarly appropriate to the particular subject matter which is under consideration before the Senate today.

Thou shalt not follow a multitude to do evil; neither shalt thou speak in a cause to decline after many to wrest judgment:
Neither shalt thou countenance a poor man in his cause.
If thou meet thine enemy's ox or his ass going astray, thou shalt surely bring it back to him again.
If thou see the ass of him that hateth thee lying under his burden, and wouldst forebear to help him, thou shalt surely help with him.
Thou shalt not wrest the judgment of thy poor in his cause.
Keep thee far from a false matter; and the innocent and righteous slay thou not; for I will not justify the wicked.

Mr. President, I am quite willing to take that passage as the text of the entire subject to be considered by the Senate; and if the Senate will apply that standard to what I believe to be the unquestionable evidence in this case, I have no doubt as to what its judgment will be in connection with the pending resolution....

Mr. President, my concluding remarks, if I may call them that, relate to a somewhat different matter, one which I think is of extreme importance. To me, the way we approach this whole matter is of the greatest importance.

I support the resolution of censure of the junior Senator from Wisconsin, not because of his personal character, as I have said, or because of his private views about human affairs. On the contrary, I support the resolution of censure because of his official degradation of a power of the Senate, by which he has gravely injured the United States and the Senate of the United States.

Here at home, the prestige and position of the Senate have been lowered in the estimation of our people. Abroad, the power and influence of the United States, which in large part depend upon the respect in which we are held, are greatly weakened by the junior Senator from Wisconsin. The power he has abused is a vital power of investigation and inquiry. This power lies at the very heart of the Senate's legislative role. To weaken it and to bring it into disrepute strike at the heart of the legislative process and of the power itself.

The investigative power is one which only the Senate itself can preserve and protect. It is not a party responsibility. The Senate alone has that power and responsibility. Here the courts have no function. The executive cannot enter. Even the Congress as a whole is not responsible. Each body of the Congress is responsible, and alone responsible, for the committees and for the Members who exercise its power in its name. In the case of the Senate the whole Senate is responsible, because the whole Senate is injured.

In the words of the Constitution—article I, section 5:

Each House may determine the rules of its proceedings, punish its Members for disorderly behavior.

Section 6 of article I of the Constitution provides, in part, as to the Members of each House, that for "any speech or debate in either House they shall not be questioned in any other place."

Mr. President, I emphasize the words "they shall not be questioned in any other place."

Mr. President, this provision of the Constitution is often said to give Members immunity from responsibility, but this immunity relates solely to the forum in which they shall be held accountable.

When the founding fathers took from a person who might be libeled from the floor of the Senate the right to have recourse in the courts, they did not mean that the floor of the Senate should become a place where falsehoods could be told with immunity. They meant to transfer to the Senate, and to the Senate alone, the responsibility for what took place on the floor of the Senate. This privilege of freedom from accountability in any other place has helped make

75

the Senate the greatest deliberative body in the world. But this privilege, like all other privileges, carries with it a heavy responsibility—the responsibility of the Senate for the conduct of its Members on the floor of the Senate. When Members have violated the canons of good conduct, have been contemptuous of the traditions of the Senate, the only place where they can be held accountable is in the Senate itself. Clearly, Mr. President, the Constitution contemplates that in cases of this kind the Senate as a whole, without regard to party, must take full responsibility for judging the conduct of its Members.

Mr. President, the junior Senator from Wisconsin is an unusual character, with extraordinary talents. It is necessary for one to see him in action, as chairman of his committee, to fully appreciate his talents; they cannot be described adequately by words. Fortunately, many millions of Americans, including, I assume, all Members of this Senate, have observed the technique and methods of the junior Senator from Wisconsin, so there is no need to attempt a description thereof.

I propose merely to recall to mind some of the instances of abuse of power which I believe fully warrant the resolution of censure submitted by the Senator from Vermont.

Mr. President, the abuses by which the junior Senator from Wisconsin has degraded and brought into disrepute the great and vital power of the Senate to investigate are not minor. His abuses have recalled to the minds of millions the most abhorrent tyrannies, which our whole system of ordered liberty and balanced power was intended to abolish.

First: He has used the position and power which this Senate has conferred upon him to infringe the rights and liberties of citizens of this republic, and he has inflicted grave injury upon them.

The first case I should like to mention is that of General George C. Marshall. I believe that General George C. Marshall is a great patriot. I think his service to his country, both in time of war and in time of peace, has entitled him to the thanks of the country which he has served with devotion and ability. . . .

Yet on the floor of this Senate the junior Senator from Wisconsin sought to identify General Marshall with "a conspiracy so immense and an infamy so black as to dwarf any previous venture in the history of man.

"The object of this conspiracy," said the Senator, "was to diminish the United States in world affairs, to weaken us militarily, finally to fall victim to Soviet intrigue from within and Russian military might without."

This attack on General Marshall was only the forerunner of other attacks on other American citizens. Nathan M. Pusey, General Ralph Zwicker, John J. McCloy, Struve Hensel, and Charles E. Bohlen have all had their loyalty impugned, their patriotism attacked, and their devotion to this country questioned.

Finally, we have the case of Annie Lee Moss, who was told—even before she had been given a chance to take the witness stand in her own defense—that the junior Senator from Wisconsin had decided that she was a Communist. She was told that if she denied the charges against her, she would be committing perjury, and that her prosecution would be recommended.

Having put a Member in a position of power where he may compel attendance upon his committee and response to his inquiry, it is the duty of the Senate to see that citizens are protected from insulting and offensive attacks by its agent. The more insignificant and helpless the citizen, the more compelling is the duty of the Senate. The Senate is not living up to this duty if it permits tactics like those used by the junior Senator from Wisconsin in the case of Annie Lee Moss to go unrebuked. I say that regardless of whether she may have been affiliated with the Communists. The procedure itself was absolutely indefensible, as will be noted from reading the record I shall present.

Second: The Senator from Wisconsin has openly invited and incited employees of the government to violate the law and their oaths of office. I think the legal position has been well stated by the chief law official of the Eisenhower Administration, Attorney General Brownell. This is what he has said:

Anyone who attempts to put himself above the law and invite government employees to turn over classified information relating

77

to our national security, in violation of statute and Presidential order, is tragically mistaken if he believes he is helping to protect our nation's safety....

I think there is no doubt that if a member of the executive branch called on the Members of the Senate, or upon the employees of the Senate, to violate their oaths of office, all of us would agree that the member of the executive branch responsible should be disciplined, punished, or perhaps even dismissed....

Third: The Senator from Wisconsin has virtually paralyzed the Voice of America and the overseas libraries by his reckless investigations. I would like to read you excerpts from an official report of the United States Advisory Commission on Information, which has been signed by Erwin D. Canham, editor of the *Christian Science Monitor,* and Justin Miller, chairman of the board of the National Association of Radio and Television Broadcasters:

The wide and unfavorable publicity that resulted from one of the congressional investigations gave the agency such a bad name that professionally competent persons were reluctant to accept employment in it.... It is not too much to say that the desirable results sought through the activities of the information agency are largely offset, if not destroyed, by this constant counterbarrage which is so generously distributed to the peoples of the world....

There is no question who is responsible for the attack on the Voice of America which has produced the result so clearly portrayed by the report of Mr. Canham and his colleagues. This is the responsibility of the junior Senator from Wisconsin....

Fourth: Mr. President, the ability of the Senate of the United States to function effectively is indispensable to the preservation of our democratic system. The tradition of this body requires that the Members treat one another with mutual respect and consideration. This body can function properly only if its Members treat one another with mutual respect and consideration. Representing forty-eight sovereign states of a great federal system with sharp diversity in religious, economic, cultural, and racial characteristics, it is not easy to restrain within reasonable bounds the conflicting opinions and personalities of the Members.

By his personal attacks upon fellow senators and apparent attempts at intimidation, the junior Senator from Wisconsin has enhanced the differences among us, impeded the work of the Senate, and tended to bring the Senate itself into disrepute in the eyes of the citizens of this country. A few examples of this kind of offense against the Senate are as follows:

New York Herald Tribune, July 28, 1953; dateline Washington D.C., July 27: McCarthy said today that Senator Monroney is "taking over the job of whitewash and cover-up of communism and corruption."

United Press dispatch, July 27, 1953: McCarthy said Monroney was welcome to the job of becoming a "megaphone on the Senate floor" through which "fellow travelers and Communists could spew forth their smear and character assassination against anyone hurting the Communist cause." But he said Monroney used the Senate floor "for smear and character assassination against members of our staff who cannot in turn use the Senate floor to fight back."

On August 20, 1951, he had this to say about the Senator from New Jersey [Mr. Hendrickson], who is certainly one of the most distinguished and honorable Members of the Senate, and I may say that I do not mean by that that the Senator from Oklahoma [Mr. Monroney] is not one of the most distinguished and honorable Members in the Senate, for certainly it is generally recognized that he is. I believe that everyone who knows the two Senators is aware of their high character.

The junior Senator from Wisconsin said this on that date about the Senator from New Jersey [Mr. Hendrickson]:

How such a man can live is a miracle—no brains, no guts, no nothing....

Fifth: The junior Senator from Wisconsin has injured the morale of the army of the United States during a period of national danger. The recent events growing out of the attacks made by the junior

79

Senator from Wisconsin on the army of the United States are too fresh in the memory of all of us for it to be appropriate for me to recount them here. I would like, however, to recall to the minds of my colleagues the statement of the distinguished senior Senator from Arkansas. Senator McClellan sat through virtually every minute of these long hearings and this is what he had to say at their conclusion:

I am compelled to say in conclusion, Mr. Chairman, that the series of events, actions, and conduct that precipitated the ugly but serious charges and countercharges that made these lengthy and unpleasant public hearings mandatory, I think, will be recognized and long remembered as one of the most disgraceful episodes in the history of our government.

Simply to say that this series of events is regrettable is a gross understatement. They are deplorable and unpardonable.

Mr. President, I submit that these deplorable and unpardonable events are but the culmination of a course of conduct which imposes upon the Senate the duty to approve the motion submitted by the Senator from Vermont [Mr. Flanders].

Mr. President, I should like to close with a paragraph from a statement by one of the leading Catholic prelates in this country, Bishop Sheil, of Chicago. It reads as follows—it is very short. I wish to close, I may say, this part of my remarks, and then I am going to offer the amendment.

But, although the church takes no position, and will not, on such a matter of public controversy, the church does take a position on lies, calumny, the absence of charity, and calculated deceit. These things are wrong—even if they are mistakenly thought of as means to a good end. They are morally evil, and to call them good or to act as if they were permissible under certain circumstances is itself a monstrous perversion of morality. They are not justified by any cause—least of all by the cause of anticommunism, which should unite rather than divide all of us in these difficult times. . . .

Mr. President, I have completed my remarks. I now send to the desk certain amendments. I intend to submit these amendments to the resolution. . . .

THE LEGISLATIVE CLERK: On line 5, after the word "condemn," it is proposed to strike the period and insert the following:

For the following reasons:

1. The junior Senator from Wisconsin, while a member of the committee having the jurisdiction over the affairs of the Lustron Company, a corporation financed by government money, received $10,000 without rendering services of comparable value.

2. In public hearings, before the Senate Permanent Investigations Subcommittee, of which he was chairman, the junior Senator from Wisconsin strongly implied that Annie Lee Moss was known to be a member of the Communist party, and that if she testified she would perjure herself, before he had given her an opportunity to testify in her own behalf.

3. Although repeatedly invited to testify by a committee of this Senate headed by the Senator from Iowa, the junior Senator from Wisconsin denounced the committee and contemptuously refused to comply with its request.

4. Without justification the junior Senator from Wisconsin impugned the loyalty, patriotism, and character of General Ralph Zwicker.

5. The junior Senator from Wisconsin openly, in a public manner before nation-wide television, invited and urged employees of the government of the United States to violate the law and their oaths of office.

6. The junior Senator from Wisconsin in a speech on June 14, 1951, without proof or other justification, made an unwarranted attack upon General George C. Marshall.

SENATE ADDRESS,
JULY 31, 1954

16. *Poison in the Mailbag*

By November, 1954, the tide had turned. The Special Subcommittee, headed by Senator Arthur V. Watkins of Utah, a Mormon elder, recommended censure on two counts. McCarthy's partisans

were in full cry; if a measure were needed to indicate the strange
sickness that the Wisconsin Senator both exemplified and fostered,
the Senate mailbag provided it. As a bacteriologist might examine
germ cultures in a Petri dish, Fulbright here places in the record
some pathological souvenirs of the time:

MR. FULBRIGHT: Mr. President ... Criticism, vigorous and personal,
is a characteristic of public life in our democratic system. All of us
are accustomed to it. I do not believe that I am any more thick-
skinned than any of my colleagues. However, formerly criticism was
based on legitimate differences of opinion about issues before the
Senate. Of late, especially since the censure resolution came before
the Senate, the character of the criticism has changed. It is no longer
criticism. It is unadulterated hate, vituperation, and abuse. It is
highly emotional, irrational, and designed to intimidate and overawe
Members of the Senate.

I shall read into the *Record* a few communications which I have
before me as examples of the character of what has come to be
known as McCarthyism. The junior Senator from Wisconsin, by his
reckless charges, has so preyed upon the fears and hatred of uninformed and credulous people that he has started a prairie fire, which
neither he nor anyone else may be able to control.

If there are ten million people in this country similar to the
authors of these letters, I believe it is something about which all of
us ought to be deeply concerned.

I may say that I have received thousands of similar communications. Some of them are so vile that I cannot use them. I shall leave
it to Senators to judge the significance of these letters.

The first letter is from San Antonio, Texas. ... In a postscript it
is stated that a copy of the letter has been sent to Senator McCarthy.
The letter is dated November 19, 1954, and reads as follows:

Dear Sir: We have asked Senator McCarthy to help us get your
name changed to "Notbright" instead of Fulbright. Also, we have
asked Mr. McCarthy to help get you in an insane asylum for your
safety as a New Deal associated with 20 years of treason. You are
judged by the company you keep. You have been a party to the

82

Roosevelt-Truman-Acheson-Hiss gang of traitors for 20 years or more, as per the records I get. We shall ask Senator McCarthy to investigate you and your leftwing gang of traitors. As per the records, your passed life has not been perfect. When you joined the only Jew to vote against 76 Senators, that proved you were the henchmen for the Jew Deal. H. H. Lehman should be deported out of this nation to Russia, or let Germany take that "bird" in and give him the gas like Hitler did, as per my opinion of his record. We know there is always some crackpot fronting for the Jew, in this case it sounds like its you, as per Mr. Fulton Lewis Jr. I'm for McCarthy 100 per cent like 80 per cent of the American people are. When you are up for reelection we want McCarthy to campaign in Arkansas against you. There will be many Senators defeated in 1956 on that very thing, McCarthyism. McCarthy is the biggest man in the United States Senate today and you can't defeat him. We are working to get 10 million names, or more, who will work against you leftwingers and the fake New Dealers and traitors. We mean to save America if we have to jail the workers against our Government. All this graft in income tax, housing, mink coats, 5-percenters, Hissism, et al. of some un-Americanism, etc. are fronting for the Jew as per their records. You and your gang of 20 years of treason, put us in three wars. Your Truman-Acheson-Hiss war was promoted to get Truman-Acheson off the hook to prevent a panic. They never intended to permit MacArthur to win that war as you well know. You and your gang put us in debt up to near $275 billion. As you know, Truman was a Pendergast gangster. That's the record of that faker and traitor as you know. When McCarthy gets out of the hospital he should get you told. We will back him 100 per cent if he will take you out to the woodshed and give you the paddle.

That letter is one example. I think it is very revealing.

I have another letter before me. It comes from Laverne, Oklahoma. It is dated November 24, 1954.... It reads, in part, as follows:

Every person that fights those that are trying to rid our (?) Government and Nation of the Reds, all shades are branded with Russia's red stick.

In other words, Mr. President, I take it that everyone who does not agree with the junior Senator from Wisconsin is a Red....

83

Here is another one, from Philadelphia, Pennsylvania, signed "Tupti." It reads as follows:

Philadelphia, Pa., November 26, 1954.

Sir: You ask for public support in this phony censure showdown. I am an ex-marine who fought in the South Pacific, to open the gates of this Nation for the commy Jews that Hitler did not kill?

You are one of the phony pinko punks connected with Lehman, Morse, Flanders, and Bennett.

Fulbright, the writing is on the wall, if that great Senator from Wisconsin is censured.

The people of this Nation will take over, and I don't mean ADA or the commy liberals that you and your stooges meet in the capital every evening. Senator Long (Huey) had the Indian sign on a great son from Arkansas, Joe Robinson. The American people are watching you with the halo around you accusing a great American, Hon. Joseph McCarthy, of Wisconsin; why did not the United States Senate censure those corrupt, rotten, racket men like Heflin, Alabama; Robinson, Arkansas; Truman, Missouri; Chavez, New Mexico; Wagner, New York (Whisky Bob); Fulbright, Arkansas.

Stand up in the United States Senate and put this in the *Record*. I will be there watching you.

TUPTI

[Laughter]...

Here is a letter from Buffalo, New York ... which reads as follows:

Buffalo, November 20, 1954

Senator Fulbright:

If you knew the contempt the people hold you and Herbert Lehman (Alger Hiss' pal) you wouldn't strut around so cocky. What did you ever do to combat communism? Nothing. You refused to vote one dollar to the McCarthy committee. A fine dirty red rat are you.

It's an old saying, and a true one: "Birds of a feather flock together." Who were the birds that voted not to allow Senator McCarthy time off to recover from his illness? I'll tell you: It was Red loving Fulbright and the rotten Jew, Herbert Lehman, the pal of Hiss.

[Laughter in the galleries]...

84

Some of the writers, Mr. President, do not have as much imagination as others. The next one is very short. It reads:

Fulbright: Tie Hyena Morse and Jackal Lehman around your foul coyote neck and jump into the Potomac.

The next letter I shall omit, because it is a little bit strong in its language....

Mr. President, here is one from Teaneck, New Jersey, having a little different approach:

November 22, 1954

Comrad Fulbright: Inclosed find two-bits toward your public schools in Arkansas.

If enough people mail money maybe Arkansas can buy books so the people of Arkansas can learn to read and write. If they could they would know Jeff Davis was not President today, and they would elect a real Democrat to be their Senator. And be sure and wear the red flag of your comrades when you vote censure against the most Honorable Joe McCarthy.

Who promoted Peress?

Mr. President, the next one is not so original. It reads:

Dear Senator Half-Bright: Now that Senator McCarthy has gone under the knife will you still say he is faking? You sir, are not worthy of being a human being. I would spit on you if I could, but you would not be worthy of my saliva.

Will you apologize, or do you think you should be censured. I honestly wonder how it is possible to look at yourself in the mirror (if you do). You are plain disgusting.

...Mr. President, I conclude with only this further comment: As I said in the beginning of my remarks, these are typical of the communications I have been receiving for almost a year. I think they evidence a great sickness among our people, and that sickness has been greatly enhanced and increased during the course of the past year....

SENATE ADDRESS,
NOVEMBER 30, 1954

17. The Purposes of Dissent: Shall We Speak Only "the Sterile Dogmas of the Street"?

On December 2, 1954, the Senate voted by a margin of 67 to 22 to condemn McCarthy, on two counts citing his disrespect for the Senate not (as Fulbright had earlier advocated) his abuse of the public. However narrow the indictment, the censure nevertheless had the effect of ending McCarthy as a political force. In a more reflective mood, on January 25, 1955, Fulbright used all his eloquence to distill the meaning of the peril McCarthy represented, to warn of our tendency to become "a society shaped in imitation of an Egyptian mummy; a society where the embalmer holds the highest place of honor; a society of fixed, painted and hard shells ..."

May I at the outset express my appreciation for the invitation to share in these ceremonies. I feel a close tie with all of you who know that works of the mind should be honored no less than works of the hand.

Elsewhere today, it seems at times that a man can be arrested for unlawful assembly when he merely collects his thoughts. Elsewhere, too, we see that action for action's sake, divorced from thought, is offered as a supreme proof of patriotism. For myself, I often feel that if men in public life read and thought a little more, and talked and acted a little less, we would the better know what to do and how to do it. ...

As for this meeting, I wavered between alternative topics I might talk about. I could not tell you how to write a book, or criticize it, or sell it. But among the many questions in which you and I as citizens of the republic have a mutual interest, one in particular towered above the others in its special significance to you as writers and to me as a public official. That question is the degree to which freedom of opinion and expression has been curtailed in our country, and the meaning this has for all of us.

As far back as the 1830's, *freedom* of discussion and the influence of the *majority opinion* thereon was a matter of real concern to thoughtful people. Alexis de Tocqueville put it well, I think:

86

I know of no country in which there is so little independence of mind and real freedom of discussion as in America.... The will of man [he said of the *majority* opinion] is not shattered, but softened, bent, and guided; men are seldom forced by it to act, but they are constantly restrained from acting. Such a power does not destroy, but it compresses, enervates, extinguishes, and stupefies a people.... The majority no longer says: "You shall think as I do or you shall die"; but it says: "You are free to think differently from me and to retain your life, your property, and all that you possess; but you are henceforth a stranger among your people. You may retain your civil rights, but they will be useless to you, for you will never be chosen by your fellow citizens if you solicit their votes; and they will affect to scorn you if you ask for their esteem.

"You will remain among men, but you will be deprived of the rights of mankind. Your fellow creatures will shun you like an impure being; and even those who believe in your innocence will abandon you, lest they should be shunned in their turn. Go in peace! I have given you your life, but it is an existence worse than death."

The sharp edge of that prophecy cuts deeply into us today, not alone because of the Senator from Wisconsin and not alone because of the driving pressure of his avowed followers. Restrictions on freedom of expression come from many sources—some of them very respectable—and in some cases for reasons unrelated to the ambitions of the Wisconsin revolutionary.

There is, for example, the narrowing effect inherent in the concentration of managerial control of the press, the radio, the movies— and, in the foreseeable future, television.

Within the last forty years, according to Morris Ernst, one third of our daily newspapers have disappeared, and more than three thousand weeklies have ceased publication. As of a recent date, ten of our states did not have a single city with competing papers, and in the whole of America there are only a few more than one hundred cities where one can find daily papers in competition. The pattern of concentration extends elsewhere. In radio, one-fifth of the stations are interlocked with newspapers. Four networks dominate national radio, while less than two dozen advertisers account for fifty per cent of network income. And in the film industry five big companies exercise a dominant influence upon the industry.

Let me make one thing plain: I am not saying that what brought this to pass was in all cases the hand of monopoly grabbing for bigness as an end in itself. In some cases, cost-account sheets *compelled* owners and managers to seek their survival by enlarging themselves through mergers. And it is to the credit of some of these that, when they found themselves in a monopolistic position, they tried to run the communications property as if it were a responsible public utility. But men of this outlook are, unfortunately, in the minority.

The general effect of what approaches monopoly control is that people hear, see, watch, read, and listen to only one side of public questions. And this in turn can adversely affect the public man to whom the guidance of public affairs is entrusted. He may know the truth and want to speak it. Yet he doubts whether his views, as transmitted to his constituents by those who control communication channels, will be fairly presented, or presented at all. So there often follows from this a chain reaction of cynicism leading to corruption. This public man, to achieve anything at all, will not use the open road, but will crowd himself into the path of low intrigue. He will not boldly scout what lies ahead for the nation. He will bend the weight of his energies to the end of having everything stand still. He will voice no prophecies of what ought to be. He will speak only the sterile dogmas of the street, and only those bits of rumor which bear the general sanction of the lords of communication.

And what of the end result to all this? It can be a society shaped in imitation of an Egyptian mummy; a society where the embalmer holds the highest place of honor; a society of fixed, painted, and hard shells; a society feeding on its dry rot, until the fateful hour when a probing finger, striking the shell from without, makes it collapse on the empty center.

This vision of the future is not drawn from the thin air or from a fevered imagination. It came after reading the report on tax-exempt foundations issued recently by the Reece Committee of the House of

88

Representatives. There, in one sentence, Chairman Reece put himself on the side of all the Pharoahs, from Rameses the First to the gentleman whose solar ship was uncovered recently. "The trustees of the tax-exempt foundations," said the Reece report, "should ... be very chary of promoting ideas, concepts, and opinion-forming material which runs contrary to what the public currently *wishes, approves,* and *likes."*

I said a moment ago that, in addition to Senator McCarthy, restrictions on freedom of expression have been imposed by the most respectable sources. Recently, for example, our military academies banned all student debate on the question of the recognition of Red China. The cadets at West Point and the midshipmen at Annapolis, who are destined to be our military chiefs, presumably could discuss how many angels can sit on the point of a needle, or any other celestially remote matter. But it was officially decreed that they should hold to the public posture of being blind, deaf, and dumb to the most tortured issue of the moment, an issue whose correct handling can determine whether the students themselves, as well as the rest of us, will live or will die.

I am indebted to the *Princeton Alumni Weekly* for another example in the same vein. The *Weekly*—scarcely a radical publication—took notice of undergraduate apathy toward political and social questions. And in listing some of the underlying causes for a phenomenon common to other colleges, it included the pressures to conform exerted by our great industrial corporations on students. To illustrate, the *Weekly* then cited from a personnel pamphlet issued by the powerful Socony Vacuum Oil Company, advising students how they should behave in college if they wished to be employed on graduation. The order of the day reads, and I quote from the pamphlet:

Personal views can cause a lot of trouble. The "isms" are out. Business being what it is, it naturally looks with disfavor on the wild-eyed radical or even the moderate pink.

Consider the implications of this text. With one hand, it gags the breath of student curiosity. With the other hand, it dangles bread before his mouth as a reward for silence, unbroken even by a moderate gurgle. It says to the student, "You will be saved only if you consider yourself a beast of burden or a beast of prey." It says to him, "We ourselves are the judge and the jury of what a wild-eyed radical and a moderate pink is. And if you ask us what it is, in the act of asking you become the very thing we don't want." And it says to him, "If you must find some way to spend your energies as an undergraduate before we take complete charge of you, there are football games, movies, and now television spectacles of magnificent dimensions which you may attend, provided they have been screened for security and do not cause you to think."

How should those of us here bear ourselves in a climate where the pressures to conform are so remorseless?

To the politician who means to be faithful to his oath of office, the answer is plain. It is to draw closer still to the letter and spirit of the Constitution. For in the degree to which he does this, he can better follow the guide lines staked out by the founders.

They were not prepared to lodge the rule of our society in the majority opinion. They knew it to be a quick and volatile thing, knew that it required a frame of law to steady it and bring it into creative focus. Neither did they say that the frame of law was itself limitless in what it could cover. They said the law itself should be limited to enumerated topics which are a proper concern of Caesar. All else—the dreams and speculations of artists, or any other manner of activity involving a connection between a man and his God— were not to be invaded by the law.

Beyond this, the founders were under no illusion about the nature of power. "Give all power to the many," they said, "and they will oppress the few. Give all power to the few; they will oppress the many. Both, therefore, ought to have power that each may defend itself against the other." And, with this in mind, the organ of government they framed was a balanced arrangement for unity and diversity, authority and liberty, security and freedom, continuity and new birth. Elsewhere, other societies have divorced these coupled terms, saying that they were incompatible and that one could survive only if the other was eliminated. And elsewhere, too, the effect of such a divorce has led directly to the dissolution of the society that was meant to prosper.

If the American politician draw close to the letter and spirit of the Constitution, he will not only gain strength and direction from what the founders first explored. He will be further reinforced when he grasps the keystone that the Constitution is superior to any majority or minority. In consequence of this, his oath of office does not require him to swing with every breeze. The oath requires of him that he should reflect the deliberate sense of the community. And this in turn means that he ought to consider himself a teacher, offering by precept and example a style and method of deliberation that can be imitated by the community at large, as it seeks on its own to know and then to do the good. It also means, as is often the case with teachers, that he must be prepared to accept banishment or destruction at the hands of the people because he has aroused their anger in the very act of serving them well.

And finally what of the writer? You have a unique responsibility to the political community of which you are a part. That responsibility arises from your talent, from your capacity to enlighten, to civilize those citizens to whose hands is entrusted the ultimate power in our society. The writer is the natural teacher of the people.

In this hurried mechanical age, the artist and intellectual are among the few who have the serenity and sense of perspective which may help us to find a way out of the fevered confusion which presently afflicts us.

Through you the political community needs to be taught how and what to laugh at, how and what to scorn or to pity; needs to be taught continuously that honor is not the same as fame or notoriety, that physical bravery is not the only form of courage. It needs to be taught the proper objects of anger or of love. It needs to be taught the nature of justice. And above all, through you, the political community needs to be taught that the capacity of the human mind has yet to be explored, that there can be new possibilities for men themselves.

ADDRESS, THE NATIONAL BOOK AWARD LUNCHEON, NEW YORK CITY, JANUARY 25, 1955

Chapter Four

DULLES: DISSENTING OPINIONS

18. Midsummer Dreaming About Russia

For nearly seven years of the Eisenhower administration, the voice of America in foreign affairs was John Foster Dulles, who quite arguably packed more power into his briefcase than any other American Secretary of State before or since. Editorial praise of Dulles sometimes verged on idolatry, but the Secretary found a pungent and insistent critic in the Senator from Arkansas. Fulbright wholly supported the great purposes of American policy, but dissented sharply against what he felt were the distortions caused by the Secretary's weakness for brinks, pacts, and sermonizing.

The elections of 1954 gave the Democrats a majority in Congress, and Fulbright became chairman of the Senate Banking and Currency Committee. In that capacity, he was absorbed through much of 1955 in a study (not an "investigation," he insisted) of the stock market. His relative silence ended abruptly in 1956. On February 25, the Senator listened incredulously as Secretary Dulles appeared before the Foreign Relations Committee, blandly dismissed Soviet policy as a "failure," and said the tide had turned against Russia. Two days later, on the Senate floor, Fulbright discussed the "midsummer dream" of Mr. Dulles.

I want to draw the attention of this body to a matter that dwarfs all other things before it. To put it plainly, the matter is this:

Will Secretary of State Dulles tell America the truth about our present peril, or will he say one thing publicly and an opposite thing privately? Will he give us a fair chance to decide for ourselves, with full knowledge of the facts, what efforts we should make for our own salvation, or will he lull us to sleep in an hour when the Soviet Union has launched a powerful diplomatic offensive against us? Will he, by his candor, rally the free world to a trust in American leadership? Or, from an apparent craving for popular approval, will he endanger the mutual trust which supports the association of free peoples?

In putting these questions before this Senate, let me make one thing quite plain. I know that no American Secretary of State walks an easy path. His motives may be pure. His patriotism may be firm. His acts may be wise. Yet the problems that crowd upon him do not lend themselves to easy answers.

Some of the problems lie wholly beyond his control. Some have been gathering force long before most of us here were born. And no one among us can dispose of them with a flick of the wrist. We may, in fact, have to reconcile ourselves to the fact that our grandchildren may be wrestling with some of the same problems that tax us here today.

For this reason, any Secretary of State merits and should get every sympathy and every ounce of support within our power to give. I, for one, as a Democrat, recall an all too recent chapter in American history. And I have no desire to repeat it.

I have no desire to vilify a Republican Secretary of State, as a recent Democratic Secretary of State was vilified because he did not reverse every world current that was adverse to America. Apart from the wrong to the person involved, we have seen all too clearly how this kind of partisanship makes the whole of America its victim.

What we want and what we will support is the truth, however unpleasant. What we want and what we will support is a Secretary of State who will not treat us as children, ready to clap in delight at every fairy story, however fanciful. What we want and what we will support is a Secretary of State who will come to us, not with packaged solutions to every ill that plagues the world, but who will come to us, instead, with a statement of facts about the nature of those ills.

Such a Secretary of State would win our respect for his courage and for the respect he himself showed for the truth.

It is my unpleasant duty to say that on Friday of last week in the Foreign Relations Committee we did not have such a Secretary of State. . . .

What could possibly induce the Secretary of State to attempt to deceive the American people about the deadly menace which confronts them?

Why did he offer us on Friday an estimate of the world situation that was more like a midsummer dream than any transaction now going on in the world of real things? To raise the question is to state the exact point at which the Secretary of State subverted what it is that makes for responsible power.

For if America were a dictatorship like the Soviet Union, Mr. Dulles would be at liberty to practice the little arts where words need not be consistent in their meaning, nor represent any realities whatsoever. Like Mr. Khrushchev or Mr. Bulganin or Mr. Molotov, he could say one thing on Friday, do an opposite thing on Saturday, and say yet a different thing on Sunday.

He could proceed this way because under a dictatorship public opinion does not have to be consulted. Whatever the people think, the means for executing policy can be extracted from them—if necessary, at the point of a bayonet.

This is not the case in these United States. The fact is that America is not the Soviet Union. Nor are our allies satellites. We and our allies have drawn together for the express purpose of preserving systems of government where an informed public opinion can be the source of public policy, the guide and the controlling force over public policy.

But I ask you: Are these systems of government well served when a Secretary of State misleads public opinion, confuses it, feeds it pap, tells it that if it will suppress the proof of its own senses, it will see that Soviet triumphs are really defeats, and Western defeats

94

are really triumphs? Will such a public opinion be prepared to make new sacrifices when the Secretary of State implies that the battle against the Soviet bid for world domination has been won? ...

Consider in closer detail what Mr. Dulles told us on Friday. Briefly, he told us that the Soviet Union was losing the cold war. And what proof did he offer?

"At this very moment, in Moscow," he said, "they are having to revise their whole program. If we had to go through such a revision and change of our whole program as they are undergoing, it would be advertised all over the world that we had failed. The fact is, they have failed, and they have got to devise new policies."

Mr. Dulles went on to say that the Soviets were not making progress in the Middle East, that the speeches of Khrushchev and other party leaders in Moscow during the recent congress [of Communist parties] indicated a failure in the foreign policy, and that, as a result of their failure, "they have got to revamp their whole creed from A to Z.

"But one thing that is absolutely certain," he said, "is that the unity and firmness and resolution of the free nations during the past few years have caused the Soviet policy to fail, and today they are trying to figure out how they are going to get a better one."

No, it is in the nature of any delusion that if it pierces the human mind, it does so because of a small truth it twists. In this light, this much is true enough: The unity of the free world, as it was first forged after the Second World War, checkmated the Soviet policy of expansion as it was pressed along rigid Stalinist lines.

Moreover, by our program of economic aid, technical assistance, and cultural exchanges, we managed to brace countless nations against the shock of subversion from within their own borders. Yet the success we achieved during this period was due in large measure to two circumstances: One was the monopoly of nuclear weapons; the other was a monopoly over the capacity to export capital for the use of underdeveloped countries.

In recent years, however, both monopolies have been broken by the Soviet Union. They have an ever-increasing arsenal of nuclear weapons and an ever-increasing capacity to deliver them onto their targets. At the same time, whether by squeezing the living standards of their own people or by other authoritarian means, apparently they have arrived at a position where they can offer underdeveloped countries capital and technical assistance for their development.

In short, they now appear to be able to imitate the best features of American policy and are pressing ahead with vigor and determination. . . .

Now I ask you in all candor: Does the skilful way the Soviet Union has posed as the champion of Asiatic peoples represent a triumph for Western diplomacy, as Mr. Dulles suggests? It does not.

Does the sight of tens of millions of people cheering Soviet leaders in India and Burma represent a dismal failure of Soviet policy? I think not.

Does the dramatic and vigorous entry of Russia into the once forbidden zone of the Middle East represent a setback for the Kremlin? It does not.

Is the shaky edifice of the Baghdad Pact a proof that all is well with the Western cause in that part of the world? I think not.

Are the cracks in Western Europe, the citadel of the Western alliance, a reason to applaud over the course American diplomacy has recently taken? I think not.

Indeed, wherever one looks, even in our own Latin American neighborhood, there is the Soviet Union on the march, confident, even cocky, wearing a false mask of new respectability, talking treacherously in soft words that are suited to parliamentary governments, and losing no chance to pre-empt the cause of peace for its exploitation.

Wherever one looks, there is the Soviet Union parading itself as the friend of the underdeveloped peoples, ready to help them raise their miserable standards of life, without requiring first that they enter into military alliances.

And wherever one looks, there is an impression of America that is a bitter caricature of what America really is and what it really wants—but caricature, nevertheless, that a good part of the world believes.

It believes it, among other reasons, for causes that can be laid straight at the door of the present Secretary of State. It believes that America can think of the fight for peace in no terms except that of military alliances and the shipment of arms....

The new strength and boldness of the Soviet policy should not be the occasion for despair, nor should it be misrepresented by those who, because of their official position, are presumed to know. If our common sense can be fortified by the truth, I believe that human liberty can still prevail over the police state of the Soviets.

SENATE ADDRESS,
FEBRUARY 27, 1956

19. The Lessons of Aswan

By the end of 1956, the midsummer dream had been rudely ended by the twin calamities of Suez and Russian intervention in Hungary, both occurring in the midst of an American presidential campaign. The tumble of events prompted the Administration to seek the so-called Eisenhower Doctrine in February, 1957, under which Congress authorized the President to grant aid to any Middle Eastern country requesting help "against overt armed aggression from any nation controlled by international communism." Though there was a stampede mood in Congress, Fulbright objected vigorously to the "blank check" doctrine which he suspected was a spurious publicity gesture (indeed, the provisions of the doctrine were never used— not even in the landing of troops in Lebanon in 1958).

Profoundly troubled by the drift of American policy in the Middle East, Fulbright offered a resolution calling for a full-scale Foreign Relations Committee study. The resolution was adopted in January, 1957, and Fulbright headed the subcommittee making the inquiry. But after seven months of patient research under frustrating limitations imposed by secrecy requirements, the Senator called off the study on July 30 and declared that it could serve "no useful purpose." The experience suggested to Fulbright how difficult it was under the complex terms of modern diplomacy for a legislator to follow the intricate details of a policy decision. The best he could do was to

97

prepare a speech against the background of his knowledge. His address, here drastically excerpted, was a detailed criticism of Secretary Dulles' decision to withdraw American aid for Egypt's Aswan Dam as a reprisal against Colonel Nasser's flirtations with the Soviet bloc.

MR. FULBRIGHT: Mr. President, the subcommittee of the Committees on Armed Services and Foreign Relations for the Review of Middle East Policy, on which I have served as chairman, has concluded that no useful purpose will be served by its continuation. The subcommittee has, therefore, recommended its discontinuation with the understanding that the Committee on Foreign Relations, pursuant to its regular procedures, will keep United States policies in the Middle East under surveillance....

Mr. President, after considerable searching thought over the past several weeks, I have decided that I should make public as much as our own security laws permit of my own conclusions about the Aswan Dam history.

On the basis of the secret and top-secret documents which the Department of State has provided—which, as I have said, apparently provide a satisfactory basis on which to judge United States policy— I have reached the following conclusions:

First: The Aswan Dam project was a sound project from the point of view of engineering feasibility, and it was a reasonable risk for economic-development loans. Sources of capital other than those involved in the offer which was made to Egypt, both private sources and other government sources, were definitely interested in pursuing the project.

The reason the United States first offered to make a contribution to the project was because it was recognized that the Aswan Dam or some other Nile River development program on a comparable scale was vital to the future of Egypt's potential development. Egypt, with its increasing population, may be expected to suffer a constantly lowering standard of living. This is likely to cause much social and political unrest in Egypt and may endanger the unstable peace of the Middle East.

Second: After many surveys and long negotiations, which were participated in by the International Bank for Reconstruction and Development, the United Kingdom, and the United States, a comprehensive plan for financing the Aswan Dam was substantially agreed upon with the government of Egypt. This plan was based on estimates that the dam would cost $1,200,000,000, a sum which would include the cost of irrigation and drainage works, powerlines, and other accessorial costs. The plan contemplated that Egypt, from its own resources, would pay for the full cost of the dam except for $400,000,000 in foreign exchange. The International Bank was willing to lend Egypt $200,000,000. The United States and the United Kingdom jointly were to grant Egypt $200,000,000, of which the United States was to contribute seventy-five per cent and the United Kingdom twenty-five per cent. These payments were to be made over the period of construction of the dam, which was estimated to be between ten and fifteen years.

For the United States this offer would have meant making contributions to the project averaging $15,000,000 a year for ten years. On December 16, 1955, the United States offered to furnish $54,600,000 toward the first stages of construction of the dam and to consider sympathetically additional financial support later. It was this offer which was withdrawn by the administration seven months later, on July 19, 1956.

Third: The administration's decision to withdraw the offer to Egypt was made against the advice of the United States ambassador to Egypt, and the president of the International Bank for Reconstruction and Development. President Eisenhower appears, according to the State Department documents, to have participated very little in the decision, except to approve Secretary Dulles' recommendation. There was apparently no consideration of the question by the National Security Council.

Fourth: The reasons given to the public for the withdrawal of the offer were not, in my opinion, valid reasons. They were as follows:

First: that other Nile riparian states had not agreed to the project. The fact, is, however, that there is no evidence that such agreement was not possible or even probable. Moreover, the lack of agreement

99

on this score was not a valid reason for withdrawing the American offer, because Egypt itself had agreed with us not to go forward with construction until agreement was reached with the government of the Sudan, the principal other country involved.

The second reason given for withdrawing the offer was that the ability of Egypt to devote adequate resources to the project had become uncertain since the time of the offer, seven months before. The fact is, however, that the major drain on Egypt's resources—namely, the mortgaging of part of her cotton crop in exchange for Communist arms—had occurred prior to the time of the United States's offer on the dam. Contrary to the statement of the Department of State, there was no substantial evidence of a radical worsening in Egypt's economic condition at the time of the withdrawal of the offer. Certainly, the International Bank had not urged that the arrangement be called off. Furthermore, there appears to have been no consideration of the imaginative use of United States surplus food supplies to counteract the inflationary effect which the commencement of construction would have had in Egypt.

Fifth: In public statements made subsequent to the announcement of the withdrawal of the offer to help with the Aswan Dam, Secretary Dulles has given as an additional reason the fact of congressional opposition to the project. There is no evidence, however, that the administration ever made any serious effort to persuade the few Members of Congress who had expressed opposition that the Aswan Dam project was sound. On the contrary, the evidence is that the administration itself began to reconsider the offer only a few weeks after the offer was made.

Sixth: The administration's judgment, based on facts known to the administration at the time of the withdrawal of the offer, seems to me to have been faulty for the following reasons:

First: the Russians had made an offer to help finance the Aswan Dam on terms more attractive than those offered by the United States, the United Kingdom, and the International Bank. There was no evidence that the administration believed that the Soviet Union was not prepared to follow through on its offer. The Secretary of State was nevertheless willing, by withdrawing the United States offer, to take the risk of massive Soviet penetration in Africa, with no compensating advantage to the United States in taking such a risk. I might say here parenthetically that it is not possible to be sure, on the basis of the documents furnished by the Department of State, whether Secretary Dulles deliberately sought to force a showdown with the Soviet Union on their offer. In this connection, we do have the evidence in Mr. Beall's biography of Secretary Dulles, in which Mr. Beall states: "It was necessary to call Russia's hand in the economic competition"... [John Robinson Beall, *John Foster Dulles* (New York, 1957)].

The second reason why the administration's judgment was poor, even on the facts known at the time of the withdrawal of the offer, was that it did not appreciate the significance to the United States of the vigor of the nationalist and neutralist drive in Egypt. I believe the Secretary of State confused Egyptian nationalism and neutralism on the one hand with communism on the other. Despite the judgment of able State Department career officials indicating that Nasser had some appreciation of the dangers of dealing too closely with the Soviet Union, Mr. Dulles seemed to believe that Nasser had become a Soviet puppet. He did not recognize that Egyptian nationalism was a powerful force which could, if recognized for what it was and carefully handled, be directed toward political freedom instead of communism.

Thirdly, the Secretary of State failed to appreciate the importance of the Aswan Dam to the economic future of Egypt. He also failed, in my opinion, to appreciate the tremendous emotional importance which all Egyptians attached to the building of the dam. He did not appreciate the effect the building of the dam would have had upon the entire Arab world as an example of our willingness to help them help themselves. The Secretary of State failed to appreciate these facts, although he had adequate reports on these points from the field.

Seventh: The administration's decision to withdraw the offer to help with the Aswan Dam was not, in my opinion, in the best interests of the United States, for the following reasons:

First: The withdrawal of the dam offer was the direct cause of the seizure by Nasser of the Suez Canal. This action led, in turn, to the Israeli-United Kingdom-French attack, to the serious deterioration in our relations with our leading allies, to the severe oil shortages in Europe, and to economic dislocations in other parts of the world. So far as cost is concerned, it was recently reported in the press that $174,000,000 has been spent under the authority of the Eisenhower Doctrine, more than our contribution to the dam would have been in ten years.

Second: The withdrawal of the offer served to increase the influence of the Soviet Union. The Soviet toe hold in Egypt has become a hammer lock on a country which otherwise might well have stayed relatively free from influence by the Communist orbit.

Third: Settlement of the conflict between the Arab states and Israel, without which no peaceful economic and political progress in the Middle East is possible, has been rendered much more difficult. To have helped Egypt concentrate on internal development, instead of foreign adventures, would have helped to create stability throughout the area.

Fourth: The withdrawal of the Aswan Dam offer has created an impression which is hard to erase, that we as a nation are interested in the economic development of other nations only if that assistance serves to put the recipient nation under the political bondage of the United States. It suggests we are not interested in the economic and political freedom of other peoples unless they are willing to adapt their policies to suit our political needs.

Fifth: Withdrawal of the offer has foreclosed what may be the primary salvation of Egypt's economic problems in the long run. The Aswan Dam—an essential element of stability in the Middle East—has been indefinitely postponed. The day when the Egyptian people might seek to build a democratic government on a solid economic base has been delayed.

Sixth: Withdrawal of the Aswan Dam offer and the consequent war in the Middle East diverted world attention from the revolution in Hungary. This, of course, is a second guess. Nevertheless, if the world had not been absorbed by the danger in the Middle East and if the Western powers had not been on opposite sides in that conflict, the Soviet Union might never have intervened in the Hungarian revolution, or the response of the West to the Soviet intervention might have been more effective. We lost a golden opportunity to promote freedom in the world of the Communist orbit, and we handed communism a key to the Middle East.

Mr. President, these are my conclusions. I believe that the documents which have been supplied to the committees of the Senate by the Department of State support these conclusions.

Mr. President, I wish it were possible to make the Aswan Dam papers public. Every time the Senate tries to make use of classified documents furnished by the executive branch, however, we encounter a fundamental problem of relationship between the Congress and the executive branch. My situation today illustrates this problem. The conclusions which I have reached cannot be subject to the jury of public opinion as long as the documents supporting those conclusions must remain classified. It is impossible for the press, for members of the public, and for students of foreign policy in the Middle East to determine whether my conclusions are sound and whether our actions, which I believe contributed directly to the seizure and closure of the Suez Canal, were reasonable or unreasonable in the light of the facts available to the Department of State....

Mr. President, to summarize, there is much evidence in the Aswan Dam papers that our policy was influenced too much by emotion and not enough by hardheaded realities. The realities require that peace be maintained in the area, that the Middle East remain free from Communist control, that the nationalism of the area be encouraged to develop in such a way as to promote economic and political freedom, that transportation through the Suez be uninterrupted, and that great power conflicts be bound to develop in such a way as not to endanger our NATO alliance....

The ill-considered decision to withdraw our offer to Egypt resulted in large economic losses to Europe and to this country, serious injury to our relations with England and France, increased hatred and fear between Israelis and Arabs, and, most important of all, the consolidation of Russian influence astride the Suez Canal and the Middle East.

Unless and until our government can develop reasonably consistent long-term policies based upon clearly understood objectives, we cannot effectively protect our own interests nor give effective leadership to the free world. . . .

SENATE ADDRESS,
AUGUST 14, 1957

20. Mutual Deterrence: "It Is Irrational Because of the Very Degree of Rationality It Requires."

On October 4, 1957, Sputnik I went into orbit, dealing a blow to American prestige abroad and American morale at home. The Soviet achievement brought to attention the remarkable technological strides made by our adversary in the field of missiles. But, while some Americans, alarmed by the "missile gap" then thought to exist, placed all their emphasis on the need for increased defense spending, Fulbright in this speech took a larger view and offered a searching critique of the theory of mutual deterrence. His was a plea for a "modus vivendi" as an alternative to "modus moriendi."

In this prescient speech—one of Fulbright's few on nuclear strategy —the Senator voiced alarm about the ceaseless spread of overseas bases. Four years before the Cuban missile crisis, he remarked: "We have treated constant Soviet preoccupation with our overseas bases as sort of an unreasonable Soviet obsession. Speaking for myself, I am frank to admit that I might find myself plagued by an obsession against Soviet bases if their ballistic launching facilities were in the Caribbean or Mexico."

As a member of the Committee on Foreign Relations, I cannot help but be impressed by a recurrent phenomenon in the conduct of the most important affairs of the nation. I may add that I cannot help but be deeply disturbed by it.

This phenomenon has appeared throughout the incumbency of the present administration. It is difficult to describe. It is difficult to pinpoint. Yet anyone who has watched closely the conduct of the government during the past few years is not likely to be unfamiliar with it. The phenomenon is what might be termed a periodic urge to inertia in the national leadership. It manifests itself in the approach of the administration to the most complex and difficult problems that beset the nation, particularly those of foreign policy and defense. Periodically, the administration is inspired, frightened, or otherwise prodded into looking at these problems. It takes them out, examines them, makes a few statements, puts them back into the bureaucratic drawers, and forgets about them.

The administration's behavior in these matters reminds me of a schoolboy who dreams great dreams of achievement. He announces his high purpose and resolve to the world. He piles his desk high with books and diligently sets about to bring the dreams to fulfilment. A half-hour later, however, the sounds of gunfire on the TV or the shouts of play outside his window become irresistible. He is off. The dreams of achievement are remembered vaguely, and the high purpose and resolve are shrugged off for another day....

Let me illustrate by citing the most recent manifestation of this urge to inertia, this craving for an easy normalcy. A few months ago, the nation and the government were shaken to the roots by the launching of the two Sputniks, by the sudden awareness that technical skills comparable, if not superior, to our own existed elsewhere, by the sudden realization that we had mistaken a boisterous optimism for an invincible superiority....

The fear-spur to action which the Sputniks provided has dulled and disappeared. Once again, the urge to inertia has taken over. Once again, the administration has yielded to its yearning for the TV and the playground.

Mr. President, that is where we are today. The President delivers his chins-up, eyes-closed homilies as the recession deepens and undermines the position of the nation at home and abroad. The urgent awareness of the need for a thoroughgoing improvement in the structure of the nation's educational system has lost its urgency in Washington, and, I daresay, elsewhere in the nation. The interminable exchange of letters concerning a summit conference goes on between Washington and Moscow. While epistles are to be preferred to missiles, the purpose of these notes—that is, the desperate need to build a more solid foundation for the world's peace—this purpose, along with the summit on which it presumably was to be pursued, has become increasingly obscured in clouds of bickering words and reservations.

All is indeed back to normal, insofar as a constructive foreign policy is concerned, insofar as positive action for peace is concerned. The administration sags in apathy. It is a dangerous apathy, compounded of a leadership that is at once aimless and feeble and a bureaucracy so fearful of change that it clings desperately to the ancient pillars of policy even as they rot away under the pressure of irresistible international developments. Aid programs as usual, cold war as usual, defense strategy as usual, foreign policies on Asia, Europe, the Middle East, and elsewhere as usual—that is what is offered. All the while, scientific changes and political changes accumulate at home and abroad to render these policies, as they are presently pursued, increasingly unreliable as guardians of the nation and international peace.

Mr. President, I have searched in hearings before the Committee on Foreign Relations, in the statements of the leading officials of the executive branch, for the reasoning which permits reasonable and intelligent men—and I assume that this administration is made up of reasonable and intelligent men—I have searched for the reasoning which permits them to accept this state of affairs, which permits them to believe that we can go on as we are for much longer without disaster. What, in short, supports in the minds of these men this apathy, this dangerous apathy, that passes for policy? ...

The answer, Mr. President, I believe is to be found partly in their lack of taste for the hard work of the intellect that must precede meaningful action. But, perhaps even more important, I believe they have found their soporific in the doctrine of mutual deterrence, for it is this doctrine which guides our basic policies today. It is this doctrine which permits the bland acceptance of business as usual, despite the mounting dangers to the nation and to the world.

In simple terms, this doctrine of mutual deterrence sees the danger of a vastly destructive war as confined solely to a conflict in which the United States and the Soviet Union participate as opponents. The doctrine assumes that, since we will not start this terrible war and the Russians will not risk massive nuclear retaliation by beginning it, a peace of sorts will be maintained so long as we keep our defense establishment, our military preparation, and our military alliances in a condition to carry out the retaliation if it should be necessary.

That is not a new concept, Mr. President. The previous administration, with slight variation, followed the same idea. We cannot know with certainty what might have happened had we not held to this concept over the years. We must assume, therefore, that it has contributed to the maintenance of peace in the past or, at any rate, that it did not contribute to total war in that period.

Does that mean, however, that what worked yesterday, when the nuclear and scientific supremacy of the United States was clear and unequivocal, will work today, when the gap in this respect between the United States and the Soviet Union has obviously closed appreciably? The question we must ask ourselves, Mr. President—those of us who have some political responsibility for the future of the nation—the question we must ask ourselves is how strong is this reed, this doctrine of mutual deterrence, on which we now stake the civilized existence of the whole human race. The question is not how strong was it yesterday, but how strong, how reliable is it today.

Let us accept for the moment the assurances of this administration that we have and we can retain the capacity for massive destructive retaliation in the event war is forced upon us. Let us close our eyes for the moment to the implication of Soviet missile achievements, the implication that, if we have not been eclipsed already, we may be eclipsed in the near future in the scientific and military field if we continue to go on as we are going. Unless we accept the assurances of the administration on this score, we do not even have the doctrine of mutual deterrence standing between us and annihilation. We have only a prayer and a smile and the good will of the Russians, which has not been, to say the least, conspicuously consistent in its manifestations in recent years.

Accepting the assurances, however, that we can stay abreast or in advance of the Russians in the total military power needed to deter, the doctrine is still no more reliable than its assumption that we will not start a war out of principle, and the Russians will not start one out of fear of retaliation. . . .

The doctrine, in short, presupposes that those in supreme political authority in the United States and in Russia will always act on the basis of reason. That is, at best, a dubious assumption for this country. On the basis of the history of Russia over many centuries, it is a highly dangerous assumption for that nation. Yet, if it breaks down seriously only once, the war of the millennium is upon us.

Nor is it only the supreme political authorities of the Soviet Union and the United States, Mr. President, who must at all times act with supreme reason under this doctrine. The same capacities must exist in individuals everywhere in the armed services of the United States and the Soviet Union, who have, by the nature of their duties and responsibilities, the potentiality for setting off this war which the doctrine of mutual deterrence is designed to prevent.

As the weapons grow in destructive capacity and the velocity of the means of delivering the destructiveness multiplies, the power to commit the act that can begin the total war inevitably becomes more widely dispersed in both countries. In law, it is now only the President in this country who can, in effect, issue the commands that would begin nuclear hostilities. In actuality, it is several of the many custodians of nuclear explosives in the military services who could touch them off in such a manner as to precipitate a war. What is true for this country must be no less true for the Soviet Union. I presume that, in theory, it is Khrushchev who would give the initial orders for hostilities to begin. But there must be in that nation and its satellites many men who finger the buttons that could send the missiles flying and thereby set off the conflict.

We have seen only recently, in the bombing of a Tunisian village, that those charged with the custody and use of military weapons can sometimes act without the express authority of those who are ultimately charged with political authority and who must ultimately accept responsibility for the use of these weapons, even though it be an irresponsible use. What happened in the French military services in Tunisia can happen in military services elsewhere.

Even with the best of intentions, weapons can sometimes be used in error, as we ourselves have seen just a short time ago in the bomb incident in South Carolina. No one gave the order to bomb South Carolina—the bomb just fell. Is it so impossible to conceive that, in the not too distant future, no one will give the order to fire the missile aimed at Moscow or the Soviet missile aimed at Washington or Chicago—it will just fire—perhaps even by a short circuit?

What I am trying to emphasize, Mr. President, is that, even though we assume that our technological-military capabilities keep abreast or stay ahead of the Russians, even though we assume that the present political administrations both of the United States and the Soviet Union wish to act in a rational fashion, the doctrine of mutual deterrence standing alone is inadequate as a safeguard for peace.

It is inadequate because it depends on a degree of technical and human perfection which nothing in the experience of mankind leads us to expect. It is, in short, irrational because of the very degree of rationality that it requires. It is irresponsible because of the very degree of responsibility it places on hundreds of men who are charged with the development, custody, and use of the deadly instruments of deterrence and the means of their delivery.

Nor is it, Mr. President, only a matter of impossible technical and human requirements that makes this doctrine of mutual deterrence untenable as an instrument of peace. Its weakness lies also in the assumption that war—*the* war, the dreaded war—will be precipitated only by the Soviet Union. The fact is that this war can begin in many parts of the globe between nations which may not be amenable to restraints by the Soviet Union or by the United States. Is anyone in this chamber prepared to say, for example, that war has become an impossibility between Israel and the Arab states? An impossibility even among the Arab states themselves? Is war in Indonesia a complete unlikelihood? Have we seen the end of a Vietnam, of China, of Korea? Are there no seeds of conflict in a divided Germany, in Eastern Europe?

In these potential areas of conflict, who is to say what degree of control Khrushchev exercises over those peoples and governments which are dominated by the Soviet Union or which look to the Soviet Union for support? Indeed, who is to say how much control we exercise over those governments allied with us, those which look to us for support?

The truth is, Mr. President, that no one can say. Communist discipline, however rigid it may be in theory, is not superhuman in practice. Khrushchev can no more guarantee the behavior at all times of a North Korean general, a Chinese Communist colonel, a Vietnamese captain than President Eisenhower can at all times persuade to restraint their counterparts among nations allied with us.

There is no need, Mr. President, to belabor the point. If the doctrine of mutual deterrence as a keeper of the peace is untenable on the grounds of the irrational and irresponsible degree of confidence it reposes in the rationality and responsibility of men in the Soviet Union and the United States in positions of power to upset it, it is equally untenable on the grounds of the degree of control which it presupposes that these two countries exercise over developments throughout the world.

Yet we cling to this doctrine for our security, Mr. President, to this dangerously illusory doctrine. We cling to it, Mr. President, and to the policies it has produced in a fashion that suggests to me the orbiting of the earth satellites. They go round and round in their predetermined paths, in the heavens, and they are destined to continue in those paths until they gradually sink of accumulated friction, or until their orbiting is brought to a catastrophic end by some cosmic accident.

Is that, then, what lies ahead for us? Are we destined to see the gradual sinking of the prestige of this nation, the steady dimming of its message to mankind, because we go round and round in the same policies, because we have not the flexibility, the imagination, or the national determination to break this inertia, move out of this orbit into new directions? Are we to see this national decline or, perhaps, even the explosion of all civilization in some cataclysmic accident?

If we are to avoid these consequences, the job ahead is not an easy one. I know that the Russian totalitarians are astute and difficult adversaries. I hope that we can be at least as astute, if not as difficult.

I know that the Russian leaders are as *inflexible* in their determination that Communist totalitarianism shall one day dominate the world as they are *flexible* in the methods by which they pursue that objective. I hope that we can be at least as flexible in the methods by which we seek the maintenance of peace and the expansion of freedom throughout the world.

The unfortunate fact is that our policies have been neither flexible nor astute in recent years. Repeatedly, the Russians have made inroads into the non-Communist world by their astuteness, their alertness, and their willingness to change methods. We forget, Mr. President, that Russian policy is not only what happened in Hungary. If it were only a question of a policy of military oppression, we would have, in my opinion, a much more easily defeated adversary. But Russian policy is also the military withdrawal from Finland; it is the Soviet signature of the Austrian Peace Treaty and subsequent military withdrawal from that country; it is also Russian acquiescence in the recent modifications in Polish communism; it is political support of the non-Communist nationalist movements in Asia and Africa and economic aid to the countries of these regions. It is, most of all, an almost continuous propaganda refrain calling for action to reduce the danger of nuclear warfare, coupled with proposals for a great variety of approaches to this fundamental international problem....

The fact is, Mr. President—and we had better face it—that, regardless of attitudes towards communism's ultimate objective, many Soviet policies and actions have evoked a sympathetic response throughout the world. These flexible policies are not going to be ignored or labeled bad by other peoples even if we choose to ignore them or to so label them. They are not going to be met by inflexibility and inertia on our part. They are not going to be met unless this administration turns off the TV, comes in from the playground, gets down to the hard work of running this government and constructing a more substantial peace, unless it sheds the sodden, dangerous apathy in which it now wallows....

There is little evidence that the administration has welcomed the range of proposals put forth by Members of this body. There is little evidence that the ideas and plans of distinguished journalists, leaders, and students have struck a responsive chord in the State Department or the White House. There is little evidence that the men and women with provocative intelligence within the working levels of the administration itself have been able to obtain adequate consideration for their suggestions at the restricted policy levels of the administration.

Indeed, Mr. President, the evidence is to the contrary. Our policies seem to be formulated while we are en route to the fires. The Eisenhower Doctrine of last year, for example, was primarily a military response to a nonmilitary threat. And today the Middle East tinderbox is as ready for the spark as ever....

There certainly is no evidence that the administration has comprehended the dangers of reliance on the doctrine of mutual deterrence. Neither is there evidence that the administration comprehends that the existence of the concept may afford new opportunities to stabilize peace.

The fact that for the first time in history great power competitors can destroy each other creates a mutuality of interest in self-survival. This mutuality of interest provides a power base for realistic, self-enforcing agreements.

It has often been said that the Soviet Union will not keep agreements unless they are self-enforcing—unless such agreements are and continue to be in the Soviet interest. If this be true—and I believe it is—it seems to me that recognition of the existence of mutual capacity to destroy each other provides the United States and the Soviet Union with a basis for agreements which might serve to reduce areas of contact that otherwise might generate the spark of war.

It is only as this nation proceeds diligently to explore these areas that it can expect to maintain the respect of mankind.

This we have not done.

Not only have we failed to press forward in a search for areas of agreement, but we have failed even to explore the proposals of others. Administratively, we are organized to brand Soviet proposals as propaganda within the hour. We do not seem to be organized to explore the feasibility of new proposals or to analyze old proposals in the light of the power reorientations of recent years, which may give them new meaning.

While I am not prepared at this time to commit myself finally to such concepts as disengagement, the fact that proposals of this kind are put forth by such able, thoughtful, and experienced men as George Kennan and Walter Lippmann suggests at a minimum that we owe it to ourselves to consider their ideas carefully and thoroughly.

The alternative to decreased tension is increased tension. The alternative to lessening tension between the Communist bloc and the free world is maintenance of the arms race, the continuation of nuclear testing, and the gradual exhaustion of such reservoirs of confidence in United States leadership as still exist throughout the world.

The alternative to *modus vivendi* is *modus moriendi*.

This requires a vigorous, unrelenting search for alternatives to destruction, whether they originate with men in the White House, the State Department, Whitehall, Warsaw, or even the Kremlin.

Not only have we failed to search for areas of agreement and to explore the feasibility of new proposals, but we have become singularly unappreciative of the feelings and fears of others, friends and nonfriends alike.

Take as an example our *obsession* with foreign military assistance programs and overseas military bases.

We have poured military assistance into any foreign country that would accept it. We have acted as if the export of military assistance were an end in itself—without significance in the political realm. But now our assistance is getting us into dilemmas of the most painful kind. . . .

The shipment of arms to any nation not practiced in the art of democratic self-government promotes maintenance of the *status quo*. Military aid to nonrepresentative governments means the use of that equipment to maintain nonrepresentative government. That aid has a tendency to pit the United States against the rising tide of self-determination and fertilizes foreign soil for the Communists to till.

And what of our overseas military bases? We now have approximately two hundred and seventy-five *major* base complexes—more than 1,400 if one counts all sites where Americans are now stationed or which are designed for emergency occupancy—located in thirty-one countries. These bases, aside from their annual maintenance costs, represent an investment of $3,700,000,000.

Many of these bases have been specifically designed to deter Soviet attack. Many are located within short range of the Soviet Union. These bases may in the past have served the deterrent purpose, and we must be grateful for that service. But these bases must certainly also provoke the Russians. Have we understood that fact? Have we made allowances for it, in our absolute unwillingness to negotiate on the subject of bases?

We have treated constant Soviet preoccupation with our overseas bases as sort of an unreasonable Soviet obsession. Speaking for myself, I am frank to admit that I might find myself plagued by an obsession against Soviet bases if their ballistic-launching facilities were in the Caribbean or Mexico. I don't think that obsession would be so very unreasonable, either.

Recently, I asked General Twining, Chairman of the Joint Chiefs of Staff, if he thought it would be "utterly unreasonable to believe that, in any negotiations, any of the bases could be traded for control of armaments."

He replied that he thought "we would all buy anything reasonable that would lead to disarmament."

I ask: Are we being reasonable? Do we believe so ourselves? Do most of the people of the world think we are being reasonable?

All the world knows that our foreign bases pose a threat for the Soviet Union. All the world knows that Soviet missiles and submarines pose a threat for the United States. All the world knows we live on the brink of disaster.

Yet we seem to operate on the theory that serious negotiation can take place only if we are safely ahead in the race. Will we ever feel ourselves sufficiently ahead to negotiate? Will the Russians?

Mr. President, I seriously doubt if either physical security or the preservation of freedom can be assured by continued preoccupation with military defense.

We put in more bases, and they make more submarines and missiles, and then we put in more bases. That is the way it is going. As General Twining said to the Committee on Foreign Relations last February, we are obviously in a race. It is a race no one can win.

SENATE ADDRESS,
JUNE 20, 1958

21. Iraq and Lebanon: "One Foot over the Brink"

The jolt of Sputnik was followed in May, 1958, by the disastrous tour of Latin America made by Vice-President Nixon—and then by the revolt in Iraq on July 14 that saw the fall of a regime closely allied to the West. A day later, President Eisenhower sent marines to Lebanon at that government's request. Our forces were still in Lebanon (their withdrawal began on August 12) when Fulbright prepared a broadside attack on the policies that he felt had brought us to the brink of disaster. His address, in the breadth of its criticism, forms Fulbright's valedictory to the Dulles era.

Mr. President, at this moment no one knows whether the United States military forces in Lebanon will be plunged deeper into the Middle East or whether an opportunity will arise in the near future to withdraw them. Certainly, it is the expressed hope of the executive branch, and, I am sure, the unspoken hope of most Americans, that these forces will be able to leave the area promptly. While they are still there, they deserve our support. The decision which put them into the Middle East was not theirs to make, though they will bear the brunt of any drastic consequences which may stem from it. The safety of the men in the Middle East is our primary concern at the moment, but if we limit our concern to considerations of the moment, we will not really solve anything. We must look at the basic causes of our troops being in Lebanon. When we do that, we find that our present trouble in the Middle East is merely symptomatic of a much more serious malady.

The truth is, Mr. President, that our foreign policy is inadequate, outmoded, and misdirected. It is based in part on a false conception of our real, long-term national interests and in part on an erroneous appraisal of the state of the world in which we live. Worse, it reflects a dangerous apathy and a quite incomprehensible unwillingness to look facts in the face....

A few weeks ago, events occurred in Latin America to remind us of the precariousness of our position in the world. There, in an area with which we had once enjoyed a most cordial, friendly, and intimate association, in this area regarded as safe, above all other, a symbolic explosion occurred, no less startling in its impact on the nation than the first Sputnik. A few years back, a former Vice-President had been greeted with almost hysterical approval in Latin America. The present Vice-President was spat upon and stoned. This, too, was a measure of how far we had fallen. This, too, gave us cause to think. What had we done? After all, this outburst of resentment and fury was directed at something besides Mr. Nixon as a person. Once again, for a brief time, we turned our attention to the serious business of what had gone wrong. Once again the soul-searching began, and once again it did not last long. We found an easy reassurance in the smug belief that only a relative handful of Latin Americans participated in the riots and that they were either Communist or Communist sympathizers. Once again the same apathetic inertia spread from the government to the people. Once again Latin America receded from the front pages of the press to the last pages.

Now it has happened again. We awaken one morning and find strange hands in control of what we believed to be the most reliable of the Middle Eastern nations, so reliable that we had encouraged it to join in a friendly military pact. Its king, who, we had been given to understand, was a good and progressive chap, is no more. We are face to face with new rulers of Iraq, who, despite the hundreds of millions we have spent on intelligence groups, are unknown factors to us. We scarcely knew whether to take them to our bosom or send them to the same mental oblivion to which we have consigned the Chinese Communists, in the naïve belief that if we failed to acknowledge their existence they would somehow go away. Next morning, we find our marines have landed in Lebanon.

It has taken this shock, Mr. President, to bring our errant attention once again to the highly dangerous conditions extant in the world in which we live. How long will our fleeting awareness last this time, Mr. President, before it disappears? Perhaps it would be well to ask ourselves: Where will the shock come next? One thing is certain: If we go on as we are, more shocks await us in the not too distant future and in many parts of the world. If we go on as we are, soon—in the fashion of the cat on the hot tin roof—we shall be skipping from one crisis to another all over the globe, unable to get our footing anywhere. We shall not even have time for another spell of apathy before we are face to face with unspeakable disaster....

It is time, Mr. President, to ask ourselves some very searching questions. Think about it for a moment. This country emerged from World War II at an unprecedented pinnacle of world power and influence. Most of the world was with us. We were looked upon from one end of the earth to the other as the great hope of mankind. Even our erstwhile enemies were ostensibly not unfriendly. In deed as well as in word, we stood for peace, progress, and the international leadership of freedom. This was the wave of the future, not communism, and no power of Soviet propaganda was able to shake that almost universal conviction. I need hardly remind the Senate that a decade later this conviction had disappeared in large areas of the world, and in many others it was gravely shaken. The first question which we must ask ourselves is: Why have we slipped? Is it Soviet propaganda which has been responsible for the change? Does the fault lie in the diabolical genius of the Russians for spreading lies and having them believed, or does it lie in ourselves?

An aphorism I heard the other day has some pertinence in this connection. A man may fail many times, this saying goes, but he is not really a failure until he starts blaming others. I suggest this is true of nations, too, Mr. President, and it is painfully descriptive of the United States government at this point in history. Everything that goes wrong is laid at the door of communism. I suggest that some of the blame belongs closer to home.

We can bewail the fact that the Russians did their homework and launched the Sputnik, but we had better look to our own failure to place greater emphasis on scientific progress and intellectual achievement. We can berate the Soviet Union for attempting to enlarge its relations with Latin America, or we can look to ourselves for losing the beneficial intimacy which we once enjoyed with that part of the world. We can denounce the Soviet Union for seeking a foothold in the Middle East, or we can examine our own failure to develop policies which win the acceptance of the peoples of that region. We can decry the Soviet Union's great influence in China, or we can look to ourselves for cutting off all our contacts with the Chinese people by emulating the habits of the ostrich. We can complain of Soviet efforts to undermine NATO, or we can ask ourselves why we have failed to give affirmative leadership to the free nations of the West. We can berate the Soviet Union for posing before the world as the defender of the ordinary man's vital interest in peace, or we can look to ourselves for our failure to give an intelligent leadership to mankind's hope for peace.

Mr. President, for years now we have taken the easy way. Let something go wrong—whether it be in China or Nigeria—and we have had a ready answer: The Soviet Union was behind it. What a perfect formula for the evasion of reality and, I may add, what a futile formula. If there is a single factor which more than any other explains the predicament in which we now find ourselves, it is our readiness to use the specter of Soviet communism as a cloak for the failure of our own leadership. The Soviet Union has indeed been our greatest menace—not so much because of what it has done, but because of the excuses it has provided us for our own failures. I am told that even now leaders of the administration go to bed with tracts from the Marxist litany in order better to understand their adversaries. Now, Mr. President, I am not averse to these studious

118

pursuits. I suggest, however, that they ought not to be followed to the point of obsession. They ought not to be used, like a hot pad, as a comforting device to provide surcease from the more chilly business of examining our policies with a view to removing the weaknesses and inadequacies which the Communists are only too happy to exploit....

I cannot believe that the Russians are any more capable than any other people. I can accept the obvious fact that they have worked harder at world domination by communism than we have for the spread of freedom. I am impelled, further, to consider the likelihood that they have been aided by the inadequacies of our own policies and, even more specifically, by the conduct of these policies. And I may add that I believe their job has become easier as the conduct of these policies has become worse and worse.

That is why I urge the Senate to put aside now this blinder, this comforting belief that the Soviet Union is the sole source of our troubles....

A principal factor involved in this process is that, in the fear of the deviltry of communism, we have cast ourselves indiscriminately in the role of the defender of the *status quo* throughout the world. Look at the image of this country through the eyes of the rest of the world. Here we are, a nation that for decades prided itself on its revolutionary tradition, on its willingness to experiment, to abandon the outworn traditions of a bygone age and move on to new horizons. We Americans conceived of our civilization as a movement, not as a condition, as a voyage, not as a harbor (as one noted historian put it). But today this dynamic nation is shrinking in the eyes of the world from the specter of revolution. Here is this nation appearing before the world as an obstacle to change at the very time when the world is in a ferment of cataclysmic change.

I do not ascribe this particular weakness in our position to the present administration. I suspect the roots of this fearful clinging to the *status quo* go back at least to the time of the collapse of Nationalist China. There is a popular concept in this country, Mr. President, that the chief trouble with our policies with respect to China was that we failed to give sufficient military and other aid in sufficient time; in effect, that we did not become sufficiently involved with the Nationalist government to sustain it. I am afraid that the opposite may be the case: that, in an urge to maintain the *status quo* in China, we gave too much and became too deeply involved with a government which had failed to meet the demands of its people for change. Those tragic events in China seem to have set a rigid pattern which has been followed almost unbrokenly ever since. Too often, when peoples elsewhere have sought to assert their God-given rights against an intolerable *status quo,* we have appeared to be on the side of those who opposed the assertion of these rights. Too often, we have found ourselves aligned against those who would strike at tyranny or corruption. We have found ourselves aligned with landlords who have exploited tillers of the soil and with militarists who have kept the people in line.

Look through the sorry record of the past ten years. What does it show? It shows aid extended indiscriminately to governments which serve the needs of their peoples and alike to those which do not. It shows aid eagerly and lavishly given to governments which profess their anticommunism, even though their peoples, with valid reason, might have been disenchanted with those governments. At the same time it shows aid reluctantly given, if at all, to governments which refuse to parrot anti-Communist lines but which, nevertheless, have deep roots in their own peoples.

Nor is that all, Mr. President. When it has been a question of spending on anti-Communist propaganda through the blatant information program, the tens of millions of dollars have poured out, willingly and without much critical judgment. But when it has been a question of exchanging students, of interchanging the best of cultural achievements between nations, there has been much rending of hair over economy and a parsimonious doling-out of the shekels. For this particular policy, the Congress must bear a large part of the responsibility.

Ever since the end of the Marshall Plan, when it has been a question of meeting the desperate needs of people elsewhere for economic and social programs, we have been pinch-penny in our approach. But when it has been a question of aid for the military establishments of other countries, the hand has gone deep and unhesitatingly into the pocket of the American people. We have on a grandiose scale provided peoples of the underdeveloped nations with the weapons of destructive warfare, and have been miserly in providing them weapons to wage war on their own poverty, economic ills, and internal weaknesses. Military aid has been on the most lavish scale. Look at what has now happened in Iraq. The Iraqi Army, which was the recipient of our arms, has thrown out the government which we regarded as the most friendly and most reliable of the Arab states in its adherence to the West. It is not at all impossible that the weapon with which the unfortunate young king was assassinated was provided, with the best intentions but with the utmost shortsightedness, under the military-aid program.

How many similar plots are being hatched in other armies which we are aiding, Mr. President? There are billions of dollars worth of arms and military supplies loose in the world as a result of this aid. Before this equipment rusts, before these supplies are exhausted, I am afraid that we are in for many other unpleasant shocks on the model of Iraq, from one end of the globe to the other. Nor is this sudden, unexpected use of military aid in Iraq the first time that has happened. How much of the equipment furnished to the Nationalist government of China was subsequently used by the Communists to kill Americans in Korea? Will we never learn, Mr. President? How many more Americans must be killed by our own foolish gifts of weapons to shaky governments before we learn?

Mr. President, I know that this administration is not solely responsible for the corner into which we are being inexorably driven in our own relations with other nations. While foreign policy in this country is basically a function of the executive branch of the government, Congress also has a share of the responsibility.

While we are asking questions about how the United States got in the world predicament in which it now finds itself, it behooves us in Congress, Mr. President, to take a look at our own part in the process. It is putting it mildly to say that Congress has not always been wise in its foreign-policy actions. This is particularly true in regard to appropriations. We have, I think, been too generous with regard to military assistance and too niggardly with regard to economic and cultural matters. This is a reflection, first, of the parochial attitude Congress frequently takes in regard to money matters, and, second, of the lack of strong political leadership in the administration....

I do not know, Mr. President, where we are heading under the present leadership of this country, which, when it is not weak and desultory, tends to be impetuous and arbitrary. I doubt that the leadership itself knows. I do know that unless there is a drastic, sweeping revision of our foreign policy and in the execution of that policy, we are heading for far greater troubles than these in which we now find ourselves. Frankly, I do not see anywhere on the horizon the will, the understanding, the initiative, or the imagination to bring about the revision which is so desperately needed in order to stop the drift to disaster. I do not see these characteristics; yet they are essential to a peaceful solution of the Middle East situation. They are essential to the maintenance of the close alliance among the Western nations. They are essential to a restoration of the sound, neighborly relations which we once enjoyed with Latin America. They are essential for stability and the growth of friendly relations with the nations of Asia and Africa and to a solution of the complex problems of the Far East.

If we are going to solve these problems, Mr. President, we must stop thinking about them in terms of a stereotyped view of the world. We must abandon the clichés and reconsider all our assumptions. One of the key questions we must ask ourselves is: What do we want the world to look like five, ten, twenty-five years from now? And, in answering that question, we must hardheadedly distinguish between what are really vital national interests and what would be nice if we could have it.

For example, what really is our policy in the Middle East? Can we live with Arab unity, or can we not? In this connection, we should determine to our own satisfaction the real relationship between pan-Arabism and communism. The assumption made by the administration that Nasser is merely a tool of the Kremlin should be tested as to its validity.

Would it not be wise for us to revive the proposal, which has been tentatively advanced on several occasions, to create a regional-development authority under the direction of Arab leaders primarily and drawing at least some of its funds from regional sources, that is, production or transportation of oil?

Should we not give careful and thorough consideration to a policy of neutralization of the area, with guarantees from all interested parties? And, as a corollary of this, would it not be wise to embargo the shipment of arms into the area?

The administration might well review the validity of the concept of the Baghdad Pact and of the Eisenhower Doctrine. If these proposals are as worthless as I believe them to be, it is high time they be reconsidered and abandoned. A fresh, new, uncommitted look should be taken at the mistaken policies we have been following, and which have led us into our present impasse.

Where are we going in the Far East? That great area is temporarily quiescent, but by no means peaceful. What is our policy? We cannot forever ignore six hundred million people on the mainland of China, but what are we doing to make it possible to deal with them on the best terms possible?

If anybody in the administration is giving serious, imaginative, uninhibited thought on a full-time basis to these and many other similar questions which I could cite, I have so far been unable to discover it. Yet there are competent people in private life throughout the country who are thinking about these questions and who, I hope, are beginning to formulate some answers. . . .

I do not pretend that there are answers to all our problems. Some difficulties in human affairs are insoluble. If this proves to be the case in regard to our present situation, we had then better begin to search for ways and means of accommodating ourselves to that fact.

But at least, Mr. President, let us try to develop a set of coherent, realistic, well-thought-out objectives and feasible policies to attain them.

SENATE ADDRESS,
AUGUST 6, 1958

Chapter Five

A WORLD IN FERMENT

22. The Bricker Amendment: "It Is an Attempt to Escape the World"

It can be fairly said that between 1954 and 1960 the dividing line between domestic and foreign affairs was largely erased, and that every significant development at home created an echo abroad. When Fulbright served as a freshman congressman on the House Foreign Affairs Committee in 1943-45, most Americans were still unaware of the extent to which the walls were closing in. By the time the Arkansas Democrat became chairman of the Senate Foreign Relations Committee, in January, 1959, both he and the country had come to learn that every domestic controversy, whether over Joe McCarthy or Central High School in Little Rock, became inevitably intermingled with world opinion.

But in 1954 the idea of Fortress America still lingered as a persistent phantom in the halls of Congress. One expression of the isolationist impulse was the Bricker amendment, designed to limit the treaty-making powers granted in the Constitution to the President of the United States. In retrospect, the fight over the Bricker amendment was the final spasm of traditional isolationism; the heir to Senators Bricker and Taft was to be Senator Goldwater, who would have America commit its arms and prestige in a provocative way in every corner of the globe. In 1954, Senator Bricker's partisans were

124

at the peak of their strength, and what should have been a great debate was taking place. Yet, as Marquis Childs wrote at the time, the discussions bore "little or no resemblance" to the great Senate debates of the past. "One speech, however," Childs added, "has been made that stated some plain truths in language of a kind that the classic debaters of the past would recognize."

The speech was Fulbright's, and it sought to place the dispute of our constitutional tradition and to recall the spirit of founding fathers who were free of "the swinish blight" of anti-intellectualism.

Mr. President, the American Constitution is one of the miracles of man's history. It was hammered out initially by great men in a series of great debates. Then it was subjected to the most searching examination in another series of debates carried on throughout the thirteen states before it was finally adopted.

Generation after generation of Americans has turned to the Federalist debates for enlightenment, not only as to the foundations of the Constitution, but also for enlightenment upon the philosophy of democratic government in the United States. The Constitution is our most brilliant, as it is our most enduring, political success. It has been a pre-eminently workable document adaptable to the incalculable social and political changes that have occurred upon this continent and in the world since it was written, nearly two centuries ago. Under it this nation has successively weathered the mightiest civil war of all time and three world wars stretching from the days of Napoleon to those of Kaiser Wilhelm II, Hitler, and Mussolini. Nor is this all. Under it also the American people have achieved more happiness and prosperity for a longer time and over a wider area than any other system ever erected by men.

The reader of the constitutional debates feels, again, a solemn pride in his country. The debaters were gifted men. They constituted, indeed, such a brilliant company as has rarely been found anywhere, and whose like we have not had since their passing. Widely and deeply educated, they drew upon all the legal-philosophical sources of the ancient and contemporary world. Themselves learned, they respected both learning and the learned. They were free of the swinish blight so common in our time—the blight of anti-intellectualism. I should like to remind you, if I may, that this blight, hitherto alien to our democracy, was endemic in Fascist Italy and Germany, as it is endemic today in Soviet Russia.

The founding fathers were children of the age of enlightenment. They believed in reason. They sought to convince other men by persuasion, rather than to try to bludgeon them into submission by force. They were serene in the belief that reason, applied to human affairs, could bring men to a better way of life and living. They had an immense contempt for the debater who descended to the low level of personalities. They detested the use of slogans and epithets, for their use is the last refuge of the mentally insecure and the intellectually bankrupt. They appealed to men's minds, not to their passions. In short, they were reasonable men seeking to establish a new state upon a rational foundation so firm that it could withstand the stress of change in decades to follow.

And here, if I may divert for a moment, I should like to say that I am tired of name-calling directed at anyone who does not agree with the other fellow. I am prepared to debate the principles in which I believe. I am not, however, prepared to indulge in any contest of name-calling, for not only is this repulsive, but it is also, as I see it, an offense to manners that govern the conduct of decent men, and it is antidemocratic in the operation of a democratic society.

The founding fathers pursued rationality in their acts and in their debates for another reason: They believed that our democratic society presupposes the code of the gentleman. It does not expect saintly conduct of men. It does, however, expect that they should conduct themselves with a decent respect for the opinions of mankind. But when they do not do so, when public men indulge themselves in abuse, when they deny others a fair trial, when they resort to innuendo and insinuation, to libel, scandal, and suspicion, then our democratic society is outraged, and democracy is baffled. It has no apparatus to deal with the boor, the liar, the lout, and the antidemocrat in general.

Under the Constitution, the United States has gone from weak-

126

ness to strength, from strength to greater strength, from isolation to world leadership, until now we are a people having an unparalleled prosperity at home and an unprecedented power abroad.

The founding fathers were, I repeat, eminently successful in their efforts. Only once was their work violently challenged. And we paid a stupendous price for that challenge in blood, treasure, and heartbreak. At that time, as you know, there were fanatics in Boston and there were other fanatics in Charleston. Men hurled epithets at one another; they refused to listen to reason; faith gave way to fanaticism; and, as Americans venomously distrusted one another, we came to a bloody civil war.

It is then no small thing to drastically alter the Constitution by an amendment that in effect throttles the President of the United States in his conduct of foreign relations. It is indeed bewildering to see the Constitution, which for so long has been the bulwark of our liberties and the primary source of our political strength, come under such violent attack as we have not witnessed since the 1850's. It is even more bewildering when one considers that, so far from being a "loophole" in our Constitution as is now claimed, the treaty-making power was perhaps the most urgent reason for calling the Constitutional Convention. Treaties made under the Articles of Confederation and the Federalist papers show the extreme care taken in the formulation of this power, and the system of checks and balances applicable to it.

But today I am less concerned with the Bricker amendment in its direct constitutional sense than I am with it as evidence of a disturbing phase of present-day thinking common to many men.

The essence of their malady, as I see it, is this: It is an attempt to escape the world. As troubles and problems, many of them apparently insoluble, pile one upon the other, an irresistible desire to escape it all wells up in their consciousness. Political scientists call this tendency to withdraw from the struggle and to pretend it does not concern us "isolationism." The psychologists tell us that it is a very natural yearning of a deeply troubled adult to return to the peace and quiet of prenatal security.

Whatever the instinct or the motive, we know that such retreat

127

from the world is impossible. Our salvation, if we are to be saved, will come from looking the facts in the face and following wise policies based upon those facts.

We often talk about adopting a tough policy in foreign affairs. I suggest that loose talk about being tough is evidence more of weakness than strength, for a strong man who really believes in himself does not try to impress the other fellow by being tough. We need, not toughness, but toughmindedness: that is, the willingness and ability to look facts in the face, however bitter they may be, to appraise them at their true worth, and then to act calmly, judiciously, and determinedly....

One reason, of course, that we should like to retreat from the world is that struggle—constant, unremitting, blood-and-sweat struggle—is the primitive law of all life on this planet. Struggle successfully, and you survive. Fail to struggle enough, and you perish. The record of mankind is replete with illustrations of tribes and nations long vanished from the face of the earth because they were unable to meet the conditions of struggle imposed upon them either by their environment or by human enemies. History records their passing, but nature does not weep for them.

Nature—pitiless in a pitiless universe—is certainly not concerned with the survival of Americans or, for that matter, of any of the two billion people now inhabiting this earth. Hence, our destiny, with the aid of God, remains in our own hands.

Mr. President, we have been given at times to adopting methods that seem strange to a civilized and enlightened people. For these methods, in essence, are those of the witch doctor in a primitive African village. He attempts to drive away the evil spirit by beating drums or by chanting cabalistic incantations. We who are brought up in the tradition of science are saddened by this spectacle, knowing how fruitless it is. But incantations can be chanted in more ways than one, and when we do it by assuming that we can banish the evil spirits of an evil world by turning our backs upon it through such concepts as neutrality or the Bricker amendment, we are merely denying our intelligence, turning our backs upon our knowledge, retreating from the facts of life, and placing our faith in methods that all history and all experience have demonstrated to be futile.

Our enemy is not the President of the United States, whether the incumbent, his successor to come, or his predecessors. Indeed, so far as President Eisenhower is concerned, it is an unbelievable spectacle to see Members of the Senate—particularly members of his own party—trying to hamstring him in the exercise of perhaps the most solemn and far-reaching obligation of his office—namely, the conduct of our foreign relations when not long ago this nation gave its life into his hands by making him the supreme commander of our military forces. And one's amazement becomes greater in the face of this spectacle seeing that recently the American people, believing not only in his high qualities as a man but also in his high abilities as a diplomat trained in the hard school of experience, elected him President of the United States at a period when the successful or unsuccessful conduct of our foreign relations may mean the life or death of this nation.

Mr. President, the Constitution charges the President with the duty of conducting our foreign relations by and with the advice of the Senate. It makes him the leading actor, not a spectator and a mere witness. And this role has been discharged by successive Presidents of the United States throughout the nearly two centuries' duration of the Constitution. It was never intended by the founding fathers that the President of the United States should be a ventriloquist's dummy sitting on the lap of the Congress.

I do not share the fears of an ignorant or wilful President or Senate, and this faith on my part is not merely an innocent trust in individuals, present and future. It is a faith in the forms of government which we have known for 165 years, in the traditions and history of the institutions of the Presidency, the Senate, and the Supreme Court, and in the ability of our people, present and future, to regulate those institutions through the processes of government, as they have in the past.

Yet we have come to this constitutional crisis—not, I believe, because Members of this Senate, whether Democrat or Republican, have little faith in President Eisenhower's wisdom and patriotism.

We have come to it, I think, because, in our desperation to escape the world that we can never escape, we are seeking some device of magic that would enable us to accomplish an impossible end.

Many years ago I read an old-fashioned oration on George Washington by Edward Everett. Everett said that "common sense was eminently a characteristic of George Washington." I could not have been more disappointed and disillusioned than by this appraisal of one of my heroes. For as a boy I naturally thought of Washington as a dashing figure on a horse leading his troops into battle, or crossing the ice-caked Delaware to strike the Hessians at night. It was years later that I realized the significance of Edward Everett's words and understood that without George Washington's common sense it might have been impossible to establish this democracy. Washington has been dead now some one hundred and fifty odd years. But common sense is as valuable now as it was in his day, even if it is apparently becoming rarer. I suggest that we could return to it with the greatest benefit to us all.

Presidents come and go. Some are wise; some are less wise. Some are strong; some are less strong. Some are gifted; some are less gifted. This is true, too, of all the men who have sat in Congress since the founding of this nation. But all our Presidents, our Congresses, and the members of our Supreme Court, proceeding with such wisdom as was given them and operating under the checks and balances of our constitutional system, erected here a system of government without parallel among civilized men....

Mr. President, I am opposed to the Bricker amendment and urge the Senate to reject it.

SENATE ADDRESS,
FEBRUARY 2, 1954

23. Little Rock: "The Legacy of an Ancient and Melancholy History"

Few controversies caused the country as much damage and Fulbright as much personal anguish as the racial strife that swept Little

130

Rock beginning in September, 1957. It had been expected that the admission of nine Negroes to previously segregated Little Rock public schools would proceed smoothly, but this did not take account of Governor Orval E. Faubus, who was in need of an issue for a third-term campaign. Whatever passions did exist were fanned by the Governor, who intruded directly into a local matter and who forced President Eisenhower to send troops to Little Rock on September 24; the ensuing uproar is too fresh in memory to require recounting here.

Fulbright was in Great Britain when emotions touched the crest, and he was widely criticized for his failure to speak out against Faubus. Caught in the net of conflicting pressure, the Senator chose a more prudent course, which, whether right or wrong, enabled him to continue to represent a state where racial feelings had been inflamed. A year later, in August, 1958, Fulbright expounded his views on Little Rock in a brief filed with the Supreme Court urging a delay in desegregation. His argument followed no stereotyped course; it was a curiously detached and philosophic analysis of the enduring Southern dilemma.

It is not the purpose here to burden the record of this court by a lengthy repetition of the facts or the legal principles developed by the attorneys for the respondents and in the opinions of the lower courts. The indulgence of this court is respectfully asked to hear an individual who is deeply troubled for the future peace and happiness of the people of Arkansas and of this nation, of all races and all creeds.

Special indulgence of this court is requested to the arguments herein set forth, not because I am a legal expert or a social scientist, but simply because for more than fifty years I have lived among the people of Arkansas, and for more than fifteen years I have represented them in the Congress of the United States, from which experience I claim some intimate knowledge of local conditions and of the mental and spiritual landscape against which the people of Arkansas live and move.

The people of Arkansas are as law-abiding, as respectful of the traditions of our Anglo-Saxon heritage as are their fellow Americans; they abhor anarchy and disorder. In truth, until the recent violence, it had been thirty years since racial disorder had troubled the people of Arkansas.

From the complete destruction of their economy during the War Between the States, the people of Arkansas have slowly rebuilt their fortunes and their standing in the nation. It may be that they are more sensitive to criticism than is the average American....

The meaningful realities of this situation are that, due to unexpected developments of an unprecedented nature, this court's original objective of procuring for Negro children education on an integrated basis cannot be provided under existing circumstances. Time is desperately needed to enable the authorities concerned to find an adjustment of this conflict.

No decision which this court can make will assure the rights of the Negro children more effectively than those decisions which it has heretofore rendered. In spite of the full force of the executive power of the federal government, even the use of the armed forces of the United States, the children did not and cannot enjoy a better, not even as good an opportunity for education under the conditions of turmoil and bedlam which result from such extreme measures. The education of all children, white and Negro, suffers from such disturbed, abnormal conditions.

The argument that to accept the decision of the district court for a delay of two and a half years is an abandonment of the integration decision of this court is without merit. Such an argument takes no account of the difference between the enunciation of constitutional doctrine and the application of that doctrine through the principles of equity. More importantly, it takes no account of the obligation of the courts to adapt their powers to the purposes for which the institution or activity affected by those powers exists....

It has become an axiom that the processes of education—and, in this country, public education—offer the solution, if any is to be found, whereby men of different races may learn to abide one another, each in the full enjoyment of his rights. If this is agreed, then the systems of education must be respected, and social experimentation in them made tolerable to their purposes.

If I may repeat, this court has observed that public education is the most important function of state and local government. (*Brown v. Board of Education,* 347 U.S. 483, 493.) To the extent that the school systems are successful, it is because local school boards, administrators, and teachers make them so. In this controversy, they are acknowledged to be men of good will. But if they are not supported by the courts, when acting in good faith, how can men of good will be expected to continue to function? It can be expected that the control of local school boards will fall into the hands of radicals and fanatics. Then neither the processes of justice nor education would be served.

The circuit court of appeals, in its opinion, had much to say about the activities of persons and governments outside this case. While these forces may be a part of the history of the case, and even if the court deems them responsible for the present circumstances, neither their recollection nor the court's despair of them affords the school board any solution to the problem of how to conduct public education in an acknowledged atmosphere of bedlam and turmoil. The court's refusal to support the good-faith position of the board can only intensify the effect of those outside forces. And, at least for the present, they are beyond the reach of this court.

The chief judge of the Eighth Circuit Court of Appeals, in a passage of profound wisdom, said:

For centuries there had been no intimate social relations between the white and colored races in the section referred to as the South. There had been no integration in the schools, and that practice had the sanction of a decision of the Supreme Court of the United States as constitutionally legal. It had become a way of life in that section of the country, and it is not strange that this long-established, cherished practice could not suddenly be changed without resistance. Such changes, if successful, are usually accomplished by evolution rather than revolution; and time, patience, and forbearance are important elements in effecting all radical changes. (*Aaron* v. *Cooper,* Eighth Circuit, supra [dissenting memorandum].)

133

That former Justice Brandeis of this court would have agreed with the reasoning of Judge Gardner is evident from his statement in Goldman's *The Words of Justice Brandeis* (1952) on page 116:

No law can be effective which does not take into consideration the conditions of the community for which it is designed; no law can be a good law—every law must be a bad law—that remains unenforced.

The failure of the majority of the circuit court to take note of these truths, in Judge Gardner's dissenting opinion, suggests that the members of the court are not familiar with the traditions, the cultural patterns, the way of life of our Southern states. Indeed, it seems clear that implicit in this whole matter is a tragic misunderstanding of fundamental human instincts and impulses.

The people of Arkansas endure against a background not without certain pathological aspects. They are marked in some ways by a strange disproportion inherited from the age of Negro slavery. The whites and Negroes of Arkansas are equally prisoners of their environment. No one knows what either of them might have been under other circumstances. Certainly, no one of them has ever been free with respect to racial relationship in the sense that the Vermonter, say, has been free. The society of each is conditioned by the other's presence. Each carries a catalog of things not to be mentioned. Each moves through an intricate ritual of evasions, of make-believe, and suppressions. In Arkansas, one finds a relationship among men without counterpart on this continent, except in similar Southern states. All this is the legacy of an ancient and melancholy history.

Under the circumstances, it is inevitable that there should have come into being what one might call a Southern mind. G. M. Young, the English historian, observed that it was dangerous for Victorian England to fail to see that time and circumstance had created an Irish mind; and it was also dangerous to fail to learn the idiom in which that mind expressed itself; and to understand that what England could never remember, Ireland could never forget.

134

History tells us that race memories long endure. They are perpetuated in myths and monuments and a mother's lullaby. They are sentimental and emotional, and when stirred up they become irrational.

We are confronted here with a problem, novel and unprecedented in the history of our country and extraordinarily complex. In our congenital optimism, we Americans believe, or affect to believe, that social questions of the greatest difficulty may be solved through the discovery and application of a sovereign remedy that will forever dispose of the problem. Yet all this flies in the face of human experience. Thus, for example, a so-called Jewish problem has endured for more than two thousand years. The Roman Catholic-Protestant problem has similarly endured since the Reformation, and one might add that the Islam-Christian problem and the Hindu-Moslem problem, among many others, plague various groups of men in this and in other countries. Millions of lives have been sacrificed to these problems, and the end is not yet.

I would suggest, then, that the problem of school integration in Arkansas is more likely—bearing in mind that flesh and blood is weak and frail—to yield to the slow conversion of the human heart than to remedies of a more urgent nature.

In this general context, we must observe a constant in the affairs of men. It is this: When their ancient social convictions are profoundly violated, or when sudden change is attempted to be imposed upon attitudes or principles deeply imbedded within them by inheritance, tradition, or environment, they are likely to react almost as by involuntary reflex, and violently.

These reflections and the inferences which may be drawn therefrom, at least as they pertain to the problem which presently confronts this court, recall to mind the words of a profound scholar, Morris R. Cohen, who wrote as follows:

The clericalist and the legalist have an undue advantage in identifying their causes with those of religion and law, causes for which humanity is always willing to make extreme sacrifices. But that identity is not complete is seen clearly in the career of Jesus of

135

Nazareth. In the days of Jesus, both clericalism and legalism were represented by the Pharisees, who carried the legalist idea into religion, and wished to control all life by minute regulations similar to those which governed the life of the high priest. To make the life of every individual as holy as that of the high priest was indeed a noble ideal. Yet it was also deadening through the mass of casuistry to which it gave rise. Jesus' protest that the Sabbath was made for man, not man for the Sabbath, cuts the foundation of all legalism and clericalism. It makes us see the profound foolishness of those who, like Cato, would adhere to the law even though the Republic be thereby destroyed. Without a legal order and some ministry of religious insight, the path to anarchy and worldliness is, indeed, dangerously shortened. But without a realization of the essential limitations of legalism and clericalism, there is no way of defending the free human or spiritual life from fanaticism and superstition. (M. R. Cohen, *Law and the Social Order; Essays in Legal Philosophy,* pages 160-161 [1933].)

For the reasons herein set forth, it is urged that this court deny the application of petitioners.

Brief of J. W. Fulbright, *Amicus Curiae,*
Aaron v. *Cooper,* August 27, 1958

24. Berlin: What Can Be Negotiated

Fulbright became chairman of the Senate Foreign Relations Committee on January 30, 1959, and it was immediately apparent that he intended to use his new influence to the full. Notice was served on the administration that every political appointment to a foreign embassy would receive the closest scrutiny. Plans were announced for a series of scholarly studies of major problems. No less important, the chairman himself in his first press conference exhorted the State Department to "move off dead center."

Besides needling the State Department, Fulbright also sought to impress upon Congress and the public that negotiation was not synonymous with appeasement. He placed himself on record as

favoring a summit meeting, and, on March 16, he tried to define
carefully the terms of dispute in the chronic Berlin crisis. His speech
caught Mr. Khrushchev's attention and contributed to the brief
thaw that made possible the Soviet Premier's American visit in
September, 1959.

MR. FULBRIGHT: Mr. President, as Mr. Khrushchev maneuvers
the Berlin situation on a giddy course toward the conference table,
the doubts and fears of our people are probably growing almost in
proportion to his capricious and thoroughly unpredictable statements.

Clearly, the executive branch must have a free hand in finding an
acceptable solution to the Berlin question. Yet it is also clear that
all Americans should have a keen appreciation of our government's
position and of just what is meant when we say we are standing
firm. They want, I should think, and surely deserve to see in a
clearer and deeper perspective the inherent character of our policy.
And this applies to our friends abroad, as well as to the American
people.

Among many responsible Europeans, there is a suspicion that we
are weakening, that we are being lured into a conference in which
all important concessions will be made by our side. They observe
that, even as we profess firmness, we are trimming our conventional
forces. A prominent French editor has been quoted as saying, "They
[meaning some French officials] think you are about to commit
treason in a war that has already started."

So it becomes urgent that not only the Russians, but the entire
world, understand our intentions—intentions which, I believe, are
shared by Republicans and Democrats alike. If we fail to make our
intentions clear, we shall have disheartened our friends and people
everywhere who value freedom, and we shall, of course, have done
our adversary a great service.

My purpose in making this brief statement, therefore, is not only
to reassure our friends, but also to make clear to the leaders of the
Soviet Union, and thereby avoid miscalculations on their part, that,
despite the free debate characteristic of a democracy, the American

people, regardless of party, stand united on the following propositions:

First: The United States will make no separate, or unilateral, deals with the Soviet Union.

Second: The United States will not be driven or enticed from Berlin or from West Germany. We intend to stay until such time as we, in concert with the governments of West Germany, France, and Britain, decide to withdraw. Such withdrawal will come only as a result of some agreement with the Russians on issues larger than Berlin which we and our allies believe is in our interest. To leave Berlin prematurely or before Russia's goad, would induce consequences of a psychological nature in both the German sectors, ranging from cynical mistrust of our reliability to despair itself. The fabric of the Western alliance would undoubtedly begin to unravel. And the neutral societies, anxiously watching this struggle of two great systems, would probably commence an unflattering evaluation of our chances.

Third: The United States cannot in honor accept, even tacitly, any proposition designed to formalize the subjugation of the once free satellite peoples. Our society owes much of its character to the eighteenth century philosophers who gave meaning and depth to the term freedom. We could no more accept the permanent subjugation of freedom in the satellites than we could consent to any compromise of freedom in Berlin or West Germany.

This is not to say that we intend to use force against the Soviets to bring about the liberation of these presently subjugated peoples. False hopes of physical intervention by us should not be encouraged.

It does mean that we deny that the Russians have any legal or moral right to dominate these subject peoples. We reject the validity of their position based solely upon superior physical power.

It does mean, we believe, that in time the public opinion of the world will cause the Russian people to relinquish their control of the once free peoples of Poland, East Germany, Hungary, Czechoslovakia, Latvia, Estonia, Lithuania, Romania, and Bulgaria.

We may even hope that, as conditions of life improve in the

138

U.S.S.R., the harsh and brutal attitude of the Russians toward their fellow men may be humanized.

These basic intentions having been stated, it is necessary to add that I see no peculiar virtue in the *status quo*. We must not, therefore, be unreceptive to fresh, soundly reasoned ideas. We welcome all responsible suggestions aimed at dissipating this glow of crisis hanging over Central Europe and the sense of futility that goes with it.

There are negotiable points. Agreements by us and the Russians on some of them might serve the interests of both nations. In Germany, we find both sides, each bristling with nuclear weapons, eying one another balefully across an unrealistic boundary. It seems to me, for example, that if both were to move back an equal distance—however slight the distance—the possibility of war, especially accidental war, would be reduced.

Much of the difficulty of making progress toward relieving tensions in Central Europe derives from the growing use of such terms as "easement," "relocation of forces," and, especially, "disengagement." If, as seems to be the case, there is a fundamental ambiguity clinging to words like "disengagement"—and even "negotiation"—it should be cleared up. These terms must not be equated with appeasement and retreat, as too often they are.

It should be clearly understood by friend and foe alike that under no circumstances will the United States disengage, or relocate its forces, except in return for a bona fide *quid pro quo*—in short, an agreement that would benefit the Western allies at least as much as it would benefit the Soviet Union.

We ought not to accept the facile axiom that the Russians have no intentions of ever coming to reasonable terms on any matter directly affecting their own interests. To endorse such dogma would be to accept an annealing of the present situation, surely insupportable over the stretch of time. To the corollary admonition —that any deal with Russia would have to be policed—we agree. Neither the United States nor any of its allies is prepared to trade an easement of the situation for any agreement that could not be effectively monitored.

Finally, as the time for negotiation draws nearer, it is essential to remind ourselves not to expect too much in the way of results. A willingness on our part to negotiate, even to relocate military forces under the right circumstances, is all to the good. However, to expect any substantial easement in the near future would be the height of wishful thinking. Indeed, it may be a matter of years rather than months before the Russians will extend a *quid* equal in value to our *quo*. As before, our duty is to strengthen our defenses and our resolve. Also, we must not be discouraged. Instead, we should chip away relentlessly at the encrusted Communist mixture of dogma, braggadocio, and fear that contributes so much to keeping world peace in a recurring state of serious jeopardy.

SENATE ADDRESS,
MARCH 16, 1959

25. *The Summit and U-2: The Question Nobody Asked*

Whatever was left of the "Spirit of Camp David," a frail wraith at best, was wholly dissipated by the bewildering events that followed the May 1, 1960, U-2 flight of Francis Gary Powers. When President Eisenhower assumed personal responsibility for the overflight, he provided Premier Khrushchev with the pretext for stalking away from the summit meeting in Paris. Fulbright sought and received Senate consent for an investigation into the debacle, and the Foreign Relations Committee held extended closed hearings. The fruit was a report that placed most of the available facts on the record, but failed to arrive at any firm judgments. To supplement the committee report, Fulbright offered his personal views in a June 28 speech that some Republicans promptly attacked as lending comfort to the Soviet Union because it criticized the administration's handling of the U-2 flights. Fulbright anticipated this criticism by noting that his words would be "twisted" and that his subtle distinction between impersonal diplomatic forms and Eisenhower's unwise candor would

140

be lost. But the main thrust of his criticism was vindicated in an objective account, The U-2 Affair (*New York, 1962*) *written by David Wise and Thomas Ross, both correspondents for Republican newspapers.*

Mr. President, on behalf of the Committee on Foreign Relations, I submit a report entitled "Events Relating to the Summit Conference," together with individual views....

As is inevitable in a case of this kind where compromise is involved, the end product is probably not wholly satisfactory to any member of the committee. Yet it is generally satisfactory to most members of the committee, and I venture the hope that it will be read and pondered by the Senate, by the public at large, and especially by the officials of the executive branch. Considering the number of cooks involved, and the diversity of their feelings about the matter, this broth has turned out rather well.

Nevertheless, Mr. President, it is with a heavy heart and with some regret that I present the report to the Senate and thereby to the people of the nation. It is never pleasant to admit error in our private lives. It is far more painful for a great nation to admit that its policies have been lacking in wisdom and foresight, and one may be sure that whoever calls attention to the errors will not be thanked for his effort.

In spite of the fact that I may well expect to receive criticism, I feel a duty to express my views for whatever they are worth.

In some systems of government, notably the Communist system, error is rarely admitted by those who govern. Infallibility of the ruler is accepted by the people, who, indeed, have nothing to say about, or any power to change, the policy in any case.

In a democratic system, such as ours, the people do have much to say about policy, and they decide who shall govern them. How, may I ask, can our people be expected to discharge their duty as citizens of a self-governing republic if they are not told the truth about their affairs? It would be easier, more pleasant, and, I am sure, more popular, to join those who pretend that all is well, that the summit meeting was a triumph for the West, and that the

Japanese fiasco only demonstrates once again the viciousness of the Communists. . . .

Mr. President, the complete report of the committee is before the Senate, but there are a few points which seem to me to require emphasis. Mr. President, to say that there is no good time for a failure is to overlook the fact that there are bad times and worse times. Certainly May 1 was one of the worst times. Little or no consideration was given to the international consequences of a failure on May 1. It has been argued that, in view of the unbroken success of almost four years, there was no reason to anticipate this failure. But, Mr. President, in an enterprise as risky as this, it is imprudent not to take into account the consequences of failure. Such consequences are routinely taken into account in thousands of decisions in the day-to-day conduct of our affairs. All of us are accustomed, in considering any plan of action affecting either our private or public affairs, to ask ourselves the question, "What happens if this does not work?" Nobody asked that question in connection with the May 1 flight.

We are told that this particular flight was in a special category, that it was seeking information of extraordinary importance which might not be available later. However, we are not told, even under conditions of the utmost secrecy, what that information was. In view of the sensitivity of some of the other things we were told, this reticence on the part of the executive branch raises the question of whether the information sought on May 1 was in fact as important as it has been represented. There is ground here for the conclusion that the alleged extraordinary importance of this information is the administration's cover story for its own costly mistake. . . .

There are three aspects of the U. S. reaction to the failure which should have been handled differently. The cover statements made about the flight were far too specific and made us look ridiculous when the full extent of Soviet knowledge was revealed. The gravest mistake was made when the President assumed responsibility for the flight. Finally, after the truth became known, the State Department and the White House assumed a self-righteous attitude which further complicated our situation in Paris.

142

The crux of the matter is found in these last two points—the assumption of presidential responsibility and the self-righteous attempts to justify the flights in terms which implied their continuation. These are interrelated, and each served to compound the mischievous effects of the other.

As is pointed out in the report, it is unprecedented among civilized nations for a chief of state to assume personal responsibility for covert intelligence operations. The traditional method would have been to allow the chief of the intelligence agency to take the responsibility. One reason intelligence agencies exist is to serve as a whipping boy in cases of this kind.

Mr. President, I am not so hidebound as to argue that any departure from precedent is a mistake *ipso facto*. We must examine the reasons for the precedents and ask ourselves why, up until the 9th of May, 1960, it had been the unvarying practice in international relations for chiefs of state to hold themselves above and apart from espionage. These reasons are sound and persuasive and go to the heart of a system of diplomatic conventions which have developed over the centuries and which make it possible for nation-states of differing characteristics to carry on amicable, impersonal relations with each other.

In this system of diplomatic forms, the chief of state embodies in his person the sovereignty and dignity of his country. It is totally unacceptable for one chief of state because of this personal embodiment to impinge upon the sovereignty of another, and much less so for him to assert the right to do so. It is begging the question to say that the sovereignty of nations is violated all the time by espionage, and that the Soviet Union is the worst offender. The violations of this type, as carried out by the covert intelligence activities of any nation-state, are institutional in nature, and hitherto have not been considered as challenging the sovereignty of the nation. This is a subtle, but an important distinction.

So long as international relations are kept on an institutional, impersonal basis, states can disagree strongly and still maintain channels of communication with each other. This is why the rather stylized language of diplomacy has been developed. This is why a diplomatic note may contain strong, even harsh, statements, but still close with the phrase "Accept, sir, renewed assurances of my highest esteem."

Within our own federal system of fifty states, even though the members are somewhat less jealous of their own dignity, are more friendly and tolerant of one another than are the members of the international community, nevertheless, similar impersonal conventions govern our conduct, even here in the Senate. We do not refer to each other even by name, but as "the Senator from X State." And we usually preface a reference to one of our colleagues with adjectives such as "able," "distinguished," or "eminent." These adjectives are used even by a senator who is describing a colleague whom he does not admire. If senators said on the floor of the Senate what they really feel about some of their colleagues, the orderly conduct of legislative business would quickly become impossible. It is against the rules of the Senate for a Member to question the motives of another senator. This derives from the fact, not that senators are different from others in their motives, but from the tradition that they represent sovereign states and from the fact that without the rule the work of the Senate would be disrupted.

It seems clear to me that if chiefs of state begin the practice of personally admitting the violation of each other's sovereignty, the orderly conduct of international affairs will quickly become impossible—as, indeed, it did become in Paris, last month.

Historically, the deliberate and intentional assertion by a head of state of the right to violate the territorial sovereignty of another nation has been considered an unfriendly act of the utmost seriousness.

It is quite unacceptable to any state to be in the position in which this government put the Soviet Union last month. Although another man would have most likely been more temperate in his choice of language, it is difficult to see how anyone could have been expected to act substantially different from the way Chairman Khrushchev acted under the circumstances which confronted him in Paris.

This is not said in defense of Khrushchev; it is said in an attempt to bring understanding of our own difficulties. Either we have got to resign ourselves to the inevitability of war, or we have got to get along, somehow, some way, with the Soviet Union. And, if we are going to get along with that country, we have got to preserve the traditional conventions by means of which we can at least talk to its representatives.

Suppose, Mr. President, that the U-2 incident had occurred the other way around. Suppose a Russian counterpart of the U-2 had come down over Kansas City on May 1. This event in itself, I daresay, would have brought speeches in the Senate powerful enough to rock the Capitol dome with denunciations of the perfidy of the Soviets on the eve of the summit conference and with demands that the President not go to Paris. But then, Mr. President, reflect how much more violent the reaction here would have been it Mr. Khrushchev had said he was personally responsible for the flight, and at the same time left the impression that he had every intention of trying it again. In this connection, it is well to remember Dwight Morrow's observation that one of our troubles is that we judge ourselves by our motives, and others by their actions.

Although it was bad enough for our chief of state to assume personal responsibility for the U-2, it was worse for us then to leave the impression that the flights were to be continued and, even more, to go to such lengths to justify the flights. I am not arguing here that the flights were not justified as an espionage operation; but the justification rested solely and simply on the need of the United States for the kind of intelligence which the flights provided. This is the kind of justification which the Soviet Union, and every other government, for that matter, can understand. But it becomes quite intolerable to go beyond this and attempt to make it appear that the flights were really the Soviet's own fault, that if the Soviets had not been so secretive, we would not have had to spy on them. This attitude of smug self-rightcousness must have been unbearably provocative to the Soviet government and contributed substantially to the violence and intemperate bad manners of their representative, Mr. Khrushchev, at Paris.

I suppose, Mr. President, that this statement will be twisted to have me saying that we must be nice to the Russians and to

145

Khrushchev and not offend him. The truth is that, in the orderly conduct of international relations, one ought not to be either nice or offensive; one ought to be impersonal and objective. Heaven knows our basic differences of substance with the Soviet Union make the conduct of our relations difficult enough, without our creating novel obstructions to the traditional means of communication and negotiation.

But a larger and rather more elusive issue is also involved here. It is one thing to say, "We tried to get intelligence, because we needed it." It is quite another thing to say, "We needed intelligence, and this gave us the right to try to get it."

If a man is starving to death, and if he robs a grocery store, we can understand his action on the basis of need; but his need does not give him a right to become a burglar. Hitler used to argue that Germany's need for *Lebensraum* gave him the moral right to commit aggression. The same kind of argument was heard from Mussolini and from the Japanese war lords of the thirties. It has even been heard from the Soviet Union. I hope it will not be heard, even by implication, in the United States.

Discussion of the wisdom of having our head of state assume responsibility for the U-2 has frequently been confused by irrelevant arguments over whether or not President Eisenhower should lie or should tell the truth. Stated in these terms, the answer obviously always is that the President should tell the truth, and that he should be commended for following the rigorous standards of honesty set by George Washington. But, Mr. President, although Washington admitted chopping down the cherry tree, he did not go on to say, "Yes, I did it, and I'm glad. The cherry tree was offensive to me, because it had grown so tall. I needed some cherries, and I shall chop down other cherry trees whenever I want more cherries."

In any event, Mr. President, my argument is not that the President should not have told the truth; my argument is that he should not, as the head of our nation, have become personally involved in the incident, one way or the other.

We have not yet seen the last of the results of the bumbling and fumbling of the U.S. government during the first two weeks of May,

1960. One result was that there was no summit conference. It is perfectly clear that the U-2 incident and our handling of it were the immediate cause of the collapse of the conference. It is irrelevant in this connection to argue that Khrushchev came to Paris with a predetermined position to prevent the conference from taking place. The determining factor in reaching this position was the U-2 incident, which had occurred two weeks before the conference. We also have the testimony of the Secretary of State that there were no indications, prior to May 1, that the Soviets did not intend to go through with the conference. And we have the testimony of former Ambassador Bohlen, now a high-ranking official in the Department of State, and our outstanding expert on Soviet affairs, and who was at Paris, that—and I quote from the report:

Had there been no plane incident, I believe the conference would have run its full course. The plane incident, the whole development connected with that, moved things into a totally new dimension.

It contributes little to our understanding of these events to say Khrushchev wrecked the conference. Of course he did. The essential point is that the U-2 was the reason he did. Secretary Gates said it was the tool Khrushchev used. Secretary Herter said it was a convenient handle for Khrushchev. This is not essentially different from saying he used it as a crowbar and sledge hammer. One might even go further and say that we forced Khrushchev to wreck the conference by our own ineptness....

Those who deplore the giving up of these flights might well reflect that the renunciation of the flights in the future was a direct consequence of the assumption of responsibility by the head of state. In the words of Walter Lippmann: "Having avowed too much, the President has had to renounce too much, much more than was necessary."

Mr. President, short of the madness of preventive war, I can think of nothing more dangerous than to resume overflights of the Soviet Union. These overflights were useful while they lasted, but they have now obviously become, as the professionals describe it, compromised.

147

Mr. President, with the completion of this report, in hand, I hope that all of us may now direct our thoughts and best efforts to the problem of improving the policy-making procedures and the executive machinery of our government. There are lessons to be learned from these experiences, if we can avoid beclouding and obfuscating them with wishful thinking or partisan bickering.

SENATE ADDRESS
JUNE 28, 1960

26. Foreign Aid: Stay the Vorpal Blade

Of all Fulbright's tasks as chairman of the Foreign Relations Committee, few were as thankless during the Eisenhower years as his chore of introducing foreign-aid legislation. Not only was the program unpopular on Capitol Hill—this Fulbright could endure—but the administration was also reluctant to adopt the reforms that the Senator urged, with the result that he frequently had to defend legislation that he himself did not wholly approve. In 1959, he tried, unsuccessfully, to make the administration adopt long-term Treasury financing of the aid program; Eisenhower opposed this as "backdoor spending." Repeatedly, Fulbright also urged that less emphasis be given to military assistance, especially in programs for developing countries. This, too, found little White House support. Nevertheless, Fulbright spoke pithily and profoundly about a program as unpopular as it is misunderstood. What follows is a characteristic example.

Mr. President, I rise to discuss the action taken by the Committee on Foreign Relations on S. 3058, the Mutual Security Act of 1960.

I do not, it will be noticed, leap to my feet ablaze with excitement and enthusiasm. My eyes do not sparkle with happy anticipation. Instead, I rise with the restraining weight of a heavy responsibility and the duty unavoidably attached to my position as chairman of the Foreign Relations Committee pulling at my shoulders. Further, I do so in the oppressive knowledge that no one in the Senate has an assignment which is less likely to arouse the sympathetic interest of the American public.

I am well aware of the fact that the mutual-security program is no more popular—or, to be accurate, no better understood—among the people of my state than it is in the nation generally. How much more pleasant it would be for them and for me if their junior Senator were today reporting from committee a public-works project easily seen as of immediate and direct benefit to Arkansas. How much more entertaining it would be if I were appearing on their television screens in the guise of St. George lustily belaboring the scaly elements of evil abroad in our land, or in a burst of patriotic fervor denouncing all those benighted "furriners" who have different ideas from ours about how to organize or manage their affairs.

Yet I can and do take the stoic's comfort to be derived from the performance of a stern but vital duty, which is essential to the security and well-being of Arkansas, the nation, and the entire free world.

I think my attitude is fully comprehensible to my colleagues. Perhaps it will be even more widely understood if I compare it with the average citizen's failure to become joyful over his life insurance policy. He does not pull out his policy every so often and look at it with tender affection. In fact, his quarterly or annual payments may be a source of distress and bitter complaint. The family man, nevertheless, feels that to reduce or dispense with that policy would jeopardize that which is dearest to his heart, the security of his family.

Mr. President, I believe that the mutual-security program is the insurance policy indispensable to this country as it carries out its international responsibilities.

I would admit that Mr. Average Citizen, while seldom enthusiastic about his personal insurance policy, might well be pleased and moved by the opportunity to attach clauses which would give him much better coverage at roughly the same cost. Many of my colleagues joined me in expressing the hope that this year's mutual-security program would come to us from President Eisenhower with just such clauses in evidence. Indeed, many of us in the last session worked hard, albeit unsuccessfully, to make the changes in the bill conceded to be necessary, even by high administration officials. We tried to give the program continuity and the ability to plan for the future. We tried to make efficient administration possible, but we failed—at least temporarily.

Unfortunately, the mutual-security program for 1960 in many ways resembles a plate of warmed-over grits. In the near absence of initiative, originality, and long-term provisions in the bill before us—symptomatic of a tired administration, as well as of election-year dictates—it is not surprising that the Foreign Relations Committee, rebuffed for its energetic pains last year, could not muster much fresh enthusiasm for what is essentially a holding operation.

At the same time, I would fully support the view that there is much nourishment in warmed-over grits, and that many would find them palatable and comforting if no more exciting fare were available.

Having, I hope, clarified my over-all position, I should now like to recall briefly some of the arguments about the bill before us. My colleagues will be glad to know that I do not intend to give a long list of facts and figures and a point-by-point recital of committee actions and changes. These are fully described and justified in the excellent committee report on their desks. Instead, I want to make a few general observations about the basic nature of the mutual-security bill.

With a slight amendment, let me recall a phrase of Plutarch's:

It is a difficult task, O citizens, to make speeches to the [pocketbook], which has no ears.

I would add "no eyes," either, for the justification of a foreign-aid program has been spelled out in detail in myriad publications for more than a decade. The arguments have been presented and wholeheartedly subscribed to by all our Presidents, Secretaries of State and Defense, Joint Chiefs of Staff, and other high officials. As was noted in the other body a few days ago, every declared presidential candidate at the present time, as well as the undeclared possibilities for the nomination, so far as I am aware, is fully committed to the importance of foreign aid. Yet each year it seems that the same fundamental arguments have to be presented to those who either fail to use their eyes and ears or refuse to believe them.

Why there should still be so little public understanding of the mutual-security program is only a partial mystery. Frankly, I do not believe it unfair to assign some of the blame to the press and other information media. Very few newspapers around the country find it to their interest to pursue educational functions. Yet many are only too happy to seize on an isolated minor instance of waste or inefficiency and use it to imply that it typifies the whole foreign-aid program, which should therefore be abolished. This is rather like having the stockholders of a big corporation demand liquidation because two out of one hundred employees in a certain category are not performing well. Then there is the classic case of the headlined big "scandal"—we had an instance of that last year—and the tiny admission of error on the next edition's back page. I would also add that few people seem to be aware of the continuing force of the mutual-security provision which prohibits undue executive branch efforts to secure public understanding of the foreign-aid program here at home.

Whatever the reasons, the fact remains that there is little understanding, or there is misunderstanding, of the mutual-security program in many areas of the national scene. I am not so naïve as to think that an attempt to counter the usual criticisms with either argument or logic will go far toward converting convinced opponents of foreign aid. But neither am I so discouraged that I shall not try to stimulate interest in the committee report among those who have as yet refrained from taking a firm position.

Before passing on to what I would consider more important factors, let me give at least a hurried "no" to the charges and epithets traditionally hurled at the mutual-security bill. There is always a sort of tragic Greek chorus ready to break into its moaning cries of "giveaway," inefficiency, blunders and baloney, waste and woe.

First, let us consider the "giveaway" charge. As in years past, my colleagues will find in the voluminous record of committee hearings testimony to the effect that roughly eighty per cent of all mutual-security funds are directly spent in the United States, and that over

500,000 jobs for American citizens have been created by the program. These estimates, made by nongovernmental experts in 1957, are still applicable and are unrefuted. But how much publicity is given and how much attention is paid to this evidence, and what is the response? One elected representative of the American people, when recently confronted with this information, figuratively folded his arms and stuck out his lower lip, and literally said, "I do not believe it." There was no further argument, and there will be none now on that score. I do not mean to imply that this is the principal justification for this program, but it is on this one score.

Next, what about waste and inefficiency? It seems that even the strongest supporters of the mutual-security program these days must go through a ritualistic ceremony of admitting and deploring the element of truth in these charges, pledging themselves anew to a crusade for improvement, and then stating somewhat ruefully that they will vote for the bill. I have considerable sympathy for this reaction, since I am far from believing that every project is equally essential and that the program now before us is the best that could be created. In fact, I know that it is not.

Yet I doubt that this defensiveness is actually necessary. I doubt that our constituents really see us or administration officials as playboys of the roaring twenties frantically scattering taxpayers' money to the winds. I doubt that we need constantly to protest that we do not condone ineptitude and careless handling of money. And I fear that, by catering to the critics' obsession with an acknowledged small amount of waste, we invite at least two dangerous reactions: One, we allow attention to be diverted from really important deficiencies in the aid program; and, two, we misrepresent Americans as being more interested in the accounting process than in preserving national security and benefiting humanity.

If anyone does not have enough imagination to comprehend the difficulties and inevitable trial-and-error methods involved in an attempt to give a primitive jungle or desert country a chance to preserve its independence, then no words of mine will serve to impart that imagination. If anyone believes that his townsmen and neighbors, in serving our country overseas, through some mysterious alchemy lose all ideals and virtues, and become bumbling wastrels, then I can only commiserate with that person for his low opinion of his fellow men, and perhaps of himself. If anyone thinks that the pure application of American business methods will lift the foreign-aid program into a paradise of efficiency, I would ask him if he has never known of a fellow citizen who went out to buy a new automobile or television set, and found he had bought a "lemon." If anyone considers that the U.S. Congress has discovered the touchstone of inspired planning and absolute efficiency, let him take a wind-swept ride on one of our impressive new subway cars, with wheels designed for a dead-straight track, and let him listen to the reproaches of those wheels as they shudder and groan through a serpentine tunnel and grind themselves into dust. But I have not heard anyone advocate the abolition of the Senate merely because of that glaring instance of ineptitude.

The sad truth, Mr. President, is that human enterprises are no more perfectible than the imperfect humans who conceive of them and carry them out. This fact happily does not in the least deter mankind in its constant battle for what it believes is progress and a better world. It has not discouraged a campaign for improved administration of the mutual-security program; indeed, our committee report, as well as that of the other body, cites marked improvements in the program....

As I have suggested, more important drawbacks exist in the mutual-security program and are of a character different from what the usual criticisms indicate. These drawbacks can generally be classified under the charge of adopting short-term solutions for long-range problems. Each year we go through the same time-consuming and exhausting process of examining the program with a fine-tooth comb. And each year the resulting legislation becomes more complex and cumbersome, as friend and foe alike hasten to add just those few more provisions that will really add up to a magical formula for preventing any waste whatsoever. In the process of detailed argument, the administration becomes more and more committed to stand by and carry out plans that events may prove to be ill-adapted to meet and overcome rapidly shifting local situations.

153

Although few programs ever undertaken by any government at any time have been so carefully scrutinized and checked, congressional critics insist upon diverting our attention from the policy issues, which properly should be our main concern, to a narrow concentration upon administrative practices. The goal here seems to be to make us over into management experts, rather than shapers of foreign policy. The committee has manfully struggled to elevate its work to the proper plane—especially with a view toward planning for the longer-range future—but has made little headway against administration timidity and congressional suspicions. . . .

Let me close by addressing exhortations to three groupings among my colleagues:

First, to those who intend to vote for S. 3058 in the belief that it is a good, sound bill and just what the doctor ordered, I pay my sincere respects with a somewhat wistful admiration for such consistency and faith.

To those who recognize that the doctor ordered it, but disagree with the nature of the prescription and want to change doctors, I would recommend the old La Guardia slogan, "patience and fortitude." I would also tentatively suggest that the medicine not be taken through clenched teeth, for fear of spilling enough to require the administration of a supplemental dose.

Finally, to those who firmly believe that the mutual-security bill is a monster to be slashed ruthlessly, I would invite them to look at page 25 of the printed hearings. They will find that the repository of all foreign-policy wisdom—I am, of course, referring to the Bureau of the Budget—has already hacked some seven hundred and fifty million dollars from the departmental requests with its "vorpal blade." Surely those colleagues will not wish to prevent the bleeding Jabberwock from staggering through one more year.

SENATE ADDRESS,
APRIL 27, 1960

Chapter Six

FROM COALITION TO COMMUNITY

---

27. A United States of Europe: "It Is Not an Idealistic Dream"

A bright strand of continuity that threads through Fulbright's public career is his conviction that free nations must hang together or that assuredly they will perish separately. The Senator had hoped that the United Nations would form a vehicle for transcending absolute sovereignty, supplanting the rule of force with the rule of law. In his disappointment with the U.N. charter, Fulbright turned his thoughts to the Atlantic community, where he saw an opportunity for achieving within a part of the world a path-breaking step toward unity.

As early as March 21, 1947, Fulbright joined with Senator Elbert Thomas of Utah in introducing a joint resolution that would have placed Congress on record as favoring the creation of a United States of Europe within the framework of the United Nations. This was two years before the treaty creating NATO was signed in Washington and three months before General Marshall, then Secretary of State, made his Harvard speech of June 5 that led to the European Recovery Program. On April 7, 1947, during the debate on aid to Greece and Turkey, the Arkansas Democrat elaborated his case for a resolution that was then regarded as a novelty and that Congress failed to adopt.

155

On March 21, Senator Thomas of Utah and I introduced a concurrent resolution providing that the "Congress favors the creation of a United States of Europe within the framework of the United Nations." On the same day a similar resolution was introduced in the House of Representatives by Congressman Boggs of Louisiana.

This is not a new idea. For centuries the leading thinkers and statesmen of the world have, from time to time, urged the creation of a federated Europe as the best method of bringing peace and prosperity to that unhappy region, and as one of the essential conditions for a peaceful world.

We know that both world wars grew out of the conflicts which are inherent in the fragmented sovereignties of Europe. We should know that so long as this senseless conglomeration of separate political and economic entities exists there is little hope for the peace and prosperity of the world. We also know that the most propitious time to move forward is just after society has been disturbed by some great upheaval, leaving it in an unstable and fluid state. Europe is in that condition today, and the time is ripe for a change. It is our job to see that the change is forward to a system of freedom and self-government, rather than backward to slavery and tyranny.

No one can tell at this time how this proposal will be received by the European countries. The practical thing to do would be for representatives of these countries to meet and draw up a tentative constitution for the consideration of their own people and the world. Only by formulating a specific proposal dealing with all the matters involved in a federal union can the ideas of the people crystallize and arrive at a reasonable judgment. If the Congress should adopt, now, Senate Concurrent Resolution 10, I think it would give impetus to the calling of such a constitutional convention.

It is, of course, certain that many people will dismiss the proposal as naïve and utopian, but we should remember that all proposals that promise any significant improvement in human affairs have always been branded utopian. The United States of America was, in the beginning, branded utopian, and its failure predicted by those who, if they were here today, would look with derision upon this proposal.

156

For several centuries, under the Roman Empire, Europe was united. Later, Charles the Great, in the ninth century, united all of Europe from Spain to the Elbe River under a single power. Europe has always been a cultural entity, and, in the great days of the Renaissance, national lines were not closely drawn. Culture was not French or German or Spanish, it was European. Since prehistoric days, the inhabitants of Europe have belonged to the same white race, whose branches are to be found also in northern Africa and western Asia. They possessed a common primitive civilization going back to the neolithic age, and the philologists tell us that, with one exception, all their languages are derived from a common mother tongue. Their political organizations and customs developed along similar lines and throughout their history were distinguishable from the servility which characterized oriental despotism.

Western Europe, exclusive of Russia, consists of a well-integrated economy and a land mass of approximately two million square miles with three hundred million inhabitants. Physically, racially, and culturally, there is no insuperable obstacle to a reasonable federation of these peoples.

There are very special reasons why the people of the United States should consider at this time the re-creation of the unity which, in ancient days, enabled the Europeans to live in relative peace and happiness. Already we have made, or are committed to make, enormous loans to the nations of Europe. We are spending hundreds of millions of dollars feeding the people of Germany and the devastated countries. We are faced in the immediate future with the further obligation of supporting Greece and Turkey at great cost. But overshadowing all these obligations is the supreme interest that we have in creating a peaceful world. The primary reason for these loans and grants is the creation of a stable and orderly world in which we may live in peace, and yet we should know that money alone will not achieve our objective.

This proposal for a United States of Europe is not an idealistic dream to bring relief to the suffering people of Europe. Americans can be, if they are of a mind to be, sound, practical businessmen. As President Truman said recently, we have already invested three hundred and forty-one billion dollars in preventing tyranny from enveloping the world. In addition, we are committed to spending six hundred million dollars annually to support Germany, to making many millions of loans to other European nations; and in the immediate future we probably shall undertake the support of Greece and Turkey. As practical people we may well ask ourselves: How do we finally work out from under these obligations?

There is no simple, all-inclusive answer to this question, but one of the essential conditions to any solution is the re-establishment of industry and commerce within the framework of a stable political system. In the Near East and in Europe a prerequisite to the revival of trade and industry is a United States of Europe. Without a prosperous Europe to consume the produce of the Near East and other countries, and without the production of Europe's industry, I can see little hope for a revival of commerce on a substantial scale.

In Moscow, at present, the representatives of the great powers are trying to find a solution to the problem of what to do with Germany. They are confronted with a dilemma. On the one hand all of Europe and the Near East is in need of the goods which Germany could produce. Without that production, the rehabilitation of those areas will be slow indeed. But, on the other hand, the great powers fear that, if the industrial capacity of Germany is turned loose to produce at a maximum, for a third time a militant Germany will emerge to attack the world....

The way out of the dilemma in which we find ourselves is the creation of a United States of Europe. There are fourteen states which are not yet dominated by the Communists. These states have a population of nearly three hundred million persons. If Germany should be reorganized as a federation of states, as she was before Bismarck, and these states then merged into a United States of Europe with three hundred million people, there would be little danger of a revival of German militarism and slight chance of her dominating the federation.

With the federalization of Europe would come freedom of commerce, the free movement of persons, a common currency, and efficient transportation. The result would be a rising standard of living and a lowering of the political rivalries and economic tensions which generate war.

If we grant that a United States of Europe is the answer to our dilemma, we may then ask ourselves: What are the prospects for its creation? It is to be expected that Russia will oppose it. Such a federation would not threaten Russia, but it would, with the return of decent living conditions, put an end to the spread of communism in Europe. Russia's opposition, exerted through her influence on the Communist parties, especially in France, is the greatest obstacle to the achievement of federation. But even in France the Communists control less than thirty per cent of the votes, and therefore, with strong leadership in the democratic parties of France, she could take the lead in promoting the union. Although France is torn by internal dissension, I cannot believe that she is through as a great nation, or that she will not develop again statesmen of the calibre of Jaurès or Briand, who advocated so eloquently the creation of a United States of Europe. If France should take the lead, and is supported by this country and England, I think a federation could be created in spite of the possible opposition of Russia....

Unless we are willing to write off Europe as our friend and supporter of democratic principles, it behooves us to use our economic power, and our talents of persuasion, to induce Europeans to create a free and democratic federation of states. Under such a union the world may again see a renaissance of culture, of freedom, and of spiritual power, which once before led the world out of the confusion and tyranny of the Dark Ages.

SENATE ADDRESS,
APRIL 7, 1947

28. Commonwealth and Continent

Fulbright's advocacy of a united Europe was not a passing gesture to the grandstand. He thought out more carefully than any other member of Congress the implications of the movement to federation

*and was already discussing the role of Great Britain and the Com-
monwealth as early as December, 1947. The occasion was the
Marfleet Lectures delivered at the University of Toronto, in which
the Senator sketched his broad design on a large canvas and considered in detail each facet of the problem. In the following brief
excerpt, he analyzes both the implications of economic supranation-
alism, then under way, and the place of the British Commonwealth
in a united Europe.*

There are many other reasons why we have cause for hope that
federation will come about. The last one to which I shall call your
attention is the compelling character of economic forces working for
union. Prior to the Second World War, Europe, over the centuries,
had developed a highly integrated economy which possessed a unique
balance of agriculture, industry, and trade. That balance was shattered by six years of campaigns. The present difficulties of Europe
are merely manifestations of the impossibility of maintaining national
particularism in the face of continental economic forces which, in
order to operate, must disregard national frontiers. The industrial
Ruhr, the coal-mining Saar, and the industrial Silesia are not German, French, and Polish alone. They belong to all of Europe and
are the heritage upon which the whole continent should build.

The Europe of the future, if it is to rise from its ashes, must find
some way by which the steel and coal of Germany, the shipping of
England, the surplus labor supply of Italy, and the many other contributions of the individual countries can be pooled for the common
continental good. A United States of Europe, I am convinced, is the
answer, and I believe that this is borne out by the Report of the
Committee on European Economic Co-operation. Here are three
significant passages.

On page 2:

(viii) The participating countries ... further stated their belief that
the establishment of a joint organization to review the progress made
in carrying out the recovery program will be necessary.

On page 12, the signatory states announced that:

The production program provides for mutual help between the participating countries over a wide field, and for a number of practical steps for specific action, such as the International Power Project. In addition, broader proposals are made for the reduction of trade barriers and the removal of financial obstacles to intro-European trade.

But the most significant passage of all is the one which deals with the obliteration of national boundaries as they may stand in the way of satisfactory arrangements for the hydroelectric plants of Italy and France. The Report says that the Committee:

...examined many projects and chose a plan which comprises six hydroelectric plants in Italy, France, and on the Austro-Italo-Swiss frontier, together with two lignite thermal plants in Germany and one geothermal plant in Italy. These projects have been selected without regard to national frontiers and involved in some cases the co-operative development of resources cutting across frontiers.

But why labor the point further? These and a whole series of measures providing for closer co-operation and the ultimate elimination of difficulties affecting trade, industry, and the free flow of goods and people across national frontiers are but the beginning of closer European co-operation, which should end in only one way—a United States of Europe.

By now several of you must be asking yourselves: Where does Britain fit into the picture? If Britain were to join a federated Europe, what would happen to her relations with members of the British Commonwealth of Nations? What would Ireland's role be in such a new arrangement? Would she remain aloof while Britain entered, or would she join side by side with Britain? Specifically, what would be the effect upon Canadian-British relations? Would there be any change in Canada's relations with Europe and with the other dominions?

The answers to these questions would tax the powers of a seer, and I make no claim in that direction. I have assumed throughout that a European union without Britain would lack realism, and for that reason British membership would be a *sine qua non* of federation. It seems to me that there are no insurmountable obstacles in the way of Britain fulfilling her obligations in both federations with injury neither to herself nor to any other state. Indeed, there is reason to believe that, by her possession of membership in both, Britain would play a larger role in the quest for world peace.

Ireland would have to decide for herself whether she would join or not, but the advantage of union would be so pronounced that she would probably join at the outset. If, for any reason, she deemed it best not to join a European union immediately, it could only be a question of time before she ultimately would join. The Irish economy is bound to that of the rest of the British Isles and to that of the continent. The isolation resulting from aloofness would cause disadvantages in trade and discriminations which Ireland would find too onerous to bear.

As for Britain's relations with the members of the British Commonwealth of Nations, the bonds which tie the group together are so flexible that there should be no difficulty in finding an adjustment which would allow Britain to be a member of both. It will be recalled that the reciprocity arrangements of 1911 between our two countries presented no serious constitutional obstacles for Canada. Empire preference could be made consistent with obligations in a new European union. In short, to an outsider there seems to be no insurmountable reason why Britain could not accept membership in a European union consistent with her position in the British Commonwealth of Nations.

If this view is correct, a Europe into which Britain was federated could offer only advantages to Canada, the other dominions, and to the world at large. Britain would be a tie between two of the most economically significant groups in the world. Her dual membership would give her the opportunity to bring the two closer together. Politically and militarily, the dual membership could eventually become a great force for peace and stability....

The criticism has been made that advocating a federation of

162

Europe is officious intermeddling by Americans. At the same time, however, we are told that we have a responsibility to use our power and our wealth to rehabilitate the stricken areas of the world. These views are inconsistent. If we grant that we have this obligation, then we must also be obliged to see that the rehabilitation is sensible and effective. There can be no obligation to re-create the same old divided Europe, from which two world wars have emerged to afflict us. Surely we have a legitimate interest in the purpose for which the products of our land and the work of our people are to be expended....

THE MARFLEET LECTURES,
UNIVERSITY OF TORONTO,
DECEMBER 8 AND 9, 1947

29. *The Benefits of Federation: "It Is an Idea Which We Have Held to for 160 Years"*

The Senator's persistent proselyting took many forms. He vainly tried to make United States encouragement of European political unity a formal part of Marshall Plan legislation in 1948 and again in 1949. He debated his idea with Secretary of State Acheson during several hearings of the Foreign Relations Committee; Acheson opposed inclusion of his amendment, on the ground that any decision on political federation ought to be left to the Europeans themselves. But Fulbright's purpose was to develop a record of debate on the subject and thereby encourage a climate of acceptance—the same tactic he followed in urging the Fulbright Resolution during World War II. Here, at the time of the formation of the Council of Europe, the Senator urges his brethren to adopt a nine-word resolution: "that the Congress favors the political federation of Europe."

Mr. President, on March 3, 1948, when the Senate was debating the Economic Co-operation Act, I offered an amendment to the preamble of that act, to express the hope that the participating countries would exert efforts to achieve political unification.

During the course of the debate it became clear that, although the then chairman of the Foreign Relations Committee, the present chairman, and other members of the committee approved the objective and purposes of the amendment, at the same time they objected to its inclusion in the bill.

I then said:

It is with reluctance that I withdraw the amendment; but, in view of the opposition of the committee and the probability that such a defeat would be interpreted as this nation's disapproval of European unity, I feel compelled to follow this course.... I still feel that unless the OEEC countries can achieve political unification during the next few years, the ERP program not only will fail to bring peace and stability to Europe, but, on the contrary, if those countries succumb one by one to the Communists, it will actually result in a tremendous subsidy, at our expense, to the growth of Communist power.

... Mr. President, I give this background for the purpose of emphasizing that, although the Senate has not specifically recorded itself as favoring European federation, there is a great deal of legislative history on the subject, and there is reason to feel that many senators believe in the necessity of European federation. I also wish to say I think that discussion is beginning to bear fruit....

For this purpose, I have introduced today, together with the Senator from Utah [Mr. Thomas], the following resolution:

In order to encourage a peaceful and prosperous order in Europe, but with no intention of imposing any particular form of political or economic association upon its people, it is hereby

Resolved by the Senate (the House of Representatives concurring), That the Congress favors the political federation of Europe.

I hope the Committee on Foreign Relations will give some consideration to this resolution when it holds hearings on the extension of the Economic Co-operation Act, and that it may give some expres-

164

sion of the belief that progress toward the goal of European federation should be accomplished with our assistance under the ECA.

At Harvard, Secretary Marshall said:

Any assistance that this government may render should provide a cure, rather than a mere palliative.

I believe that the revival of European economic prosperity alone, without some permanent form of political federation, is a mere palliative and not a cure. I do not believe that the relatively small and independent political sovereignties of Europe, as they now exist, can, under modern political and economic conditions, retain their independence or economic prosperity without aid for very long.

If the same old prewar Europe of many small, independent states is economically rehabilitated, I do not think we shall have achieved anything of lasting value, commensurate with the sacrifices that we shall have made. Europe reconstructed can protect herself from neither alien domination nor internal quarrels. Standing alone, none of the sixteen nations can withstand the determined pressure of the Russians. While they may think they can take refuge in neutrality, the last war has proved how futile that is.

For centuries—from the grand design of Henry IV, in 1610, to Winston Churchill today—many of the greatest statesmen of Europe have called for European federation. It is no longer a philosophical longing or an idealistic dream. The ancient prejudices about sovereignty are beginning to dissolve, and a United States of Europe has actually become a matter of practical politics, as was demonstrated on last Friday [by the formation of the Council of Europe].

I believe that we should promote the idea of European federation with all our powers of persuasion and, provided the Europeans are willing, with all our economic and industrial strength.

My efforts to obtain an expression of the Congress endorsing European federation have met with one consistent objection: that it is an unwarranted interference in the affairs of other countries. I think the announcement by the Brussels powers will do much to dispel this notion. I am not, by this resolution, attempting to force an alien notion upon the free governments of Europe. I am rather attempting to record this nation's endorsement of a great movement, and to urge its further development before it is too late....

The world today wants to know where we stand. Many Europeans believe we may once again withdraw from Europe. The Russians believe it and are striving to bring it about in Berlin and Germany and all over Europe. They hope that we shall become so disgusted, disillusioned, and tired of the ever-intensified war of nerves that we shall give up and go home. We are trying to convince Russia and Europe now that we will stay.

I believe that we can and will stay—but only so long as we believe that by our defense and assistance we can accomplish something which gives hope of progress toward lasting peace. From our own experience we can, and do, believe in the principle of federation as a means of assuring domestic tranquillity, common defense, and general welfare. It is an idea which we have held to for 160 years, in which we have faith for the future, and which, I am convinced, the people of Europe can adapt to their own great security, prosperity, and happiness.

It is, I believe, of the greatest importance that the people of Europe be given a goal, a hope for the future. The unity of Europe, solid and permanent, is such a goal. It is a goal which I believe will inspire them to great creative acts and to great sacrifices, such as they have performed in the past and which I am sure they can achieve again, to their own benefit and to the benefit of the world.

SENATE ADDRESS,
JANUARY 31, 1949

30. *A Marriage That Makes Sense*

From 1949 through 1957—the year that the Treaty of Rome created the European Economic Community—Fulbright did not miss an opportunity to abet the progress of union. Through resolutions, speeches, and articles, the Senator lent his support to each step on the way. When Great Britain decided, in July, 1961, to apply for full membership in the Common Market, a dream shared by the

166

Arkansas legislator, by now chairman of the Senate Foreign Rela-
tions Committee, seemed near realization. In a speech in London,
Fulbright illumines the import of the British decision and warns
that failure to join could lead to German domination of Europe.

The single most encouraging trend in recent years toward the
strengthening of the free world is the movement toward European
unification, and the single most important event within that trend
is the decision of the United Kingdom to seek admission to the
European Economic Community. Such losses to Communist imperialism as have been suffered by the free world are counterbalanced, and perhaps more than counterbalanced, by the growing
unification of the resurgent nations of Western Europe and by the
gradual development of a broader Atlantic community consisting
of nations which possess a great preponderance of world resources
and industrial productivity.

Some years ago a distinguished British statesman suggested that
the unification of the proud and ancient nations of Europe was
analogous to a shotgun wedding between a man and woman who
had cordially disliked each other since childhood and who were now
being told that a forced union could somehow resolve their strife.
Now, however, the movement has developed considerably among
the continental nations, and the Common Market is a striking success. As Great Britain contemplates joining the European Economic
Community, I would suggest a different analogy, that of *The Taming
of the Shrew,* the tale of an explosive courtship that culminated in
marital bliss. I refrain from suggesting which party is the tamer
and which the shrew.

The announcement by Prime Minister Macmillan on July 31 of
the decision of the United Kingdom to seek membership in the
Common Market was an epochal event in the history of this island
kingdom and also for Europe, for the Commonwealth, and for the
free world. It marks the culminating step in the departure of the
British nation from its ancient tradition of "splendid isolation." It is
analogous in its historical significance to the final repudiation of
isolation by my own country during World War II.

Britain's entry into the European Economic Community will not only contribute to the economic growth and welfare of Britain and Europe; it will mark a significant step toward the evolution of a genuine community of the North Atlantic—a community that of necessity must include the United States—and perhaps, as well, a step toward the emergence of a broader concert of free nations. This, in my judgment, is the real significance of the Prime Minister's announcement of July 31....

Britain's participation in the Common Market will have long-term benefits for the entire free world and immediate benefits within the European community itself. Without Britain there can be little doubt that West Germany, with its great industrial machine and skilled and energetic population, will play the pre-eminent, if not the dominant, role in the European community. I, for one, can contemplate this prospect with little enthusiasm. Germany, it is true, has come far since the fall of the Third Reich toward earning an honorable place in the society of democratic nations. West Germany, nonetheless, is a fledgling democracy, not yet ready for a role of leadership in the free world. France, on the other hand, is a venerable and respected member of the community of free nations, but she is governed under new and untested institutions and is much preoccupied with problems in North Africa. Only Britain, I suggest, has the long experience, the ancient institutions, and the over-all political maturity for leading Europe into a new era....

European union has been intermittently and tentatively encouraged by the United States, but with distinctly less constancy and conviction than I, for one, would advocate. The closing of ranks in Europe will not diminish the burden carried by the United States, but will permit the sharing of an ever-increasing burden which the industrially advanced free nations must bear in helping the world's underdeveloped countries. The U.S. cannot by itself bear the responsibility of maintaining freedom wherever it continues to exist, of narrowing the gap between the rich and the poor societies, of matching stride for stride a totalitarian adversary dedicated to the destruction of all free societies and their absorption into the Communist imperial system.

168

The ability of any one of the European countries, by itself, to shape the course of events elsewhere in the world is limited indeed. This was made dramatically clear in Asia in the late forties and early fifties, and is equally true in Africa today. The United States, despite a chain of heavy commitments stretching around the world, frequently finds its efforts frustrated, and exercises only marginal influence in many areas.

The United States, a united Europe, and the Commonwealth, however, through sustained and co-ordinated effort, can profoundly influence the course of events elsewhere in the world. And, in cases where events might defy their collective efforts, they should be able, acting jointly, to minimize the effects of these events upon themselves. In a world beset by forces of upheaval and the specter of nuclear war, Europe now offers a vision of hope and progress. The prospects are bright that such dangerous traditions as French-German rivalry may finally be dissolved; that Britain may actually cast aside her historic role of Europe's detached monitor and invite Europe and the Commonwealth to shape a common destiny; that stability, prosperity, and steady growth may have placed Europe and the Commonwealth on the threshold of an enterprise that can produce their greatest achievements and greatest glory.

ADDRESS BEFORE THE SEVENTH
COMMONWEALTH PARLIAMENTARY
ASSOCIATION CONFERENCE,
LONDON, SEPTEMBER 30, 1961

31. For a Concert of Free Nations

By 1961, the phrase "grand design" had become virtually a cliché, and from the first faltering steps to a broad Western alliance the free nations had come to the threshold of a true Atlantic community. Fulbright presented his mature views on this broad theme in an article in Foreign Affairs *that has already become one of his seminal public papers. He assays the imperfections of the United Nations,*

169

looks back to the concert of Europe and ahead to the concert of free nations in a statement that opens generous vistas in a troubled world.

I

The Soviet Union has demanded that the United Nations be reorganized on the "troika" principle, with equal executive power given the West, the Communist bloc, and the neutral states. Each would wield a veto. This proposal quite clearly aims to emasculate the United Nations and in particular reduce the office of the Secretary-General to the same impotence which blights the functioning of the Security Council.

In this situation it has been suggested that a general conference of U.N. members be called to review and possibly revise the charter. I believe that a review conference at this time would be an exercise in futility. Quite obviously, the Western powers—and, hopefully, many of the neutrals—will reject the Soviet scheme. And the Russians can hardly be expected to agree to any Western proposals for strengthening the organization when their own objective is diametrically opposed to this.

Whatever inadequacies there may be in the U.N. charter, the problem is not basically a legal matter, but one of power politics in a divided world. Instead of engaging in an arid and irrelevant exercise in legalities, we would be far better advised to seek feasible means of building a cohesive community of free nations. This objective should be pursued as far as possible within the United Nations. In large measure, however, it must be pressed outside of the U.N., through instrumentalities that reflect a limited but real community of common interests.

Despite the existence of a very imposing array of international organs of consultation and co-operation, the free nations of the world seem chronically unable to unify and co-ordinate their policies. They are at the same time confronted with an adversary who has repeatedly demonstrated an impressive capacity to mobilize diverse resources for the achievement of single-minded objectives. The question quite naturally arises whether some new machinery or system can be devised through which the free nations can advance their common interests with a far greater degree of co-ordinated effort and shared responsibility than has yet been achieved in the postwar era.

We have created extensive international machinery since World War II: the United Nations, a global system of alliances, and, most recently, the Organization for Economic Co-operation and Development. Despite the existence of these and other organs, the United States continues to bear a disproportionate share of the burden of world responsibility—a burden, I fear, which overtaxes even our own considerable resources. Throughout the world, both allied and uncommitted nations display a distressing tendency to stand aside, even when their own vital interests are involved, and leave it to the United States to act, while reserving for themselves the right to criticize or to condemn. . . .

It is thus imperative that we strive for a broader unity, a unity which is oriented to our needs, but rooted in our capacity. While the United Nations will remain a symbol of our aspirations, we can hope at the most, as things stand, to build a viable community of the free world. The question is whether we have yet done all that we can to develop it. Although such a community must for the foreseeable future be limited to the free nations, it can set its sights on universal values.

II

Prescriptions for the future, if they are to prove effective, must be rooted in the experience of the past. It is more than an academic exercise, therefore, to look back in history for models and examples of a viable spirit of international community.

Such a spirit prevailed in remarkable measure in nineteenth century Europe. In the wake of the Napoleonic Wars, Europe developed a primitive but effective system of public law based on the treaty structure erected by the Congress of Vienna. In order to provide permanent security against a resurgence of French militarism and aggression, Britain, Austria, Russia, and Prussia formed in 1815 a quadruple alliance, of which Article 6 provided for "periodic meetings of sovereigns or their ministers" for preserving the peace and stability of Europe. France, the defeated aggressor, was granted remarkably generous terms and within three years of her defeat was brought into the system of consultation. Thus emerged the concert of Europe, an oligarchy of great powers, but none the less a genuine community of nations who identified their common interests in preserving a rough balance of power and the basic integrity of the treaty structure.

The Vienna settlement opened a century of relative peace. The guiding rule of the concert, never made explicit but none the less effective, was that no change in the treaty structure could be made without the consent of the five-power oligarchy. Thus, for example, with "due process of law," the concert decreed the independence of Belgium in 1830, a definite regime for the Turkish straits in 1840, the independence of Bulgaria in 1878, and, as late as 1913, the concert successfully imposed a settlement of the Balkan wars.

The role of Britain in the concert of Europe is especially instructive. As the leading financial, industrial, and naval power, Britain accepted special responsibilities for the enforcement of the public law of Europe. She initiated something of a Marshall Plan after 1815, providing loans and subsidies to revive the war-torn economies of the European powers. Britain was the "holder" of the balance of power, and her weight was thrown, when necessary, to the support of the weaker side in continental controversies and against the potential violator of treaties. When forcible changes in treaty requirements were unavoidable, as in the case of Russia's denunciation in 1871 of the naval restrictions imposed upon her in the Black Sea at the end of the Crimean War, Britain insisted upon a conference to put the stamp of legality on a foregone conclusion and thus to avoid a dangerous precedent.

The point which is most instructive for America in our own time is that Britain led but did not dominate the concert. She was not the mistress of Europe but its *primus inter pares*. Her role, in short, was not to exercise sole responsibility, but to lead a system of shared responsibility. The *Pax Britannica* was thus a multilateral system which depended at least as much on its members as on its leader.

The concert of Europe represented a limited community and a fragile system of law, but it kept the peace for a hundred years—a splendid achievement by contrast with the far more structured and sophisticated international machinery of the twentieth century.

Nevertheless, the concert had major flaws, and these ultimately proved fatal. It was, first of all, an oligarchy of great powers, which imposed its will on the lesser states with little regard for their desires and aspirations. Secondly, the concert at times showed little understanding of the rising forces of democracy and nationalism in nineteenth century Europe. Indeed, the eastern powers—Austria, Russia, and Prussia—were quite hostile to these forces and sought in vain to use the concert as an instrument to suppress them and to "make Europe safe for autocracy." Thirdly, the absence of established machinery of obligatory consultation reduced the workings of the concert to hazardous uncertainty. Sir Edward Grey, the British Foreign Secretary, tried desperately and vainly to invoke the concert in the crisis of the summer of 1914. The chaos of telegrams frantically exchanged among the chancelleries of Europe at that time persuaded Grey that, if the concert of Europe had had some established machinery of obligatory consultation, war might have been prevented.

The most serious handicap to the effectiveness of the concert of Europe, however, proved to be the disintegration of the international community of shared values on which it rested. During the first half of the nineteenth century, nationalist movements were also liberal and democratic, and Europe was increasingly dedicated to the rule of law. This trend was arrested and then reversed by the rise of a new form of nationalism—militant, aggressive, and ultimately xenophobic. The prime mover of the new nationalism was Germany, whose unification and pre-eminence were won by the arms of autocratic Prussia. After the defeat of France by Prussia in 1871, Germany became the predominant nation in Europe, dedicated to Bismarckian "blood and iron." Europe in the late nineteenth century was prey to militarism, secret alliances, and nationalist rivalries. The demise of the concert of Europe in 1914 reflected the gradual enfeeblement and final disintegration of the community which had given Europe its happiest and most productive century.

Out of the ruins of the old European order, British and American statesmen devised the League of Nations—a radically new idea for the creation of a world-wide community of law. The British conceived of the League of Nations as an enlarged and improved concert, but Woodrow Wilson thought of it as a universalized application of the Monroe Doctrine, which he regarded as a partnership of American states for the advancement of democracy in world affairs. British thinking was empirical in terms of European experience, a latter-day effort to bring in the new world to redress the balance of the old. Wilson's conception was universal and idealist, generalizing the Monroe Doctrine as he conceived it into a world moral order. These two views were not mutually exclusive. The British hoped to revive a community that had disintegrated; the Americans hoped to build a new one. Both looked to their own deeply rooted traditions of ordered society under the rule of law.

The chief British contribution to the Covenant was a system of obligatory consultation, peaceful settlement of disputes and sanctions against violators. The objective, inspired largely by the disastrous experience of 1914, was to enforce delay and an attempt at peaceful settlement before nations actually resorted to war.

The major American contribution was Article 10, a mutual guarantee of political independence and territorial integrity among the members of the League. Article 10, said President Wilson, was the "backbone of the whole of the Covenant." It represented the guarantee which is the *sine qua non* of any valid system of collective security, an obligation inherent in membership, flowing directly from the Covenant, and not dependent upon the decisions of any organ of the League.

The founders of the League believed that it reflected the birth of a new world order and that its very processes would guide a nascent community to full maturity. Wilson had no illusions as to the existence at that time of a genuine international community, but he firmly believed that the historical moment had arrived for such a community to be born. The League, said Wilson in presenting the

Covenant to the Peace Conference on February 14, 1919, would depend ultimately on the "moral force of the public opinion of the world." "Armed force," said the President, "is in the background in this program, but it is in the background, and if the moral force of the world will not suffice, the physical force of the world shall. But that is the last resort. . . ."

The year 1919 was perhaps the high-water mark of democracy in world history. The victory was won by democratic nations, unshared with great totalitarian powers. It marked the occurrence of an epochal opportunity to lay the foundations of a world community of law—not to create a community full-grown, for that is the work of generations, but to give birth to a prospect of world peace under world law.

The opportunity so briefly presented in 1919 was lost, and lost completely, by the generation of statesmen who governed during the interwar years. It is not necessary here to rehearse the tragic annals of that era: the retreat of America to isolation; the capitulation of the League to Japanese aggression in Manchuria, Italian aggression in Ethiopia, and German aggression in Europe. The result was World War II, more devastating than the first war. By 1945, the statesmen of the West were ready to retrieve the errors of the interwar years. They had the will perhaps, but the opportunity of 1919 was not to be repeated. The victory of 1945 was shared by a dynamic new totalitarianism, one which rejected the values which underlay both the nineteenth century concert and the Covenant of the League of Nations.

III

Under these conditions the United Nations was conceived and created, an organ of international community far more ambitious than the League and launched under far less auspicious circumstances. There is no mystery in the failure of the United Nations to fulfil its promise. That promise rested on the assumption that President Roosevelt brought back from Yalta in February, 1945—that we had achieved unity "in spirit and in purpose" with our allies.

Events proved that hope illusory, and with it went the promise of a genuine system of collective security on a world-wide scale.

There are at least three preconditions of a viable system of collective security: (1) a *status quo* on which the principal powers agree; (2) the availability of overwhelming force to those nations who support the *status quo* or at least oppose change by violence; (3) a high degree of political and moral solidarity among the great powers. These are the minimum conditions of a minimum international community. None of them existed at the end of World War II. The success of the United Nations depended upon the presence of all of them.

The United Nations charter reflects the ambivalence of excessive aspirations toward a world community and the existence in the world of conflicting powers and ideologies. In the words of the distinguished international lawyer, Julius Stone:

The very ambition of the charter turned it into a two-faced instrument. One face looks nobly towards the beginnings of a super-state well beyond the League of Nations; the other looks grimly backwards to the anarchic self-help of the old world, well before the foundation of the League of Nations. Which was the real face? (Julius Stone, *Legal Controls of International Conflict*. New York: Rinehart, 1954. P. 280.)

The answer, unfortunately, is the "second face." The global community which the charter assumed exists today neither in fact nor in prospect. If the social fabric essential to institutions does not exist, even the most brilliant statecraft cannot create it.

The "first face" of the charter appears in the peace-enforcement powers of the Security Council, an organ vested with full authority to apply all sanctions, including the use of force, against any nation which commits a "threat to the peace, breach of the peace, or act of aggression." The Security Council has the theoretical power to decide on such measures, and all members of the United Nations are bound under Article 25 to "accept and carry out" these decisions.

The veto reduces these powers to a nullity because it renders the great powers immune, leaving the enforcement of the peace to their fiat. The charter was never intended for use against the great powers. They were the policemen, set above the law, whose compliance with the charter depended not on law but on their own consent, and on the illusion of their unity "in spirit and in purpose."

The history of the United Nations has been in large measure a history of retreat from false hopes and of adjustment to the reality of a divided world. The veto in fact is an accurate reflection of that reality. Its removal would not result in a genuine system of collective security. More likely, it would mean the end of the organization. The veto is the reflection, not a cause, of conflict. In its absence, a great power would not comply with the charter, but would rebel against it. The real problem is one not of legalities but of power politics in a divided world.

The veto represents the "second face" of the charter; it is a clause of escape and evasion. So does Article 51, which recognizes an "inherent" right of individual and collective self-defense. As Western statesmen have repeatedly pointed out, their system of defense alliances is wholly valid under the charter, clearly licensed by Article 51. But NATO is an essential instrument of collective security precisely because of the failure of the U.N. It is not a realization of the charter, but a substitute for it, authorized by a clause of escape and reservation.

The primitive parts of the charter, those which look to anarchic self-help, have proven viable because they reflect reality. The grand innovation of an authoritative international executive quickly broke down because it defied history and falsely assumed the existence of a community of the great powers.

The gradual transfer of authority from the Security Council to the General Assembly has been an effort to adjust to reality by retreating to looser and more traditional forms of co-operation. Such was the intent of the Uniting for Peace Resolution of November, 1950. The Security Council has all but ceased to function, and it was the General Assembly which dealt more or less successfully with the Suez crisis of 1956 and quite unsuccessfully with the Soviet suppression of Hungary. The difficulty with the General Assembly is that it is a most unwieldy body and one which bears no relationship to the realities of world power. A body in which Guatemala or Bulgaria exercises the same voting power as the United States or the Soviet Union can scarcely be expected to serve as a reliable instrument of peace enforcement or even of consultation.

The anarchic face of the U.N. dominates. Its forward-looking face is but a shadow and a promise. It seems quite clear that, if we are to develop a working concert of free nations, we must look elsewhere for a model and an instrumentality.

IV

By far the most impressive achievements of policy co-ordination among sovereign powers have occurred in wartime. In both world wars the Western powers, particularly Great Britain and the United States, achieved a high degree of co-operation along specific functional lines in the common war effort.

During the First World War the Allied and Associated Powers dealt through international agencies with such problems as the co-ordination of military strategy, the allocation of shipping, and the maintenance of supplies of food and raw materials. The Supreme War Council, for instance, under Marshal Foch, was virtually an international cabinet for the conduct of the war. Before the war was over, some European statesmen began to think of it as a "rudimentary league of nations." A number of other functional international organs operated with great success during the war and the Peace Conference.

Impressive achievements of close co-ordination, indeed unification, of policy were achieved by Great Britain and the United States in World War II. The grand strategy of the war was planned in constant and intimate consultations between President Roosevelt and Prime Minister Churchill, and the British and American armed forces were put under a joint command known as the Combined Chiefs of Staff. Under the direction of the political leaders of the two countries, the Combined Chiefs of Staff, sitting in Washington, formulated and executed policies and plans relating to the strategic conduct of the war, allocation of munitions, and transportation requirements. A close working relationship developed between the top British representative, Field Marshal Sir John Dill, and General George Marshall, who together made major policy decisions in an informal manner. The Allied war effort was also unified by a system of combined boards, whose task was to muster the full economic resources of Great Britain and the United States and Canada.

The combined boards, as well as the Combined Chiefs of Staff, were created and carried on in an atmosphere in which the common purpose of defeating the enemy overrode all other motives. Survival itself depended upon common effort and a united front. National and group interests were readily subordinated by the two English-speaking nations, with their common interests, their similar outlook, and their community of democratic values. Underlying the ability of British and American officials to work closely together was a sense of community derived from long association and a common heritage. It is significant that at no point was the Soviet Union brought into the system of unified conduct of the war.

The experience of the joint war effort points to the efficacy of a functional approach toward the building of an international community. Common efforts to deal with specific concrete problems are likely to be more productive in the long run than comprehensive and spectacular attempts at world constitution-making.

In times of clear and present danger, custom, inertia, vested interests, and traditional viewpoints give way to the needs of the times. The problem that now confronts us is whether they will give way in a time of ominous danger, but danger which is vague, ambiguous, and lacking in dramatic urgency. That is the nature of the peril which confronts the free world. Unless we can forge something like the unity of purpose and common action that we so successfully forged in wartime, we may well fall victim if not to cataclysm then to creeping catastrophe.

V

In a speech on June 10, 1961, to a rally of Young Conservatives, Sir Anthony Eden called for a "political general staff" of Western leaders to enable free countries to stand up to "the monolithic mass which is the Communist world." In a pessimistic assessment of the cold war, Eden declared: "There must be much closer unity within the West before there can be effective negotiation with the East." Ordinary methods of diplomacy within the free world are inadequate, said the former Prime Minister. "Something much more thorough is required." Citing the experience of the Combined Chiefs of Staff in World War II, Eden said that all would have been confusion and disarray without them. "This," he said, "is exactly what has been happening between the politically free nations in the postwar world. We need joint chiefs of a political general staff." Citing the advances of Communist power in recent years, Sir Anthony observed: "This very grave state of affairs will continue until the free nations accept together the reality of the danger that confronts them and unite their policies and resources to meet it."

While I fully agree with Sir Anthony's contention, I think that we must carry the analysis further, bearing in mind that, while common peril may be the measure of our *need,* the existence or absence of a positive sense of community must be the measure of our *capacity*.

While it is hazardous to project the trend of history, it seems clear that a genuine community is painfully emerging in the Western world, particularly among the countries of Western Europe. At the end of World War II, free Europe was ready for a new beginning. The excesses of nationalism had brought down upon Europe a generation of tyranny and war, and a return to the old order of things seemed unthinkable. Under these conditions, a new generation of Europeans began to discover the bonds of long association and shared values that for so long had been subordinated to nationalist xenophobia. A slow and painful trend toward unification has taken hold, a trend which may at any time be arrested and reversed, but which may also lead to a binding federation of Europe. It may well be that the unification of Europe will prove inadequate, that the survival of free society will require nothing less than the confederation of the entire Western world.

The movement toward European unity has been expressed in two currents: federalism and functionalism, one looking to the constitution of a United States of Europe, the other building on

180

wartime precedents of practical co-operation for the solution of specific problems. Thus far the advances made have been almost entirely along functional lines.

Many factors contributed to the growth of the European movement. In 1946, Sir Winston Churchill, who had spoken often of European union during the war, advocated the formation of "a kind of United States of Europe." Had Churchill been returned to office in 1945, it is just possible that Britain, instead of standing fearfully aloof, would have *led* Europe toward union.

In 1947 and 1948, the necessity of massive co-ordinated efforts to achieve economic recovery led to the formation of the Organization for European Economic Co-operation, to supervise and co-ordinate the uses of American aid under the Marshall Plan. The United States might well have exploited the opportunity provided by the European Recovery Program to push the hesitant European nations toward political federation, as well as economic co-operation, but all proposals to this effect were rejected by the United States government at the time.

Another powerful factor in the European movement was the threat of Soviet aggression. The Communist coup in Czechoslovakia in 1948 was followed immediately by the conclusion of the Brussels Treaty, a fifty-year alliance among Britain, France, and the Benelux countries. And of course the Soviet threat was responsible for NATO, the grand alliance of the Atlantic nations....

If a broader Atlantic community is to be formed—and my own judgment is that it lies within the realm of both our needs and our capacity—a ready nucleus of machinery is at hand in the NATO alliance. The time is now ripe, indeed overdue, for the vigorous development of its nonmilitary potentialities, for its development as an instrument of Atlantic community. What is required is the full implementation of Article 2 of the Treaty, which provides:

The Parties will contribute toward the further development of peaceful and friendly international relations by strengthening their free institutions, by bringing about a better understanding of the principles upon which these institutions are founded, and by promoting conditions of stability and well-being. They will seek to eliminate conflict in their international economic policies and will encourage economic collaboration between any and all of them.

As Lester Pearson wrote in 1955:

NATO cannot live on fear alone. It cannot become the source of a real Atlantic community if it remains organized to deal only with the military threat which first brought it into being.

The problem of NATO is not one of machinery, of which there is an abundance, but of the will to use it. The NATO Council is available as an executive agency; the Standing Group, as a high military authority. The unofficial Conference of Parliamentarians is available as a potential legislative authority. This machinery will not become the instrument of an Atlantic community by fiat, but only when that community is a state of mind—a conviction that goals and values are widely shared, that effective communication is possible, that mutual trust is reasonably assured.

An equally promising avenue toward Atlantic community may lie through the development and expansion of the O.E.C.D. Conceived as an organ of economic co-operation, there is no reason why O.E.C.D. cannot evolve into a broader instrument of union if its members so desire. Indeed, it might be a more appropriate vehicle than NATO for the development of a parliamentary organ of the Atlantic nations, because it could encompass *all* of the members of the Atlantic community, including those, like Sweden and Switzerland, who are unwilling to be associated with an essentially military alliance like NATO.

Underlying these hopes and prescriptions is a conviction that the nations of the North Atlantic area do indeed form a community, at least a potential community. There is nothing new in this; what is new and compelling is that the West is now but one of several powerful civilizations, or "systems," and that one or more of the others may pose a mortal danger to the West. For centuries the North Atlantic nations dominated the world, and as long as they did they could afford the luxury of fighting each other. That time is now past, and the Atlantic nations, if they are to survive, must develop a full-fledged community, and they must also look beyond the frontiers of "Western civilization" toward a world-wide "concert of free nations."

VI

The burden of these reflections is that a broader unity among the free nations is at the core of our needs. And, if we do not aspire to too much, it is also within our capacity. A realistic balancing of the need for new forms of international organization on the one hand, and our capacity to achieve them on the other, must be approached through the concept of "community." History has demonstrated many times that concerts of nations based solely on the negative spur of common danger are unlikely to survive when the external danger ceases to be dramatically urgent. Only when a concert of nations rests on the positive foundations of shared goals and values is it likely to form a viable instrument of long-range policy. It follows that the solution to the current disunity of the free nations is only to a very limited extent a matter of devising new machinery of consultation and co-ordination. It is very much a matter of building the foundations of community.

It is for these reasons that proposals for a "new world order," through radical overhaul of the United Nations or through some sort of world federation, are utterly fatuous. In a recent book called *World Peace Through World Law,* two distinguished lawyers, Grenville Clark and Louis Sohn, call for just such an overhaul of the U.N., basing their case on the world-wide fear of a nuclear holocaust. I believe that these proposals, however meritorious in terms of world needs, go far beyond our capacity to realize them. Such proposals look to an apocalyptic act, a kind of Lockean "social contract" on a world-wide scale. The defect of these proposals is in their attempt to outrun history and their assumption that because something may be desirable it is also possible.

A working concept of the organic evolution of community must lead us in a different direction. The failures of the U.N. and of other international organs suggest that we have already gone beyond what was internationally feasible. Our problem, therefore, is to devise processes more modest in their aspirations, adjusted to the real world of sovereign nation-states and diverse and hostile communities. The history of the U.N. demonstrates that in a pluralistic world we must develop processes of influence and persuasion rather than coercion. It is possible that international organization will ultimately supplant the multistate system, but its proper function for the immediate future is to reform and supplement that system, in order to render pluralism more compatible with an interdependent world.

New machinery of co-ordination should not be our primary objective in the foreseeable future—though perhaps the "political general staff" of Western leaders proposed by Sir Anthony Eden would serve a useful purpose. Generally, however, there is an abundance of available machinery of co-ordination—in NATO, in O.E.C.D., in the U.N., and elsewhere. The trouble with this machinery is that it is not used, and the reason that it is not used is the absence of a conscious sense of community among the free nations.

Our proper objective, then, is the development of a new spirit, the realization of a potential community. A "concert of free nations" should take its inspiration from the traditions of the nineteenth century concert of Europe with its common values and accepted "rules of the game." Constitutions of and by themselves mean little; the history of both the League of Nations and the United Nations demonstrates that. But a powerful sense of community, even with little or no machinery, means a great deal. That is the lesson of the nineteenth century.

A realistic "concert of free nations" might be expected to consist of an "inner community" of the North Atlantic nations and an "outer community" embracing much or all of the non-Communist world.

The North Atlantic nations represent an almost-existing community, and, because they do, they can press forward in the development of supranational institutions. Because their community is fragile, these institutions for the time being should be functional rather than federal, piecemeal and pragmatic rather than general.

In practice, this would mean the further development of NATO as an organ of political and economic co-operation, the vigorous implementation of the O.E.C.D., and the expansion of existing organs of European integration, with Great Britain, Canada, and the United States moving toward full participation.

The "outer community" poses much more difficult problems, because it is a *potential* community, still far from realization. Our objective must be to bring it into existence, a task which will take time and patience. The problem here is to persuade the new and underdeveloped nations that, for certain purposes at least, their interests and objectives coincide with our own. Their aspirations for economic development, for military security, and for freedom are all objectives which represent our interests as well as their own. The way to persuade these nations of this community of interests is for the West to assist them in their realization. In practice, this means a unified Western program of economic assistance for sound development programs, rigorous respect for the sovereignty of newly independent nations, and a growing practice of consulting these nations on specific common problems.

Such a policy also means the encouragement of a greater sense of responsibility among the underdeveloped nations than now exists. If their economic development programs are unsound, we must not be "blackmailed" into providing lavish aid for fear they will otherwise go to the Communists. When we consult them on matters of security, we must make it clear that their security as well as our own is involved, and they must accept responsibility accordingly.

In all these ways we can work toward a "concert of free nations," a community rooted not only in common peril but also in common values and aspirations. Such a community falls far short of the stable *world* order we desire. Its merit is that it represents a realistic accommodation between our needs and our capacity.

Freedom is not its own defense. Its survival in this century will require the construction of a new community of unified effort and shared responsibility. In the words of the Spanish philosopher Salvador de Madariaga:

The trouble today is that the Communist world understands unity but not liberty, while the free world understands liberty but not unity. Eventual victory may be won by the first of the two sides to achieve the synthesis of both liberty and unity.

"FOR A CONCERT OF FREE NATIONS,"
Foreign Affairs, OCTOBER, 1961

Chapter Seven

THE KENNEDY AGENDA

32. Lacking: A Consensus

In 1960, everything seemed to happen at once. It was the year of the U-2, the Congo upheaval, and the United Nations session at which Khrushchev banged his shoe while Castro taunted America from a Harlem hotel. It was a presidential year, and no less than three members of the Foreign Relations Committee—John F. Kennedy, Hubert Humphrey, and Stuart Symington—were prominent contenders for the Democratic nomination.

Fulbright gave his formal support to yet another senator, Majority Leader Lyndon Johnson, but his relations with Senator Kennedy were cordial. After the Los Angeles convention, Fulbright played a useful supporting role in the campaign by publicizing the Eisenhower Administration's refusal to make public the "prestige" polls taken by the USIA—polls that evidenced a lack of confidence abroad in American leadership. But the election itself did not yield a clear verdict; the close vote meant that the country had a new President but not a new consensus.

In December, the President-elect was assembling his cabinet and Fulbright was among those considered for Secretary of State. The choice went to Dean Rusk. While the whole story of the appointment is not yet public, Fulbright was not overwhelmed by disappointment. He felt he was better suited to his job in the Senate, he approved the selection of Dean Rusk, and on the whole he was heartened by the direction taken by the New Frontier.

Party success, however, was not an end in itself to Fulbright, and he reserved the right to speak his own mind as a senator. His relations with the White House were cordial but not intimate, and from the beginning Fulbright's attitude to the new Administration was that of qualified approval. Fulbright was especially troubled by the lack of new mood in the country to match the new temper in Washington. In April, he elaborated his views in a lecture before the American Philosophical Society.

I have often said—and still believe—that a nation can conceive and execute a foreign policy that is responsive, courageous, and creative only to the extent that its people succeed in cultivating these same qualities in themselves. Thus, diplomatic style is necessarily a reflection of national style.

It is not enough to be powerful militarily and economically. An inept, clumsy national style can undermine military strength. Style and power are indivisible; they march together. One looks to history in vain for a situation in which the problems were of comparable weight and gravity to those that the United States must shoulder in the Sixties. Stated broadly, the responsibility is one of leadership. And it is not a problem just for the President and the Secretary of State, supported by the leadership in Congress. It is a collective one, dependent finally upon a consensus of a majority of our people.

The President, who is deeply read in the history and philosophy of democratic societies, tried to make this clear from the beginning. In Los Angeles last July, he defined his new frontier "not as a set of promises," but as "a set of challenges." He said, "it sums up not what I intend to offer the American people, but what I intend to ask of them. It appeals to their pride, not their pocketbook—it holds out the promise of more sacrifice instead of more security."

As we know, scarcely half of the electorate responded affirmatively to the challenge stated in those terms. The response to the challenge was, to say the least, tentative. Yet in that same speech in Los

188

Angeles, the President said, correctly, that the new frontier of which he spoke is here, "whether we seek it or not."

That is, indeed, the case. What remains to be seen is whether the national mood will merge with the national responsibility. That was really the central issue of the campaign. And it has by no means been fully resolved.

Erasmus, in *The Praise of Folly,* observed that he "who grasps the helm of great affairs...is one who is exposed to all eyes, and like a favorable star he has power, by the good influence of his conduct, to bring salvation in human affairs. or like a fatal comet he may bring destruction in his train."

The recent dramatic exploits of the Russians into the realm of the stars lends new meaning to Erasmus' observation...

It has often been said by Americans, with a kind of detached diffidence tinged with a touch of self-righteousness, that the leadership of the free world has been thrust upon us, that we did not seek it.

It may well be true that we have *not* been an ambitious, power-seeking nation, although I suspect these assertions of innocence may be inspired by the desire to avoid the responsibility and burdens which go with power. But, in any case, even if true, it is irrelevant to the question of our present responsibility, in the words of Erasmus, "by the good influence of our conduct to bring salvation in human affairs."

In contrast to our tentative or even reluctant approach to power, the Russians boldly and aggressively grasp at every opportunity to expand their empire. I am not suggesting that we do likewise. I am suggesting that, as the leader of a free, pluralistic society of nations, we recognize and accept the leadership, that we engage *all* our faculties, in the contest. It is not enough to pay the bill, however burdensome that may be upon our taxpayers. Beyond this, we must strive to understand with our minds and our hearts the peoples with whom we are associated in this struggle.

Many thoughtful men have commented on the reasons for the unwillingness, or inability, of Americans to perceive the full sweep of their responsibilities. Some have put the problem in a deep historical perspective, suggesting that the national mood, like a pendulum, swings back and forth, with the citizenry making its full commitment to national problems only in times of crisis. Others speak of dreadful anxieties brought on by the psychology of life in the nuclear age, which cause people to turn their minds away from the uncongenial urgencies of the time.

Probably there is some validity in both of the theories that are offered to explain America's apathy. The national style is the sum of many attributes, attitudes, and characteristics. Among the most significant is the failure, by a large proportion of Americans, to identify what they regard as their own best interests with the national interest....

This is a large country, larger by far than any contemplated by Erasmus. Divided as it is along regional, cultural, and economic lines, national consensus is an elusive goal. The various economic and sectional interests have often seemed to be in conflict, and, except in time of national crisis, they have rarely been brought together into a purposeful whole. Thus, whatever the pressures on the economy, we can rely on labor unions to demand broader welfare programs—on farm organizations to seek high subsidies—on the business community to lobby for a more congenial tax structure. We can also rely on many millions of Americans to identify their points of view with organizations that reflect their social and political attitudes.

It has been suggested that the size and complexity of the United States is such that it is beyond the comprehension of the citizens, that the nation is too abstract and remote a concept to arouse and attract their loyalty. In time of crisis such as war, this has not been true, but it is true that we have in this country an unprecedented number of organizations, thousands of them which seem to attract the energies and the devotion, a part of which at least, in smaller countries, is accorded the nation ...

In the President, we have an articulate and vigorous advocate of the national interest and of the national responsibility. For that, I am very grateful. Yet, as I suggested earlier, the programs of a

President under our system are as strong and responsive as the people themselves are strong and responsive. And it is the task of those others of us who are obliged to serve the general interest to speak out in informed and thoughtful terms on the problems that are truly national—those which lie with equal weight on all regions of the country and all sectors of the society. In doing so, we will necessarily be competing with an infinity of special interest—and with the so-called public opinion manipulators, who represent not only domestic clients of every description, but foreign governments as well. The total of effort and investment devoted to opinion-manipulating, or molding, in this country now represents one of the major undertakings. It pervades our national life. Books on the subject are found on the best-seller lists. Many newspapers and radio stations accept uncritically the handouts given them by the opinion-makers. Motion picture houses offer short subjects, as well as newsreels, which frequently contain material created and donated by these image-makers, and in their concern with narrow interests, they have helped to blur the national interest, and hence the national style as well. And they have had a disturbingly compliant, unskeptical society to work with.

It is plain that since the Korean War days, Americans have suffered what in athletic circles is known as a let-down. Since then, individual prosperity in our country has risen, by and large, while the nation itself has been diminished, in terms of both prestige and relative strength. We have created the richest society in the material sense that the world has seen. We are more than merely affluent. We are the acquisitive society. Our consumption is staggering. We have at our disposal a kaleidoscopic array of things to buy. There is irony in this, but little that can be rationalized into optimism. Because it is doubtful that the old, empirical attitudes that have accompanied this affluence are relevant to our present role as defenders of western civilization ...

The decay in our civilization is pervasive—visible to anyone who can look above his private interests and preoccupations. It is visible in institutions, such as labor unions and large business corporations.

Recently, we had a glimpse of how the free enterprise system, of which we speak so proudly, can be manipulated and stultified by corporate executives, who, among other things, are not above conspiring to violate the law and to gouge the public.

The decay is more than moral. As much as anything, it appears to be a spreading decline in taste and in a sense of values. To take one example, the American bemusement by size has become, if anything, more conspicuous. Santayana pointed to our "singular preoccupation with quantity." And Tyrone Guthrie, according to a recent article in the *New Yorker,* has noted our easy assumption "that a big country, a big building, or a big potato is not just bigger than a small one; that there is inherent virtue in jumbo size."

To me, the irony of this involvement with size, as I observed earlier, is the unwillingness or inability of so many Americans to identify themselves with something as vast as the United States. Bigger cars, bigger parking lots, bigger corporate structures, bigger farms, bigger drugstores, bigger supermarkets, bigger motion-picture screens. The tangible and the beautiful shrink. Left to wither is the national purpose, national educational needs, literature and theater, our critical faculties. The national dialogue is gradually being lost in a froth of misleading self-congratulation and cliché. National needs and interests are slowly being submerged by the national preoccupation with the irrelevant...

It may be that the accelerating deficiencies in American life were inevitable. Americans are a ruggedly positivist and determinist people. We have shaped an environment to our will. Our concern with cause and effect—with the palpable, the negotiable, and the functional—stimulated enormous growth in the first century, or so, of our history. This growth has materialized into what we call the American way of life, with its implicit offer to every citizen of a life not only free from want, but even more bountiful.

Preoccupied with this way of life, Americans have failed to develop a philosophical and cultural base to sustain it. This is the more perplexing when we consider the rich cultural and philosophical heritage that we possess, along with the strong cultural influences

192

to which we have been exposed. We often complain that we are misunderstood and unappreciated abroad. The problem, to a considerable extent, lies with our terms of reference. They do not faithfully reflect our heritage, the principles and ideals that we profess ...

That is a pessimistic evaluation. Perhaps it is too bleak. In any case, I do not pretend to have the answer to the problem of preparing our society for the difficult and taxing days ahead. But I would fully subscribe to the tone of the President's inaugural address. "Ask not what the country can do for you, but what you can do for your country." This classic phrase may have touched the American conscience. The reaction to the Peace Corps is interesting, and should probably offer some encouragement. In Washington, many people believe that the Peace Corps concept is aimed not so much at the needs of less developed countries, as at the need to generate enthusiasm among Americans for their own responsibilities. The ultimate contribution of the Peace Corps to its stated objectives may be relatively small, even negligible; but, as a device to dramatize certain problems and bring a sense of idealism and purpose to these problems, it may have significant effect.

I wish I could say that the burden of the new Administration's program was in line with the tone of the President's possibly historic first statement. It is not, though, and of necessity probably could not be. Nevertheless, in Washington at least, there is an impression that strong leadership and direction have been returned to the conduct of our affairs. And this, I think, is the first step toward the goal of developing a national appreciation of this country's true position and function in the society of nations.

I return to the thought with which I began that the leadership of the President, of any President, is not enough in the democratic, pluralistic society which we have created on this continent. His leadership can be effective only if he is able to bring about, with the help of all of us, a consensus among our people. Since we are not an authoritarian society, this can be accomplished only by an unparalleled effort on the part of everyone, to understand and to work as never before, for the restoration of an appreciation of

quality, of beauty, of intelligence and integrity in our national sense
of values.

THE PENROSE LECTURE, AMERICAN
PHILOSOPHICAL SOCIETY,
PHILADELPHIA, APRIL 20, 1961

33. *The Cuban Memorandum*

*April was the month of the Cuban invasion. There is no longer
any secret about Fulbright's role in cautioning the Administration
against the invasion. It has been a matter of record that the Senator,
on his own initiative and without access to any confidential files,
made his views known to the President both in a memorandum and
at a top-level meeting in which the invasion plans were given a
final discussion.*

As narrated by Sidney Hyman in the New Republic *(May 14,
1962), Fulbright happened to speak with the President late in
March. Mr. Kennedy heard that the Senator was planning to leave
for Florida on March 30 to spend Easter with a relation; since the
President himself was flying to Palm Beach the same day, he
invited Fulbright to join him on the plane.*

*Fulbright saw in this chance encounter an opportunity to discuss
the invasion rumors that had been appearing in the press. He asked
Pat Holt, a Foreign Relations Committee staff member, to draft a
memorandum outlining Fulbright's reasons for judging the rumored
plan unsound. The next day he boarded the presidential plane and
gave a copy of the reworked memorandum to the President. On
the return trip to Washington, a few days later, the President again
discussed the question with Fulbright and asked him to attend a
meeting that same afternoon (April 4) at the State Department.*

*The meeting was fully described as early as June 24, 1961, in an
article by Stewart Alsop in the* Saturday Evening Post. *As Alsop
reported, the discussion went round the room and the President's
advisers, including the military and CIA Director Allen Dulles,
pronounced the plan feasible. It developed that Fulbright, the only*

outsider present, was the only person to oppose the invasion plan on both moral and practical grounds. Fulbright was also the only person present, as Hyman notes, who owed nothing to the President and did not have to concern himself with his status as an adviser should the invasion plan succeed.

The first public mention of Fulbright's role came in a garbled story by Rowland Evans in the May 4 issue of the New York Herald Tribune, *which bore the mischief-making headline: "Why Fulbright's Glaring at the White House—and a Cuban Secret." This prompted President Kennedy to remark at his May 5 news conference that he felt that Fulbright was "a valuable citizen and I think his counsel is useful and I think he should say what he thinks."*

Subsequently, the story was accurately recounted and the substance of the memorandum summarized in columns by Marquis Childs and Walter Lippmann, in a New York Times Magazine *article by E. W. Kenworthy, as well as in the articles by Alsop and Hyman already cited. The text of the memorandum follows:*

The question of United States policy toward Cuba involves a choice of two practical possibilities:

1. Overthrow of the Castro regime.

2. Toleration of the Castro regime, combined with efforts to isolate it and to insulate the rest of Latin American from it.

To these might be added a third possibility—reformation of the Castro regime. But Castro has had so many opportunities to reform and has rebuffed all of them that this course seems more theoretical than real. Perhaps, however, it should not be rejected out of hand until the President has consciously satisfied himself, through whatever private channels are available, that it is a futile course to pursue.

The Overthrow Policy

It is possible for a regime to be overthrown either from within or without. Despite signs of dissatisfaction within Cuba, the preponderance of the evidence points to the conclusion that the Castro regime is actually strengthening its control of the island, through familiar police-state methods. One cannot, therefore, count on a collapse of the Castro regime or its forcible overthrow through unaided internal forces.

Almost daily, however, the press carries stories, and in some cases pictures, of Cuban exiles undergoing military training at secret bases in Florida, or "somewhere in the Caribbean," or in Guatemala, for an invasion of Cuba. It is an open secret that the United States government has pressured Cuban exiles to get together and that the U.S. is supporting, or at least tolerating on U.S. soil, the activities of the exiles looking towards a return to Cuba. It may be argued that all of this is supposition and none of it can be proved; but for the Latin American public—and the U.S. public, too, for that matter—it does not have to be proved. Millions of people still think the United States instigated the Castillo Armas invasion of Guatemala in 1954; but the U.S. hand in that enterprise was far better covered than it is today with regard to the Cuban exiles. Furthermore, as the Cuban exiles intensify their activities aimed at overthrowing Castro, the more difficult it will become to conceal the U.S. hand.

If Cuban exiles mounted an invasion of Cuba, if they then proclaimed a revolutionary government, if this government appealed to the United States for help, if it were recognized by the United States and given help—all these things would put a coating of legality on the enterprise, but they would do nothing to lessen effectively the universal popular impression that the whole operation was a brainchild and puppet of the United States.

Most Latin American governments are probably sufficiently outraged, or scared, or disillusioned with Castro to be willing to look politely the other way while these things were going on. But the United States problem in Latin America is not with governments; it is with people, particularly with workers, peasants, and students.

The argument is made that Castro must go in order to keep his influence from spreading further among these groups. But Castro's influence has already gone far beyond the personal appeal of Castro as an individual. It has been converted into *Castrismo,* which can be

196

expected to persist as a doctrine of radical social reform with heavy anti-Yanqui overtones long after Fidel Castro ceases to be the dictator of Cuba. For the United States to overthrow Castro behind a façade of Cuban exiles would merely add fuel to the appeal of *Castrismo*. Such an action would be denounced from the Rio Grande to Patagonia as an example of imperialism and as the conclusive answer to those who felt that the 1960 election presaged a change in U.S. policy. We would undoubtedly also confront a serious situation in the U.N.

To a large degree, all of this would counterbalance the advantage which would be attained by removing Havana as a source of propaganda, funds, and agitators. Thus, so far as insulating the rest of the Hemisphere is concerned, the United States would not find the overthrow of Castro, in the manner described above, a pure gain. It might even find it a net loss.

There would, of course, be other advantages in the removal of Castro. It would open the way to negotiations for the restoration of confiscated American properties, or for the payment of compensation for them; and it would reopen Cuba for American traders, tourists, and investors. The extent of these advantages can easily be over-emphasized, however. It is naïve to expect that American business and American landholders ever return to the *status quo ante* in Cuba. One cannot completely unscramble the omelet.

Consideration must also be given to the nature and the composition of the government which succeeds Castro. It must be one capable of securing and maintaining genuine popular support— which is to say it must be left of center. Castro probably has such support now, and any successor would have to do more than give lip-service to the social goals of the Castro revolution.

The leaders of the Democratic Revolutionary Front are a rather uncomfortable coalition, representing what is widely thought to be a shotgun marriage. They include some able men, and they exclude Batista supporters; but they also include some pre-Batista politicians who can scarcely be expected to have more success in governing Cuba now than they had before. The Front, in short, is without the kind of leadership necessary to provide a strong, vigorous liberal government. It includes no Muñoz Marín, no Betancourt, no Lleras Camargo.

If the Front comes to power in Cuba, it—and through it, the United States—will inherit a country virtually bankrupt and in an advanced state of social disorder. The task of putting together the pieces will be long, arduous, and expensive, with no guarantee of success. If it were not successful, the United States would be blamed; if it were partially successful, the United States would be blamed for its shortcomings, not only in Cuba but elsewhere.

Although no estimate of the cost of Cuban rehabilitation can now be made, it would be substantial. Consideration should be given to the question of whether the same amount of money could not be put to better, more productive use in other countries of the Hemisphere.

The prospect must also be faced that an invasion of Cuba by exiles would encounter formidable resistance which the exiles, by themselves, might not be able to overcome. The question would then arise of whether the United States would be willing to let the enterprise fail (in the probably futile hope of concealing the U.S. role) or whether the United States would respond with progressive assistance as necessary to insure success. This would include ultimately the use of armed force; and if we came to that, even under the paper cover of legitimacy, we would have undone the work of thirty years in trying to live down earlier interventions. We would also have assumed the responsibility for public order in Cuba, and in the circumstances this would unquestionably be an endless can of worms.

One further point must be made about even covert support of a Castro overthrow; it is in violation of the spirit, and probably the letter as well, of treaties to which the United States is a party and of U.S. domestic legislation.

The charter of the Organization of American States provides, in articles 15 and 16:

No State or group of States has the right to intervene, directly or indirectly, for any reason whatever, in the internal or external affairs of any other State. The foregoing principle prohibits not only armed force but also any other form of interference or attempted threat against the personality of the State or against its political, economic and cultural elements.

No State may use or encourage the use of coercive measures of an economic or political character in order to force the sovereign will of another State and obtain from it advantages of any kind.

Title 18, United States Code, sections 958-962, and Title 50, United State Code, appendix, section 2021, *et seq.* generally prohibit the enlistment or recruitment for foreign military service in the United States, the preparation of foreign military expeditions in the United States, the outfitting of foreign naval vessels for service against friendly powers, and the furnishing of money for military enterprises against foreign states.

The Convention on the Duties and Rights of States in the Event of Civil Strife, signed at Havana in 1928 and ratified by the United States in 1930, binds the parties:

To use all means at their disposal to prevent the inhabitants of their territory, nationals or aliens, from participating in, gathering elements, or crossing the boundary or sailing from their territory for the purpose of starting or promoting civil strife.

It should be noted that a protocol strengthening this Convention was signed by the United States in 1957 and transmitted to the Senate with a request for advice and consent to ratification in 1959. Among other things, the protocol provided, in Article 5:

Each Contracting State shall, in areas subject to its jurisdiction and within the powers granted by its Constitution, use all appropriate means to prevent any person, national or alien, from deliberately participating in the preparation, organization, or carrying out of a military enterprise that has as its purpose the starting, promoting or supporting of civil strife in another Contracting State, whether or not the government of the latter has been recognized.

The Senate gave its advice and consent to ratification July 30, 1959. But the U.S. instrument of ratification has never been deposited with the Pan American Union, and the protocol is therefore not in effect so far as the United States is concerned. The clear inference is that the delay has been caused by sensitivity to the fact that the U.S. would be in violation of the protocol if it completed ratification.

Aside from this protocol, however, the other treaties to which the United States is a party and the domestic statutes which have been cited clearly are intended to prohibit the kind of activity now being carried on by Cuban exiles. To give this activity even covert support is of a piece with the hypocrisy and cynicism for which the United States is constantly denouncing the Soviet Union in the United Nations and elsewhere. This point will not be lost on the rest of the world—nor on our own consciences for that matter.

THE TOLERATION POLICY

It is argued that, recognizing the disadvantages of intervening in Cuba through an exile front, the disadvantages of not intervening are even greater. In this view, it is held that the longer Castro stays in power the harder it will be to dislodge him and the shakier the situation will become in Central America and the Caribbean.

There are, admittedly, difficulties in this area, and these difficulties are compounded by Castro's activities. But, as indicated above, they might be compounded even more by ill-concealed U.S. action against Castro. They might be alleviated by other steps designed on the one hand to isolate Castro and on the other hand to insulate the area against his influence.

Castro has already isolated himself to a degree, especially so far as governments are concerned, and this process can be expected to continue. But in general, the insulation process must be carried out before great results can be expected from a policy of isolation. This is to say that the social and political fabric of the area must be strengthened very materially before vigorous action can be expected in the OAS.

This is a slow and difficult process, and the question arises: Can it be done? Can we afford the time? The answer is yes, on both counts, provided that the Soviet Union uses Cuba only as a political and not as a military base ("military" is used here to mean missiles and nuclear weapons, not small conventional arms).

Remembering always this proviso, the Castro regime is a thorn in the flesh; but it is not a dagger in the heart. Its existence represents a great blow to the prestige of the United States. Conversely, it is a great boon to the Soviet Union. It also serves the Soviets as a base for agitation in the rest of Latin America, though removal of this base would by no means exclude the Soviets from the Hemisphere so long as they have their embassies in Mexico, Montevideo, and elsewhere. Nor would it remove the cause of social and political unrest in the area.

Neither, however, is Cuba all net gain for the Soviet Union. It is a long way away. It is expensive in terms of rubles and of Soviet resources.

It was said above that the fall of the Castro regime from internal causes could not reasonably be expected, but this is true only so long as the Soviet Union is willing to pay the price of keeping Castro in power. This price is likely to become progressively higher.

If the Castro regime remains in power, its agitation and propaganda elsewhere in the Hemisphere and particularly in Central America and the Caribbean is certain to continue and is more likely to increase than to diminish. But as was pointed out above, the sources of social and political unrest in these areas predated Castro and, in the absence of corrective action, will also outlive him.

The real question concerning the future of the Castro regime and its effect on the United States is whether Castro can in fact succeed in providing a better life for the Cuban people; in making Cuba a little paradise, a real Pearl of the Antilles; and whether he can do a better job in this respect in Cuba than the United States and its friends can do elsewhere in Latin America. In all honesty, one should be wary of dogmatic answers on this point. But if one has faith in the human values of the United States, and if that faith is supported by vigorous and intelligent action, then there is no need to fear competition from an unshaven megalomaniac. To look at the other side of the proposition, it would be a fatal confession of lack of faith in ourselves and our values if we decreed that Castro must go because he might succeed.

It will not be easy in any circumstances to shore up the countries of the Caribbean and Central America, and Castro will make it more difficult. But the disadvantages of a policy of overthrow are a good bit clearer than the disadvantages of a policy of toleration, isolation, and insulation.

The Act of Bogotá and the Alianza para Progreso provide the basis for a solid policy of insulating the rest of the Hemisphere from Castro. But more needs to be done, primarily along political lines. In Mexico, in Costa Rica, and throughout the continent of South America except for Paraguay, there are political leaders with whom the U.S. can work, despite the difficulties which some of them pose. The great lack in the Caribbean and Central America is indigenous political leadership. This is a field which requires our urgent attention.

The United States has sadly neglected the political orientation of its economic aid programs. Far too much attention has been given to the economic content and consequences of such programs and far too little to their prospective political results. Insofar as they had political content at all, these programs have usually been keyed to supporting a given government in power, and too often it has been a traditional, oligarchical government on its way out. Too many American ambassadors have counted themselves successful if they were on a first-name basis with the incumbent President, only to wake up some morning to find the President in exile and a totally unknown group running the country. Virtually nothing has been done to help up-and-coming politicians by way of orientation and training in political techniques. Too little has been done by way of helping underdeveloped countries to develop the kinds of political institutions which, in the United States and Western Europe, act as shock absorbers and ease the peaceful transition of political power.

Tentatively, the question may be raised as to whether this important and hitherto-neglected field provides an opportunity to make use of the talents of the Cuban exiles in a more productive way than invading their homeland.

Would it, for example, be possible to approach some countries in Central America about the possibility of putting Cuban exiles into those countries to help in this respect? Could some of these exiles be used by President Betancourt of Venezuela?

It is to be noted in this connection that Tracy Voorhees, in his last report to President Eisenhower in January, recommended that ways be found to use Cuban exiles in technical assistance in the ICA program in Latin America.

The point to be emphasized here is that the Cuban exiles must be given something constructive to do or they will deteriorate as human beings. Many of them are now receiving military training. How many of them are now receiving political training to go along with it? Such political training would be necessary even if they invaded Cuba; it ought to be possible to put such training to good use elsewhere in the Hemisphere even if they don't invade Cuba.

For example, there is the International Institute of Political-Social Studies in San José, Costa Rica. The Board of Directors of this Institute consists of Rómulo Betancourt, President of Venezuela; Víctor Raúl Haya de la Torre, leader of the APRA Party of Peru and potentially that country's next President; José Figueres, former President of Costa Rica; Eduardo Santos, former President of Colombia and publisher of one of that country's most influential newspapers; and Normas Thomas. Has the possibility been explored of using this Institute to train Cuban exiles in political action work and then scatter them throughout the area?

There have been reports of Castro agents infiltrating, agitating, and training in the mountains of northern Peru. Has thought been given to sending Cuban exiles into the same area?

This paper is written in full knowledge of the difficulties which will attend any large-scale program for the use of Cuban exiles such as is suggested. Latin American governments may well oppose the idea.

Yet, at least so far as Central America is concerned, we must some time break out of the vicious dilemma in which we are now trapped.

This is the dilemma of governments in power which perhaps give lip-service to social reform but which do not really have it in their hearts. We must make it clear to them that the time for conversion is growing short; that if they are converted to the cause of genuine social reform, we will help them; but that if they are not, we do not propose to be overthrown with them.

One perhaps extreme possibility would be to offer to the governments of Central America some, or all, of the advantages now enjoyed by Puerto Rico in its relationship to the United States. Nationalism in these countries is so strong that we could not take over their foreign affairs; but we could offer them the advantages of a customs union, of FHA housing programs, and of tax incentives, in return for real land reform and progressive income taxation. Alternatively a more vigorous policy should be pursued to encourage economic integration and political federation of those countries among themselves.

Finally, it is suggested that emissaries of the Administration consult Governor Luis Muñoz-Marín of Puerto Rico before taking irrevocable steps in the Caribbean. Depending on the outcome of these conversations, it might also be well to consult former President Figueres of Costa Rica, former President Santos of Colombia, President Lleras of Colombia, Prime Minister Beltrán of Peru, Mr. Haya de la Torre of Peru, and President López of Mexico. President Betancourt of Venezuela is left off this list because he has such an *idée fixe* about Trujillo. López might also well be left off, because the Mexicans are so traditionally isolationist in these matters. On the other hand, consulting López would undoubtedly flatter him.

CONCLUSION

American property interests in Cuba have been lost, probably most of them irretrievably. But there remain roughly eight billion dollars in American investments elsewhere in the Hemisphere, plus an incalculable American political interest.

This political interest could be irreparably damaged by ill-con‹

sidered, ill-concealed action vis-à-vis Cuba. The doctrine of non-intervention badly needs redefinition, but in its present state it is the keystone of all Latin American policies toward the United States. It got that way for historical reasons—U.S. interventions have generally been on the side of élite groups and the status quo. To most Latinos, "nonintervention" does not mean that you don't intervene on their behalf. The trouble is, that we have rarely, if ever, really intervened on the side of the people of Latin America. Such intervention is implicit in the Act of Bogotá and it might be well be faced by all concerned. In the meantime, however, to revert to the Teddy Roosevelt style of intervention in Cuba, however artfully or ineptly, would set us back another two generations.

Cuba is no longer important to the United States for its own sake, but only for its effect on our Hemisphere position. Whether we like it or not, we in truth engaged in a kind of competitive co-existence with Castro to see whose system can produce reform and progress more quickly.

We have on our side the best group of Latin American governments, overall, that we have ever had. On the continent of South America, only Paraguay is not moving with the times. Elsewhere, the picture is reversed. Except for Mexico and Costa Rica, the picture in Central America and the Caribbean varies from gloomy to desperate. However, it might perhaps be possible to use our still-strong influence on such presidents as Ydígoras in Guatemala, Villeda in Honduras, and even Somoza in Nicaragua to move them a little along the path to salvation.

In the meantime, building in the countries where there is leadership to work with, we can establish areas of strength that can themselves exert a considerable influence—and do so more effectively than we can.

We cannot realistically expect much help from the OAS in the near future, but this is not to say we can never expect such help. We can afford to be patient enough to await that day.

MEMORANDUM,
MARCH 29, 1961

205

34. Laos, Vietnam, Latin America: Should We Abandon Our Principles?

As summer began in 1961, a new and shaky Administration was in "disarray" in the Olympian judgment of the London Times. *In June, while the humiliation of the Cuban debacle still burned, Mr. Kennedy conferred with Premier Khrushchev in Vienna and President de Gaulle in Paris, and found that both adversary and ally could be inflexible. A new Berlin crisis was looming, the news from Laos was disheartening, and the struggle in Vietnam increasingly uncertain. It was a moment when gnawing frustration lent appeal to the extreme right's call for an adventuristic policy; there was a need for calming, reflective words. On June 29, the Senator rose on the floor to deliver an address simply entitled, "Some Reflections upon Recent Events and Continuing Problems."*

Madam President, for the past two months the attention of the world has been engaged by a series of dramatic events. In their wake, a great many Americans have been left shocked, confused, and frustrated by unmistakable blows to the prestige of the United States. First, a Soviet flier orbited the earth in a space vehicle. Then came the misadventure in Cuba. This was quickly followed by a further decline in the Laos situation, which has set the stage for what may be an unhappy denouement to that affair.

On the heels of these events, there has emerged another Berlin crisis, one that probably is more serious than any of its predecessors. I do not now intend to explore the elements of the Berlin situation. It is at this moment under the most serious study by this government and our European allies.

My fear is that many Americans, including some whose judgment is generally good, are drawing the wrong conclusions from the earlier events I mentioned. From the Soviet space achievement, they conclude that we must dramatically expand our man-in-space program, whatever the cost. The lesson of Cuba, they suggest, is that

206

the objective was the correct one, but that the means employed were inadequate. And they further suggest that any means by which we can block Communist encroachment in our hemispheric garden is the proper course of action. From the events in Laos, many of these voices argue that a political settlement in the present circumstances will simply yield up another country to communism; that we must prevent with any available means the formation in Laos of a government that includes Communist participation.

What these voices are saying is that the United States is the strongest country in the world, and should not hesitate to commit its strength to the active defense of its policies anywhere outside the Communist empire. This is dangerous doctrine; nothing would please Communist leaders more than to draw the United States into costly commitments of its resources to peripheral struggles in which the principal Communist powers are not themselves directly involved.

As a nation, we are understandably prone to be more responsive to dramatic events than to the hard, continuing struggle itself. This is a susceptibility that is common to free societies, but much less a problem to totalitarian societies. As a nation, we are a ruggedly pragmatic people, accustomed to disposing of problems swiftly and resolutely. Yet it may be that the simple trial-and-error methods that accompanied our growth are not relevant to our present role as defenders of Western civilization.

As leader, we must recognize that the struggle with our Communist adversary has entered a critical phase. Our position has been steadily receding over the past several years. We can no longer afford errors. Henceforth, we must endow our actions with greater wisdom, judgment, and consistency than has been the case in recent years. This is a large order. We are caught up in a swirl of events. Wisdom and judgment derive from reflective thought. It is difficult to bring these qualities to bear on events that often develop with bewildering speed. The answer, of course, is policy. We must develop policies against which we can properly evaluate our initiatives and our responses to critical events. We must also develop style. It is one thing to enunciate policies, and another to make them credible. It is style, our performance as a nation and a great power, that determines the credibility of our policies. In the present struggle, style is as important as power. They have a one-to-one relationship.

Cuba, Laos, the Soviet cosmonaut—none of these by itself is a threat to our national security or to the long-term success of our policies. But by exaggerating their significance and reacting to them injudiciously we disfigure our national style and undermine our policies. . . .

It may be that the time has come to reappraise some of our basic assumptions. Throughout much of this century many Americans assumed—wrongly—that the transgressions and affronts to world order committed by aggressive forces were none of our business. With the collapse of that assumption, a good many of us have swung in the other direction and to the opposite conclusion that we can— and should—impose our design for living upon the uncertain but aspirant societies of the world. This assumption is also illogical. However admirable our design may be, it cannot be imposed.

In the struggle with communism, there is a double standard. The Communists seek to impose their design on other countries. Their tactics most often are a brew of terror, subversion, and saturation propaganda, mixed with promises, of which a number are translated into meaningful assistance. The United States seeks not to impose its hegemony upon others, but to help others remain independent and safe from foreign domination. It is suggested with some frequency that U.S. policies would be improved by an infusion of the more mischievous tactics employed by the Communists; that with some application we could beat the Communists at their own game. This, I think, totally misses the point and the real nature of the struggle. The fact is that our greatest strength—indeed, our greatest asset in the struggle—is this double standard. Ours is a permissive system, challenged by one that is totalitarian. Our system guarantees certain basic rights to the individual, and it is these that have made the United States the focus of man's best hope for a way of life that is consistent with his quest for freedom and dignity.

It is not our affluence or our plumbing or our clogged freeways that grip the imagination of others. Rather, it is the values upon which our system is built. These values imply our adherence not only to liberty and individual freedom but also to international peace, law and order, and constructive social purpose. When we depart from these values, we do so at our peril. The world, as we have come to realize, also recognizes the double standard and demands from the United States a higher order of conduct than is expected from others. Whether this distinction will be an asset or a liability in the struggle with communism, remains to be seen. Certainly the answer rests with us. If we are faithful to our own values, while following an intelligent, courageous, and consistent line of policy, we are likely to find a high measure of the support we seek abroad. But if we fail our own values and ideals, ultimately we shall have failed ourselves.

In glancing over the shards of past civilizations, the eye pauses wistfully over the glory radiated by Periclean Athens. As if plotted by one of its own dramatists, the seed of the tragedy that befell Athens and the other city-states can be traced to the highest moment of Athenian brilliance. Shortly after the start of their brief ascendency—and well before the outbreak of the Peloponnesian War—the Athenians made a distinction between themselves and those who depended on their leadership and benevolence. They denied to these others the elevated and enlightened attitudes which inspired the genius of their own society. Thus, the Athenians lost the respect and good will of those who might have supported them in the struggle against Sparta.

The highest achievements of our society are also the products of ideas first put forth in the world by these old Athenians. And as Athens was the leader of a league of city-states, so is the United States the leader of a number of societies who seek primarily the continuing right to be free to choose for themselves.

Some may object that, as a practical matter, the fire spread by communism can be fought effectively only with fire. I disagree. The United States must remain strong and firm. But the United States, in order to prevail, must also help others toward the fulfillment of their own highest purposes. The United States cannot guarantee the borders of a neutral country against infiltration, or its villages from subversion. But the United States can become a pivotal force in enabling well-intentioned governments of independent countries to bring about the economic and social reforms that their societies are understandably enough insisting upon. Given such reforms, subversive efforts fail, and terrorists are unable to intimidate unsympathetic peasants and villagers backed up by alert government forces. The late President Magsaysay of the Philippines understood the elements of the problem, and in his country disposed of it decisively.

Mao Tse-tung, who directed the most stupendous of guerrilla operations, is a high authority on the subject. In his treatise on guerrilla warfare, he wrote: "Guerrillas are like fish, and the people are the water in which the fish swim. If the temperature of the water is right, the fish multiply and flourish."

In colonial Indochina, the temperature was right; the French spent eight years trying to defeat the Vietminh guerrilla army. They invested seven billion dollars in this war, which cost the lives of 100,000 French and Vietnamese soldiers. At one stage, the French committed a force of a half million men to the fighting. But France bore the heavy burden of its colonial record and its unconcern with political and social reform. Inevitably, France lost.

In Laos, the Communist Pathet Lao guerrillas have also found the temperature of the water agreeable. Here, however, the situation lacked the element of inevitability. Somewhat quixotically, the United States sought to make an armed anti-Communist bastion of Laos. This was a mistake. Laos is a primitive country. Most Lao are rooted in the past. Theirs is the pace of the meandering Mekong River which nourishes their lands. Most are concerned, not with an entity known as Laos, but with their families, with the life in their villages, and with their religion. They are a disarmingly gentle people, for whom conflict is disagreeable. They keenly dislike killing each other. It is likely that many more people are presently losing their lives in the terror-ridden countryside of South Vietnam each month than have died from all the strife in Laos.

I say that our policy in Laos was a mistake, because it was not related to the needs of the country or to the nature of its people and their interests. In a landlocked country of mountains, rain forests, and river delta—a country profoundly backward, even by regional standards—the United States attempted to establish an anti-Communist force in the form of an elaborately outfitted 29,000-man army and a tame government.

The situation in Laos has wobbled ever since between tragedy and farce. Just as there was never any pro-Communist motivation among most Lao there was no anti-Communist motivation, either. And the United States utterly failed to inspire it. The illusion that we could make a bastion of Laos cost us more than three hundred million dollars. The cost to our prestige cannot be measured.

South Vietnam is a different case. The people are anti-Communist. That would seem to raise a question If the temperature of the water is not right, how is it that the Communist Viet Cong guerrillas in South Vietnam have managed to gain a foothold in much of the countryside? The answer appears to rest with the regime of Vietnam's President Diem.

The regime in Vietnam has been strong in a situation where strength has been essential. It has been courageous and diligent in bringing order and economic progress out of the chaos that attended the country's birth. It can point to a record of steady accomplishment. Yet the regime has lacked something in benevolence and has shown impatience toward a people who have suffered a great deal. Opposition, including that of anti-Communist elements, has been vigorously suppressed. It is a regime that of necessity has been authoritarian, but one that also has been perhaps unnecessarily severe. On balance, however, it should be said that the accomplishments of this regime are overlooked by many observers and commentators, who all too frequently have accepted uncritically the most abusive gossip and propaganda circulated about President Diem and his administration.

The term "qualified success" could be used to describe the American performance in Vietnam, as well as the Diem regime. Our aid programs have enabled the country to endure and to achieve modest progress. Yet the emphasis has been too heavily weighted on the military side. If there has been any assessment by us of Vietnam's long-range economic problems—any coherent effort to measure programs against economic targets—I am not aware of it.

Ultimately, Vietnam's struggle for survival as an independent country will be determined by the economic and social progress that flow from the programs and policies of its government. Paramilitary operations might influence, but would not determine, the outcome. Neither would a costly, protracted, and inconclusive military struggle in Laos determine the outcome in Vietnam. For the United States, the proper course is to continue sustaining and supporting efforts of the Vietnamese army to cope effectively with the foe in being— tough bands of hit-and-run Communist guerrillas—while devoting at least as much effort to assisting and guiding the Vietnamese people in their struggle for dignity and economic independence....

The tempo of Communist subversion in southeast Asia has been stepped up briskly in the past several months. We can hardly expect a respite; indeed, one can safely assume only that the struggle for independence in southeast Asia has entered a decisive stage. The pressure will be relentless. Some countries, especially the politically nonaligned, have not yet been exposed to the weight of the problem, but they are acutely conscious of the danger.

Were I the leader of one of these countries, I would adopt the following policy toward the United States. I would repeat and clarify my determination to remain free of political alignment with either power bloc. I would seek economic and technical assistance from the United States, and remind the United States that if I choose to accept limited aid from the Communist bloc I am not unaware of communism's ultimate plans for my country. But I would discreetly point out that the United States cannot with guns, tanks, jeeps—or even with dollars—keep communism out of my country. The United States, I would add, can help me keep communism out of my country by imaginatively and dispassionately supporting my efforts to promote the welfare of my people. If communism should attack my country from without, I would call upon the United States and its allies for whatever military support they could make available. If communism should commence a campaign of terror and subversion inside my country, I would seek from the United States technical military assistance so that I might cope effectively with this Communist device. And I would seek still further direct economic assistance so that I could quicken the pace of progress in my country.

If I were one of the so-called neutralist leaders of a newly independent country, I—like most of this group—would have silently identified my hopes for the future with American leadership. And despairing of consistently wise American leadership, as I often would, I might impart this thought to my American colleagues. The Soviet revolution occurred more recently than the American. And its heirs are adroit in trimming their sails to the revolutionary winds of change around the world. Yet much of the world remembers what the American Revolution has accomplished. And the countless millions who do remember—whether in Vietnam, Iran, Cuba, or elsewhere—hope and insist that the spirit and intelligence that inspired America's revolution will animate America's foreign policy....

SENATE ADDRESS,
JUNE 29, 1961

35. *Total Victory: A Slogan Clinically Examined*

Fulbright's preceding speech seemed eminently sane to some; to others, it expounded fearful heresy. On July 13, Senator Barry M. Goldwater spoke for the radical right in deploring Fulbright's assertion that it would be dangerous for the United States to be drawn into peripheral struggles. "I suggest," said Goldwater, "that a far more dangerous doctrine is the one advanced by the Senator from Arkansas—one that would make of 'nonintervention' under any circumstances a national policy ... It is really astounding that our government has never stated its purpose to be that of complete victory over the tyrannical forces of international communism."

On July 24, Fulbright replied to the Senator from Arizona.

Mr. President, I should like to comment briefly today on certain themes contained in the remarks concerning our foreign policy made by the junior Senator from Arizona [Mr. Goldwater] on July 13. The Senator's views are, as usual, forthright and provocative. They

213

are of special significance, in that the Senator is an acknowledged spokesman and leader of opinion in his party.

The Senator says that our fundamental objective must be "total victory" over international communism. I must confess to some difficulty in understanding precisely what "total victory" means in this age of ideological conflict and nuclear weapons. Certainly the term is a stirring one. It has a romantic ring. It quickens the blood like a clarion call to arms, and stimulates the imagination with a vision of brave and gallant deeds.

It would be beneficial and instructive, I think, if those who call for total victory would spell out for us precisely how it might be achieved and, more important, what we would do with a total victory once we had won it. Is it to be won by nuclear war—a war which at the very least would cost the lives of tens of millions of people on both sides, devastate most or all of our great cities, and mutilate or utterly destroy a civilization which has been built over thousands of years?

Or can total victory be won without war—by some brilliant stroke of diplomacy or by arguments of such compelling logic that the Communists will acknowledge the error of their ways and abandon their grand imperialistic design? Perhaps the advocates of total victory believe that we can achieve it by abandoning our efforts toward disarmament and engaging in an unrestricted nuclear arms race, even though such a policy would provoke similar measures by the Communist powers.

The Senator from Arizona suggests that the periphery of freedom "is growing steadily smaller in direct ratio to our failure to act from strength." What would a policy of strength involve? Does it mean a military invasion of Cuba which would destroy the Castro dictatorship, but which would also alienate the rest of Latin America and necessitate the stationing of Marines in Cuba to protect an American-imposed regime against Fidelista rebels and guerrillas? Does it mean the commitment of American forces to interminable guerrilla warfare in the jungles of Laos, a war in which all the advantages of geography would be on the side of the Communists?

Even more perplexing than the question of how to win a total victory is the problem of what we would do with it once it was won. Would we undertake a military occupation of Russia and China and launch a massive program to re-educate two-hundred million Russians and six-hundred million Chinese in the ways of Western democracy?

Political objectives must be framed in terms of time and circumstance. In the Middle Ages, when military combat took the form of jousts between chivalrous knights, total victory was perhaps a reasonable objective. One combatant bested the other with his sword or lance or mace, and that was the end of it. In our own time the chivalrous encounter has been relegated to the football field or the boxing arena, and it is a dangerous illusion to confuse the rules of a college football game with those that apply to the arena of world politics.

We have had total victories in the past, and their examples offer little encouragement. We fought the First World War to make the world safe for democracy, and prosecuted the Second World War to achieve the unconditional surrender of our enemies. Both world wars ended in total victory, but the world is far less safe for democracy today than it was in 1914, when the current era of upheavals began. One of the principal lessons of two world wars is that wars, and total victories, generate more problems than they solve. Apparently we have not yet fully accepted the fact that there are no absolute solutions, that we can hope to do little more than mitigate our problems as best we can and learn to live with them.

As I said in my remarks of June 29, there is a double standard in the struggle between communism and the free nations. While Communist tactics include terror, subversion, and military aggression, the world demands a higher order of conduct from the United States. Our policies must be consistent with our objectives, which are those of constructive social purpose and world peace under world law. Were we to adopt the same mischievous tactics as those employed by the Communists, the principal target of these tactics would be our own principles and our own national style.

The Senator says that world opinion "is an area of official concern which has no reason for existing," that world opinion actually countenances international communism. The Senator does an injustice to the hopes and aspirations of peoples throughout the world and he credits communism with a far greater appeal than it actually has. It is not communism which appeals to the hearts and minds of the emergent peoples of Asia, Africa, and Latin America. These people hope for peace, for a decent material life, and for national self-determination. Only insofar as communism succeeds in identifying itself with these aspirations does it win prestige, allegiance, and respect.

World opinion is eminently worth courting—because the hopes of millions of people for world order and for economic and social reform are our hopes as well. Where world opinion seems to us to be feeble or ill-informed, our proper task is to seek to develop and inform it, not to dismiss it as unworthy of our concern.

We have much to learn, as well as to teach, from the opinions of peoples throughout the world. Our own judgments are not infallible, and there is much to be gained by a decent respect for the opinions of mankind.

World opinion is a civilizing force in the world, helping to restrain the great powers from the worst possible consequences of their mutual hostility. To disavow and override the opinions of other peoples because they do not always agree with our own is to destroy a potentially powerful force for peace and to return to the laws of the jungle.

The Senator says that I favor a policy of "nonintervention." I am indeed opposed to policies that would overextend the United States, especially when such policies find little or no support elsewhere in the non-Communist world. By refusing to permit our national strength to be sapped by peripheral struggles, we maximize our power to honor our obligations and commitments all over the world. We are committed to military and political alliances with many nations and we are committed to assist many more nations toward the fulfillment of their legitimate political, economic, and social aspirations. Such policies are the diametric opposite of any doctrine of nonintervention. Their basic concept is one of intervention—but not indiscriminate military intervention in response to every provocation and every disorder, regardless of its character and cause. The latter approach is one of long-range intervention in depth, one which employs all of the instrumentalities of foreign policy, the political and economic as well as the military. Its object is the realization of our national interests and not merely the piecemeal frustration of Communist ambitions.

There are limitations to foreign policy. We are neither omniscient nor omnipotent, and we cannot aspire to make the world over in our image.

Our proper objective is a continuing effort to limit the world struggle for power and to bring it under civilized rules. Such a program lacks the drama and romance of a global crusade. Its virtue is that it represents a realistic accommodation between our highest purposes and the limitations of human capacity. Its ultimate objective is indeed total victory, not alone for our arms in a nuclear war or for the goal of a world forcibly recast in our image, but rather for a process—a process of civilizing international relations and of bringing them gradually under a world-wide regime of law and order and peaceful procedures for the redress of legitimate grievances.

SENATE ADDRESS,

JULY 24, 1961

36. "Where There Is Sugar, You'll Find Flies"

Fulbright was preoccupied with state politics through much of 1962, and campaigned steadily until the July 31 primary gave him a two-to-one victory over an extremist opponent. However, he did not neglect one item of Senate business. The year before, Fulbright had become concerned with the spread of lobbying by registered American agents in behalf of foreign governments. He began collecting material with the aim of conducting a full committee inquiry into nondiplomatic relations. During 1962, he guessed, accurately, that the renewal of the Sugar Act might create public controversy about foreign lobbies. Under the sugar program, American consumers pay out some five hundred million dollars yearly in indirect subsidies to support a noncompetitive domestic industry and to dole out premium prices to overseas producers. When Castro's Cuba lost its sugar quota, foreign producers saw an opportunity to divide up a lucrative market. Foreign lobbying was especially intense in Washington when the House Agriculture Committee reported out a bill awarding quotas to fifteen new foreign areas. Along with Senator Paul H. Douglas, Fulbright had a record of opposing the entire sugar quota program. Both Senators led the fight against the House bill and did succeed in setting aside part of the old Cuban market into a "global quota" where no premium prices would be paid. Fulbright used the occasion to dramatize the need for an inquiry into foreign lobbying; the investigation was duly authorized. In abbreviated form, here is Fulbright's indictment of a program that invites a swarm of flies.

Mr. President, there is another side of this sugar program that needs public discussion. Some years ago, when I was dealing with questionable activities in a small branch of this government, a wise man wrote me that "Where there is sugar, there you'll find the flies."

Mr. President, the lobbyists on Capitol Hill working on the sugar bill are thick as flies. It would be one thing if they were all associated with domestic interests, who themselves are knowledgeable in the ways of this city and prepared to handle any situation. The fact is that many of them are Americans representing foreign nations who for the most part are naïve about the working of the legislative branch of our government.

In 1956, when the sugar bill was up for revision and hearings were held there were only four foreign lobbyists heard. This year, no less than twenty-two appeared before the House committee. It is not only the proliferation of foreign lobbyists that disturbs me, but also the type of contacts and amounts of their fees.

The law firm of Dawson, Griffin, Pickens, and Riddell, for example, signed a letter contract with the Indian Sugar Mills Association on May 21 of this year that could bring that law firm $99,000 in fees and $15,000 if the House sugar bill is passed. There were only fifty days remaining before a new sugar bill was expected, yet this law firm was signed for almost $100,000 almost entirely to aid in promoting India's effort to get a sugar quota.

Another lobbyist worth noting is Rocco C. Siciliano, a former special assistant to President Eisenhower, whose law firm represents the Sugar Association of El Salvador for a fee of $10,000. Mr. Siciliano reported to the Senate Finance Committee that he specifically was hired to lobby this particular sugar bill. The interesting fact here is that for that fee—a very substantial one in El Salvador's terms—Mr. Siciliano was hired less than a week ago, on June 21, only nine days before the current legislation is to run out and by which time it is generally expected we would have approved a new measure.

There is another type of lobbyist working on this bill for foreign nations. He is one who is getting a basic fee and then something additional based on the amount of sugar he gets for his client...

Mr. President, if this foreign sugar lobbying were limited to large fees and persuasive talking it would be one thing. But the fact that the Sugar Act up to now has placed Congress in the position of deciding where U.S. sugar will come from has worked to undermine our State Department in the eyes of the nations with whom they deal. In all sugar-producing countries, including the twenty-two with lobbyist representatives, it has been the Administration's policy to have the United States ambassador indicate that the Administration program will place the United States on a global quota basis. Yet these nations have gone ahead and hired outside representation in an effort to have Congress change the Administration's position.

Should the Administration and the President be reversed on this issue, and quotas be granted to all these countries thanks in part to nondiplomatic representations to Congress, the prestige of our nation will be severely dimmed. For these countries will then be tempted to think that if lobbying works in sugar, why not try it in other areas—perhaps military or foreign aid.

Mr. President, I would like to sum up the current program this way: the Secretary of Agriculture has been given the power to set the domestic prices of sugar and control its growth, processing, and marketing. About the only thing he cannot control is how much of it each one of us consumes. The program has kept a floor under domestic sugar prices, which have steadily risen since the Act became law. It has brought increased income to growers, so much so that almost every farmer in the nation is tempted to get a quota. It has necessitated a consumer subsidy of mounting proportions, one that could go to two and a half billion dollars over the life of the proposed legislation. Through quota premiums to foreign producers it has encouraged inefficient foreign production that almost rivals our own domestic inefficiency. It has also caused serious diplomatic problems among nations with whom we are friendly and has fostered a foreign sugar lobby that if successful could stimulate similar activities in other fields which could grow into a serious hindrance to the regular conduct of foreign affairs.

SENATE ADDRESS,
JULY 22, 1962

Chapter Eight

POLITICS IN UNIFORM

─────── ∿∿∿ ───────

37. The Military Memorandum

*The selection that follows is easily among the most controversial,
the least read and most influential of the Senator's major utterances.
During 1961, Fulbright began diligently to collect material on the
strange alliance that had sprung up between some military officers
and the zealots of the extreme right, who saw internal Communist
infiltration as virtually the only peril to the republic. The public
became aware of this breach of American military tradition when
Major General Edwin A. Walker—ironically, the officer in command of the federal troops during the Little Rock school crisis—
was reprimanded for his eccentric troop-indoctrination program at
an overseas base.*

*On his own initiative, Fulbright submitted a memorandum to the
Secretary of Defense detailing the abuse of a National Security
Council directive permitting military personnel to arouse the public
on cold-war issues. The problem touched close to home; the first of
eleven specific incidents described in an attachment to the memo-
randum concerned "strategy for survival" conferences held in Little
Rock and in Fayetteville, the Senator's home town. News of the
Fulbright memorandum prompted an uproar when Senator Strom
Thurmond of South Carolina demanded its text "within the next*

hour." Fulbright responded by placing the entire memorandum, here complete except for its four attachments, in the Record.

Mr. Fulbright: Madam President, I have been surprised in the past few days by a display of intense interest in a memorandum on propaganda activities of military personnel which I have submitted to the Secretary of Defense.

Perhaps I am naïve. I must confess that I was unaware that the subject was one which could arouse great controversy. The memorandum was based on my strong belief in the principle of military subordination to civilian control. There has been a strong tradition in this country that it is not the function of the military to educate the public on political issues. Military officers are not elected by the people, and they have no responsibility for the formation of policies other than military policies. Their function is to carry out policies formulated by officials who are responsible to the electorate. This tradition is rooted in the constitutional principle that the President is the Commander in Chief of the armed forces and that, therefore, military personnel are not to participate in activities which undermine his policies.

Madam President, I did not think that this constitutional tradition was controversial.

The memorandum was a personal one. The Committee on Foreign Relations did not act upon it in any way. It was transmitted to the Secretary of Defense as a personal correspondence.

Madam President, I must confess to still another misapprehension. I was unaware that it was the custom, the practice, or the right of senators to demand access to the private correspondence of their colleagues. Although I should not have thought it my duty to open my private files, I would have been quite willing to show the memorandum in question to any senator who courteously requested to see it. I was not willing, however, to comply with an ultimatum such as I received from the junior Senator from South Carolina on July 21 demanding that he be provided with a copy of the memorandum "within the next hour." Aside from the fact that I had no copy of

222

the memorandum available at that time, I was unwilling to open my private papers in response to so impertinent a letter.

Madam President, I have now been apprised of the misapprehensions under which I was laboring. Apparently the constitutional principle of civilian control of the armed forces is indeed a subject of political controversy. In view of this fact and in order to dispel the fears of those who have persuaded themselves that the memorandum contains material which is sinister, subversive, or sensational, I have decided to release the text of the memorandum. I therefore ask unanimous consent that it be printed in the *Record* at this point.

MEMORANDUM: PROPAGANDA ACTIVITIES OF MILITARY PERSONNEL DIRECTED AT THE PUBLIC

There are four attachments [1] to this memorandum from which the following conclusions are made:

1. Under a National Security Council directive in 1958, it remains the policy of the U.S. government to make use of military personnel and facilities to arouse the public to the menace of the cold war.

2. Basic material for implementing the policy, under the title of "American Strategy for the Nuclear Age," prepared and disseminated by private organizations with close military connections, and being distributed as a master curriculum for strategy seminars, is by no means representative of the President's announced strategy for the nuclear age. Although scholarly, and worth attention as elements of strategy, its total effect can be said to be contrary to the President's program.

---

[1] The attachments were: (a) a summary list and description of eleven instances of education and propaganda activities of military personnel; (b) an article, "School for Strategy," by Gene M. Lyons and Louis Morton, from the March 3, 1961, issue of the *Bulletin of Atomic Scientists;* (c) an article by Cabell Phillips headed "Right-wing Officers Worrying Pentagon" from the June 18, 1961, *New York Times;* and (d) a copy of a letter from Brigadier General Fred C. Weyland, Deputy Chief of Legislative Liaison, Department of the Army, dated June 12, 1961, and sent to Senator Joseph S. Clark, explaining Pentagon policy on politics in uniform.

3. In at least eleven instances of what apparently are implementations of the National Security Council policy, the actual programs, closely identified with military personnel, made use of extremely radical right-wing speakers and/or materials, with the probable net result of condemning foreign and domestic policies of the administration in the public mind.

The purpose of this memorandum is to give some indication of the dangers involved in education and propaganda activities by the military, directed at the public, and to suggest steps for dealing with the underlying problem.

The attached list of instances of military participation, in varying degrees, in programs having as at least part of their purpose to educate or propagandize the public, as well as the military, does not purport to be exhaustive. It was gathered from newspaper reports, interviews, and other sources. It is believed there have been other similar cases, perhaps many others, and that still more may well be in process of formation.

As a generalization, the instances described in the attached list involve the participation of military personnel in programs on the nature of the Communist menace and proper methods of combating it. Under such names as "alerts," "seminars," "freedom forums," "strategy for survival conferences," "fourth dimensional warfare seminars," and perhaps others, military personnel of various services and rank have participated to such a degree as to identify themselves with the fact of the program and, at least to some extent, its content.

The content no doubt has varied from program to program, but running through all of them is a central theme that the primary, if not exclusive, danger to this country is internal Communist infiltration. Past and current international difficulties are often attributed to this, or ascribed to "softness," "sell-outs," "appeasements," etc. Radical right-wing speakers dominate the programs.

The thesis of the nature of the Communist threat often is developed by equating social legislation with socialism, and the latter with communism. Much of the administration's domestic legislative program, including continuation of the graduated income tax, expansion of social security (particularly medical care under social security), federal aid to education, etc., under this philosophy would be characterized as steps toward communism.

This view of the Communist menace renders foreign aid, cultural exchanges, disarmament negotiations, and other international programs as extremely wasteful, if not actually subversive. This is a most moderate characterization.

Whether these instances are representative of programs implementing the National Security Council directive is not known, but the pattern they form makes it strongly suspect that they are. There are many indications that the philosophy of the programs is representative of a substantial element of military thought, and has great appeal to the military mind. A strong case can be made, logically, that this type of activity is the inevitable consequence of such a directive. There is little in the education, training, or experience of most military officers to equip them with the balance of judgment necessary to put their own ultimate solutions—those with which their education, training, and experience are concerned—into proper perspective in the President's total "strategy for the nuclear age."

THE DANGERS

These propaganda activities may well become important obstacles to public acceptance of the President's program and leadership, if they are not already. However, this is by no means the limit of the danger.

The view of the menace of the cold war described above already has great appeal to the public. In the future it may well have much greater appeal. This opinion is based upon an appraisal of the cold-war struggle now and in the future, never better described than in the President's inaugural address when he spoke of "the burden of a long twilight struggle, year in and year out," which, he also said, may not be solved "in our lifetime on this planet."

The American people have never really been tested in such a struggle. In the long run, it is quite possible that the principal problem of leadership will be, if it is not already, to restrain the desire of the people to hit the Communists with everything we've got, particularly if there are more Cubas and Laos. Pride in victory, and frustration in restraint, during the Korean war, led to MacArthur's revolt and McCarthyism.

This problem of democratic attitudes toward foreign policy has never been better stated than by de Tocqueville, who wrote:

Foreign politics demand scarcely any of those qualities which a democracy possesses; and they require, on the contrary, the perfect use of almost all those faculties in which it is deficient.... A democracy is unable to regulate the details of an important undertaking, to persevere in a design, and to work out its execution in the presence of serious obstacles. It cannot combine its measures with secrecy, and it will not await their consequences with patience. These are qualities which more especially belong to an individual (a dictator) or to an aristocracy (or an oligarchy or presidium).

He also wrote of "the propensity which democracies have to obey the impulse of passion rather than the suggestions of prudence, and to abandon a mature design for the gratification of a momentary caprice."

It is probably the view of most Members of Congress today that if foreign aid were laid before the people in a referendum, it would be defeated. The question arises: How will it be five or ten years from now? Even the most devoted adherents do not expect immediate or dramatic results, particularly since, in contrast with the European recovery program, foreign aid will be operating primarily upon primitive economies. Yet, in the meantime, all the paraphernalia of our international programs must be at least tolerated by the people during the "long twilight struggle."

The radicalism of the right can be expected to have great mass appeal during such periods. It offers the simple solution, easily understood: scourging of the devils within the body politic or, in the extreme, lashing out at the enemy.

If the military is infected with this virus of right-wing radicalism, the danger is worthy of attention. If it believes the public is, the

226

danger is enhanced. If, by the process of the military "educating" the public, the fevers of both groups are raised, the danger is great indeed.

Perhaps it is farfetched to call forth the revolt of the French generals as an example of the ultimate danger. Nevertheless, military officers, French or American, have some common characteristics arising from their profession, and there are numerous military "fingers on the trigger" throughout the world. While this danger may appear very remote, contrary to American tradition, and even American military tradition, so also is the "long twilight struggle," and so also is the very existence of an American military program for educating the public.

This memorandum has not attempted to deal with the basic traditional and constitutional question of military efforts to propagandize the public—although the violation of these concepts alone should be sufficient basis for challenging the National Security Council policy and its implementation.

Fundamentally, it is believed that the American people have little, if any, need to be alerted to the menace of the cold war. Rather, the need is for understanding of the true nature of that menace, and the direction of the public's present and foreseeable awareness of the fact of the menace toward support of the President's own total program for survival in a nuclear age. There are no reasons to believe that military personnel generally can contribute to this need, beyond their specific, technical competence to explain their own role. On the contrary, there are many reasons, and some evidence, for believing that an effort by the military, beyond this limitation, involves considerable danger.

RECOMMENDATIONS

1. With reference to the National Security Council directive of 1958, suggested revision is based upon its description in attachment 3 (*New York Times* article of June 18, 1961), from which the following is excerpted:

227

President Eisenhower and his top policy leaders decreed that the cold war could not be fought as a series of separate and often unrelated actions, as with foreign aid and propaganda. Rather, it must be fought with a concentration of all the resources of the government and with the full understanding and support of the civilian population. It was decided in particular, that the military should be used to reinforce the cold-war effort.

This policy should be reconsidered from the standpoint of a basic error: that military personnel have the necessarily broad background which would enable them to relate the various aspects of the cold-war effort, one to the other.

2. The White House and the Defense Department should cease treating propaganda activities of military personnel as problems of discipline in individual cases or of co-ordination of such cases from a press or public-relations standpoint, and begin the process of formulating directives which will bring such military activities under effective civilian control.

So long as the cases are treated individually as disciplinary cases, there may well be considerable public sympathy with the individual concerned, as a person, or with his expressed viewpoint. However, if appropriate directives are established, as general propositions, without reference to specific cases, the broad principle of civilian control should be accepted—or, to take the converse, disagreement with the principle would be difficult to sustain.

3. The organization, mission, and operation of the National War College should be reviewed in the context of the cold war and the limitations on the role of the military in the President's program. If its function is, as stated, "To enhance the preparation of selected personnel of the armed forces and the State Department for the exercise of joint and high-level policy, command and staff functions and for the planning of national strategy," the questions arise whether it should operate under the Joint Chiefs of Staff, and if its administration should be so largely dominated by the military, as at present.

4. The relationships between the Foreign Policy Research Institute, the Institute for American Strategy, the Richardson Founda-

228

tion, the National War College, and the Joint Chiefs of Staff should be re-examined, from the standpoint of whether these relationships do not amount to official support for a viewpoint at variance with that of the administration. These relationships may give one particularly aggressive view a more direct and commanding influence upon military and civilian concepts of strategy than is desirable.

5. Long-range studies, preferably dominated by a board of civilian educators, should begin the development of a program for exposure of promising military officers to broader educational opportunities, perhaps requiring completion of graduate studies in history, government, and foreign policy at universities as a condition to high ranks

6. With respect to the problems illustrated by the case of General Walker, it is suggested that a civilian committee be appointed to review troop-education activities of military personnel from the standpoint of their necessity and, if found to be, to develop procedures for bringing the content of such programs and, if possible, their actual operation under civilian control.

SENATE ADDRESS,
AUGUST 2, 1961

38. Who Is Really "Soft on Communism"?

The squall on the right intensified; Fulbright swiftly became the major target for self-styled patriots who made patriotism a refuge for silliness. The Arkansas Democrat replied to his critics with a speech before the military themselves at an opening session of the National War College and the Industrial College of the Armed Forces. But his response was addressed to more than an audience of soldiers and contains what may become a classic statement on the sources of frustration that have helped to spawn the fanatics of the radical right.

The extreme difficulty of defining the proper relationship between military and civilian authorities in a democracy derives basically from the stubborn refusal of the world of reality to accommodate itself to the tidy compartments of theoretical logic. It has always been difficult, and in the modern world of nuclear weapons and cold war it is all but impossible, to separate military problems from general policy; to designate one neat area labeled "question of military policy to be decided by generals" and an altogether separate area of "questions of politics to be left to the politicians."

David Lloyd George once declared, "There is no greater fatuity than a political judgment dressed in a military uniform."

The reply might well have been: "No, except a military judgment dressed in civilian clothes." The real answer, if not in Lloyd George's time, then certainly in our own, is that the problems of national security are so inseparably related to problems of diplomacy, economics, and technology that lines cannot be drawn and decisions must be made jointly. The politician must acquire knowledge and sensitivity to every aspect of national security, including the military, while military officers are under a heavy obligation to bring to the performance of their tasks much of the wisdom of history and statecraft.

The military profession is now involved intimately in national policy processes. This involvement is not the result of any conscious quest for political power on the part of the military, but rather the inevitable product of the new world-wide commitments of the United States and of the revolution in military technology. Power in a democracy is inseparable from responsibility. Accordingly, the military establishment is under the most compelling obligation to exercise the power which has been thrust upon it with wisdom and restraint.

There has been considerable public and rather vitriolic discussion and controversy in recent weeks regarding a memorandum which I submitted to the President and to the Secretary of Defense concerning the sponsorship by military personnel of public meetings primarily devoted to highly controversial political issues. I have been more than a little surprised that this private memorandum has aroused such animated arguments about the involvement of the military in politics and above all has brought into question the principle of civilian control of the military establishment.

This latter principle, rooted in our Constitution and in many centuries of Anglo-Saxon tradition, has served the republic well. It is indispensable to the preservation of democratic government, and it is equally indispensable to the preservation of the professional integrity and effectiveness of the military. As President Kennedy pointed out in his press conference on August 10, nothing would do more grave damage to the prestige and integrity of the armed forces than their embroilment in transitory partisan controversies.

The memorandum which I submitted to the Secretary of Defense was based upon my strong belief in those principles. Its purpose was certainly not to silence military officers who choose to express their own views in public and who are subject to the discipline of their superiors and their own sense of duty and propriety. Nor was the memorandum prepared for the purpose of criticizing private individuals or organizations for holding or promulgating any opinions whatsoever. There is no question of the right of groups of private citizens, such as chambers of commerce, to organize programs of any character, to select speakers freely, and to discuss any topics they choose. The memorandum was directed solely at the impropriety of officers of the armed services permitting their prestige and official status to be exploited by persons with extreme views on highly controversial political issues.

The memorandum set forth instances of military sponsorship of attacks by radical extremists on the policies of our government. The point cannot be overstressed that it is not these verbal attacks which are at issue, but their sponsorship by military authorities. These acts of official sponsorship are far more significant than the few cases in which military officers—often retired or reserve officers—took the platform themselves.

Nor does it matter whether the extremist views expressed were those of the left or of the right. The instances cited in the memorandum happened to be cases which reflect the extremism of the right. I would have been equally concerned had I known of military participation in attacks from the extreme left.

Nor was I concerned with disciplining individuals or groups. It is the constitutional right of all Americans, civilian and military, to hold whatever political views they are led to by conviction and conscience, be they moderate or extreme. Military men in their official status, however, are committing not only themselves as individuals but the prestige of the armed services when they promote or appear to sponsor partisan political meetings. They are therefore doing a disservice both to the American people and to the armed services when they lend their support to any groups or organizations which espouse policies that run counter to those of the Commander in Chief of the armed forces and which have the effect of generating distrust and suspicion among our people.

The memorandum contained a specific recommendation that the Defense Department issue general directives to bring under over-all control the activities of military officers in lending the weight of their official status to organized expressions of extremist opposition to the policies of our government. No disciplinary action against individuals was called for. The primary objective of my recommendation was to insure that military personnel adhere to the obligation, which is inherent in their duty as soldiers, to refrain from public expressions of criticism of the over-all political policies, as distinguished from the technical military policies, of the government and of their Commander in Chief.

Wherever there is power there is the possibility that it will be used and the danger that it will be misused. This assumption, expressed in Lord Acton's maxim that "power corrupts, and absolute power corrupts absolutely," is common to all effective democracies. This principle is one of instinctive distrust of power itself wherever it exists. It has nothing to do with the motives of any group or individual who may wield it. It has been directed against big business, big labor, and big government, and now, inevitably, it is directed against our big military establishment.

There are powerful barriers in the United States to the rise of a political military establishment: the country's long history of antimilitarism; the recruitment system which creates a corps of officers nurtured in this history; the officer-rotation system; the strong bonds of our professional soldiers to the political and social values of the democratic society from which they are drawn; and, finally, the

232

longstanding tradition, which is tightly woven into the whole fabric of American military custom, that the officer corps should be non-political.

The roots of the American military tradition lie deep in the history of the Western world, particularly that of the English-speaking countries. Since the emergence of the modern state-system in Europe, and perhaps even further back in the Middle Ages, the military, like the church, in most Western countries has enjoyed special status, prestige, and perquisites. With its special privileges went special responsibilities. Like the church, the military, in the United States, Great Britain, and other countries, gradually discovered that the retention of its special status and its effectiveness in performing its mission were best served by rigorous abstention from the controversies and intrigues of politicians. There emerged thus a tradition of disciplined abstention from political activity. In the few instances in the modern history of the West in which this tradition did break down, the military, like the church in similar circumstances, found itself beset by hostile reactions and the weakening of public confidence.

The military remains in accord with the basic values of our society. There are no fundamental disagreements, such as prevail in France, for example, between the professional soldier and the rest of society with respect to the written and unwritten rules—the general political consensus—of our society. Generally the military profession is a fair representation of all of the major elements of American society. The principle of civilian supremacy thus remains intact even in the face of an enormous expansion in the power and influence of the armed forces.

In the most democratic of societies, however, there are differences in spirit and mood between the professional soldier and the politician or statesman. The politician must move tentatively in an atmosphere in which goals and means often become mixed. Only in the most general terms does he have predefined objectives, and excessive precision will only make movement difficult. The soldier works differently. His objectives are defined clearly in advance; he will then state his requirements and dispose his forces so as to gain the object.

233

As one student of military affairs recently expressed it: "In military arrangements flexibility is a necessary evil and ambiguity may easily cost lives; in politics flexibility is the first rule and ambiguity an essential instrument."

In considerations such as these lie the wisdom and justification for civilian supremacy and military professionalism. As long as democratic government is honest and efficient and as long as the military adheres to nonpolitical professionalism, there can be no impairment either of democratic institutions or of the integrity of the military establishment.

The problem of maintaining military obedience to civilian authority is fortunately not one which in any basic sense threatens such settled communities as the United States or Great Britain. None the less, by reason of the differences in training and outlook between the soldier and the politician, the possibility of mutual distrust or even hostility is ever present in a time of grave threats to the national security. Our military leaders are experts in the complex technical questions of national defense. Their counsel, with its admirable qualities of expedition and decisiveness, is indispensable to political leaders. Politicians, on the other hand, must concern themselves with a wide variety of nontechnical factors, including the interplay of diverse interests in a pluralistic society. This involves interminable bargaining and compromise—a process which may often strike military experts as inefficient or even dangerous to national security. In the higher reaches of the defense hierarchy, the expert who knows what should be done finds himself at the mercy of the politician who knows what can be done.

Under these circumstances, it can readily be understood that dedicated and patriotic soldiers are subjected at times to a great temptation to descend into the arena of political conflict. Few of our military leaders have done so—a fact which evidences their wisdom as well as their restraint. The few who have raised their voices in public partisan controversy have inadvertently done a disservice both to the American people and to the military establishment itself.

The effectiveness of our armed services depends upon the maintenance of their unique prestige and integrity. These will remain intact only so long as the services adhere to their tradition of non-political professionalism. No group or institution can participate in political debate without itself becoming an object of partisan attack. It is precisely because of its status as a nonpolitical institution that the military in the past has enjoyed the virtually unanimous support of the American people and has thus been beyond partisan assault. It will be recalled that the late Senator McCarthy, who succeeded in frightening or humiliating many reputable groups and individuals, took a fatal step toward his own undoing when he directed his irresponsible charges against the U.S. Army. The prestige of the army was such that the people rallied to its defense. It is my hope that the armed services will never yield to misguided temptations which can only shatter the high esteem in which they are held. The preservation of that esteem is essential to the success of the armed forces in fulfilling their assigned mission and essential also, therefore, to the defense of the republic.

The appeal of certain ideas espoused by the radicals of the right is not difficult to understand. To a nation beset by onerous challenges and responsibilities, they offer deceptively quick and simple solutions. They tell us that we have only to proclaim our dedication to total victory over world communism and to root out subversives—real and imaginary—at home and our problems will be solved. They tell us that our system of alliances and our military and economic commitments abroad are unnecessary and dangerous, that they somehow "play into the hands of the Communists." Instead, they offer us clear and simple solutions—ringing declarations about foreigners and rooting out the disloyal at home. And those who disagree with them, they say, are "soft on communism."

It seems to me that it is these extremists who are advocating a soft approach. Their oversimplifications and their baseless generalizations reflect the softness of those who cannot bear to face the burdens of a continuing struggle against a powerful and resourceful enemy. A truly tough approach, in my judgment, is one which accepts the challenge of communism with the courage and determination to meet it with every instrumentality of foreign policy—political and economic as well as military—and with the willingness to see the struggle through as far into the future as may be necessary. Those who seek to meet the challenge—or, in reality, to evade it—by bold adventures abroad and witch hunts at home are the real devotees of softness—the softness of seeking escape from painful realities by resort to illusory panaceas.

The most astonishing of the propositions of the radical right is their contention that the internal Communist menace is the primary problem of the cold war. They thus credit a wretched handful of Communists in the United States with greater power and influence than the Soviet Union and Communist China with their vast military and political power. I think that this viewpoint is patently absurd. It reflects an amazing lack of confidence in the wisdom and good sense of the American people and their ability to identify and reject Communist propaganda. If this proposition were true, we would be wasting billions of dollars on the armed forces themselves, funds which instead should be transferred to the FBI to fight internal subversion. In fact, the FBI has for years received all of the funds it has requested of the Congress. The internal danger exists and requires constant vigilance, but it would be a tragic irony if, in false and panic-stricken mistrust of our own free society, we were to neglect the overriding danger—that of world-wide Sino-Soviet imperialism.

Implicit in much of the propaganda of the radical right is the assumption that our free society is permeated with corruption and decay. It is said, for example, that the schools and churches of this country are infiltrated with Communists. I recently received a propaganda sheet from an organization which calls itself "conservative" that declared among other things that "any Member of Congress who votes for foreign aid should be defeated for participating in an act of treason." I do not understand how an organization can be regarded as conservative that in effect charges the majority of the Members of every Congress since World War II and three Presidents with treason.

Extremists and irresponsible pronouncements are being widely heard in the land. In a recent speech at a Fourth-Dimensional-Warfare Seminar in Pittsburgh, sponsored by the Chamber of Commerce of Greater Pittsburgh in co-operation with various local military organizations, a retired rear admiral developed the theme that American foreign policy since World War II has consistently played into Soviet hands, that the United States is militarily incapable of surviving surprise Soviet attack, and that negotiations with the Russians for disarmament are in fact appeasement. In a speech last week a prominent elected official denounced Mr. Kennedy's bunch of muddle-minded advisers. Contending that our foreign-assistance program aided the Communist cause, he assailed as irresponsible elements those who favor the independence of the emergent nations of the world. And he declared that it was fatuous nonsense for American foreign policy to take cognizance of some nebulous thing we call world opinion.

The extremists of the right call themselves conservative. In my judgment their views are not conservative, but radical—radical because they fail to distinguish between democratic social progress and totalitarian communism, regarding the former as a step toward the latter. The true conservative is one who wishes to conserve the historic values of our society. He recognizes that the world does not stand still and that, because it does not, we must at times modify and reform traditional practices through orderly processes of change in order to adapt them to new conditions. Social progress is thus seen to be the indispensable means of preserving traditional values in a changing world.

Far from being a step toward communism, social progress through orderly and constitutional procedures is one of the best defenses against communism. The reforms which were undertaken in the United States in the 1930's are believed by many to have thwarted the Communist movement which might have thrived on the mass suffering caused by the depression. Governmental action, for example in the creation of the TVA or the Arkansas River development program, is not, in my opinion, a step toward communism. We are now encouraging the nations of Asia, Africa, and Latin America to undertake basic economic and social reforms because experience has shown that social progress is the key to stability and popular support for governments, and that these in turn form the most solid barriers to Communist penetration.

Those who have faith in our free people and our free institutions must dismiss the wild charges of extremists as malicious and absurd. Only if our society is in an advanced state of disintegration is it as susceptible to Communist infiltration as the radicals of the right contend. I, for one, believe that our free society is strong and stable, and that it is strong because it is free. Because this is so, we need not be fearful of Communist propaganda. The American people can be counted upon to reject it as they have always rejected totalitarian doctrines.

Those who contend that our free society is permeated with corruption and subversion are in fact espousing a line that the Communists themselves would be the first to applaud.

Indeed, the radicals of the right, whose avowed intent is to save our society from destruction, are painting the same picture of ineptitude and decay that the Communists, whose aim is the destruction of our society, would want the American people to believe.

There is a tendency in the history of democratic nations for overly emotional groups and individuals to react to threats from foreign totalitarian powers by permitting themselves to entertain illusions regarding totalitarian forms of an opposite tendency. Thus, for example, when we were threatened by the right-wing totalitarianism of Nazi Germany, a few Americans suddenly professed to see democratic virtues in the Communist absolutism of the left. Now that we are endangered by Communist imperialism instead, a few Americans have fallen prey to the delusion that the radicalism of the right is not totalitarian at all, but is in reality the true philosophy of freedom.

It is my belief that all forms of radical extremism, left or right, are anathema to freedom and democracy. Indeed, the totalitarian left and the totalitarian right have far more in common with each other than either does with genuine democracy. The unholy alliance of left and right is an old combination in certain countries of continental Europe. Together they have formed the "disloyal oppositions" which have beleaguered the democratic center in postwar France and Italy. It is illuminating to note that the Weimar Republic in

238

Germany was destroyed by Nazis and Communists acting in league for their common purpose of destroying the democratic republic. The experience of these countries reveals that the totalitarianism of the left and the totalitarianism of the right have a single common bond: their shared hostility to democracy and freedom.

The United States has been virtually free, throughout its history, of the destructive presence of a powerful disloyal opposition. With the exception of a few marginal groups, our political parties and our people have shared a virtually unanimous faith in constitutional government and free institutions. We have enjoyed the immense benefits of political consensus among a people who were born free and who never in their history have had a serious or prolonged flirtation with any form of absolutism.

It is this incontestable fact of history that reduces the shrill charges of the radical right, and of the radical left as well, to palpable nonsense.

Now, as in the past, the success of our national policies must be rooted in the basic unity and consensus of the American people. This consensus, in a time of overriding danger, must of necessity consist in unified national support of our elected leaders, and especially the President of the United States, the Commander in Chief of our armed forces. "Although the rod of fire may be passed about," wrote the historian Herbert Feis, "it comes back to him. It is his 'yes' or 'no' that settles history." The President alone, in his role as teacher and moral leader, can arouse the American people from apathy and indifference and inspire them to the efforts and sacrifices that must be made if we are to survive in this century of peril. In the past the American people have never failed to unite behind their chosen leaders to overcome external dangers. By their reckless charges that the evils that threaten our survival are not external, but are within our society, the extreme right-wingers generate distrust and suspicion and, in so doing, threaten to shatter the basic unity of the American people and to undermine the consensus in which vigorous and successful national policies must be rooted.

The problem was admirably expressed in a recent editorial which appeared in the conservative *Arizona Daily Star,* of Tucson, Arizona.

"It is one of the unfortunate characteristics of American life," the editorial pointed out, "that too many of our good citizens and government officials have a definite inclination to think in terms of reckless absolutes, when it comes to foreign policy. Americans like to think in terms of freedom and democracy, as if they were something that could be bequeathed automatically by us to all nations of the world. Similarly, we are prone to boast and threaten and talk in terms of total war. If it is not that, we must have total peace. Tragically, we think that by total war we can bequeath to the world total peace." The editorial further pointed out that "there is a vast difference between telling the masters of the Kremlin that we will stand by our rights in Berlin with all of the might and power our country can mobilize, and in making irresponsible threats. It is one thing to make war to defend our rights; it is quite another thing to go out on another futile crusade, and expect total victory to give us what we want."

Americans, unfortunately, tend to take a single-factor approach to world politics. Prior to World War II, we thought of international relations too much in moral and legal terms. Since 1945 we have increasingly shifted our thoughts to the terms of military strength and balance-of-power alliances. Actually, a successful foreign policy has many facets: military, political, economic, cultural, moral, and ideological. All of these must be used, not independently and consecutively, but interdependently and simultaneously. Realism in world politics consists in knowing how and when to shuffle the various factors in the face of changing dangers and opportunities.

No one understood the subtleties and complexities of foreign policy better than Winston Churchill, who wrote:

Those who are prone by temperament and character to seek sharp clear-cut solutions of difficult and obscure problems, who are ready to fight whenever some challenge comes from a foreign power, have not always been right. On the other hand, those whose inclination is to bow their heads, to seek patiently and faithfully for peaceful compromise, are not always wrong. On the contrary, in a majority of instances, they may be right, not only morally but from a practical

240

standpoint. How many wars have been averted by patience and persisting good will. How many wars have been precipitated by fire-brands. How many misunderstandings which led to wars could have been removed by temporizing.

The realities of American foreign policy lie in the fact that the world has undergone revolutionary changes since World War II and that the end of this historical upheaval is not yet in sight. To live in a world of revolution, and to attempt to shape the forces of change toward constructive purposes requires patience, discipline, and sustained effort. Only by the cultivation of these qualities can the American living in the 1960's hope to escape the defeatism and despair that arise when initial efforts fail to produce total victory.

The basic principles of American foreign policy for a world in permanent revolution were shaped in the years immediately following World War II, or more specifically in the spring of 1947 in what has been called the fifteen weeks. During those weeks, the historic principles of American foreign policy were radically overhauled. The landmarks of that transformation were the Truman Doctrine and the Marshall Plan. Through these instruments the United States acknowledged its permanent involvement in the affairs of the world. The responsibilities of the United States were now extended beyond the confines of the Western Hemisphere to the far outposts of the free world.

The revolution in American foreign policy was expressed in the policy of containment, which implied the permanent commitment of American resources around the perimeter of the Soviet empire. The Marshall Plan implied the involvement of the United States in world affairs in an even more intimate way. The United States now recognized its responsibility to help nations which were threatened with economic disaster and, beyond that, its responsibility to help develop a viable international economic and political order.

These were days of imagination and innovation in our foreign policy. The crisis of the 1960's derives from our failure to adapt the now classic policy forms of 1947 to new conditions and new challenges.

The conditions of the world have been greatly altered since the immediate postwar period. Four fundamental changes have occurred.

First: The balance of military power has changed radically. In the years following the war, we forged a system of alliances which, with our monopoly of atomic power, provided substantial protection for the nations threatened by Communist imperialism. That protection has now diminished, and it has been replaced by a highly unstable nuclear stalemate, which Winston Churchill has called the "balance of terror."

The second great transformation of recent years is the impressive recovery of Western Europe to booming economic well-being and substantial political stability as well. The military dependence of Western Europe on the United States remains, while in the political field it has diminished, and economic dependence has all but ended.

The third significant change has been a fundamental alteration in Soviet foreign policy. Ten years ago, one of the greatest assets of our own foreign policy was the heavy-handed tactics of Stalin. Whenever Western efforts slackened or Western unity cracked, Stalin could be counted upon to take some drastic action which would galvanize the West to renewed efforts and unity. Khrushchev's foreign policy is of a quite different nature. His tactics are far more varied. Besides using diplomatic and military pressures wherever these seem promising from his point of view, Khrushchev seeks to subvert the entire non-Communist world through the impact of Soviet power and economic and technological accomplishments. The Khrushchev approach is more skilful, more insidious, more subtle, and, therefore, far more challenging to the nerves, the patience, the resourcefulness, and the dedication of the West.

The fourth overriding change of our time is the rise of the former colonial and semicolonial nations of Asia, Africa, and Latin America. These nations, most of which are uncommitted and all of which are caught up in the emotional fervor of nationalism, are now the great prize in the struggle between East and West. Their political and economic stability, and their continuing freedom from Communist subversion and domination, are now among the foremost objectives of our foreign policy.

It is against the background of these great transformations that we must reassess the foreign policy of the United States for the decade ahead. The crisis of our foreign policy at present derives from the failure to devise adequate responses to these four great changes in the world situation.

The policies devised in 1947 have been largely successful. With only a few exceptions, the power of the Soviet Union and of Communist China have been militarily contained. Such losses as have been suffered are counterbalanced, and perhaps more than counterbalanced, by the growing unification of the resurgent nations of Western Europe and by the gradual development of a broader Atlantic community, consisting of nations which possess a great preponderance of world resources and industrial productivity.

We must now focus our efforts on the insidious challenges of psychological penetration, of political subversion, of economic conquest, of the use of foreign aid and trade as political weapons. To meet these threats we have already begun to devise, and we must now go on to perfect, new and varied instruments of foreign policy that go far beyond containment and military alliances.

Foreign policy in our time is inseparable from domestic policy. It is more accurate to think of every aspect of public activity as part of national policy. How we conduct ourselves in Cuba, Laos, Berlin, or Montevideo is indicative of our maturity or lack of maturity as a nation. But our neglect of education, our tolerance of criminal activity, our impulsive reactions to the criminal hijacking of an airplane are also indicative of our maturity or lack of it, of the trustworthiness of our national—or foreign—policy, and of the integrity of our "national style."

We must view the nation, not as a set of compartments in which foreign and domestic affairs are neatly divided, but rather as a unified whole. And, in this view of things, we must understand that it is only as we are ready to sacrifice many of our personal and group interests and predilections that we have a chance of surviving as a society, not by luck but by our own efforts. In short, it is our character as a people, rather than any arid collection of predetermined formulas and prescriptions, that will determine our capacity to meet the Communist challenge.

The overriding question is whether this nation is prepared to accept the permanent and inescapable responsibilities of having become a major power. We have clung too long to our youth as a nation, during which our foreign policy consisted in a series of exhilarating and successful adventures. Our history—from the minutemen to the Alamo, from the conquest of the West to the charge up San Juan Hill—was an unbroken chronicle of victory and success. But that was in the days of our youth, and we live now in a far more difficult and more dangerous world—a world in which we must come of age. Neither God nor nature has preordained the triumph of our free society, and it would be a tragic mistake to assume the inevitability of our survival.

History plays cruel tricks. It allowed us to believe that the triumphs of our past were the product of our vigor and resourcefulness alone. What we failed to perceive in our past was the presence of another element: the element of an improbable run of luck, the luck of a rich and unspoiled continent far removed from the centers of power politics and world conflict.

That immunity from the conflicts and afflictions of the Old World ended fifty years ago.

Woodrow Wilson knew it. He perceived the ultimate fact of this century of American history: not that America must come out into the world, but that the world had come in on America. "There can be no question," he said in his address to the Senate of July 10, 1919, "of our ceasing to be a world power. The only question is whether we can refuse the moral leadership that is offered us, whether we shall accept the moral leadership that is offered us, whether we shall accept or reject the confidence of the world."

America rejected the confidence of the world in 1919. We preferred to count on a continuation of the good luck that had never before failed us. It was a thoughtless and unsuccessful gamble, for which both we and the world have already paid an incalculable price. None the less, there are those among us who are still bemused with the dazzling illusions of our lost youth.

Our prospects have narrowed greatly since the lost opportunity of forty years ago. I do not know how long it will be before they finally dim into darkness if we do not finally reconcile ourselves to the burden of continuing and onerous responsibility in a harsh and dangerous world. Our power is inseparable from continuing trusteeship, and this trusteeship, as Wilson perceived, derives not from choice but from inescapable compulsion: "the compulsion of honor, the compulsion of interest, and the compulsion of humanity..."

Our proper objective as a nation must be, as it was to Woodrow Wilson, "to make a society instead of a set of barbarians out of the governments of the world." Advancement toward this objective will require persistent effort in the face of inevitable frustrations. More fundamentally, it will require the cultivation of qualities that are associated with maturity rather than youth: qualities of wisdom, as well as resourcefulness; persevering determination, as well as righteous dedication; and, perhaps most of all, moral courage in place of adolescent bravado.

The purpose of our foreign policy is the very gradual improvement of human life on earth. Our success is not guaranteed, and, if our efforts are to be coherent and sustained, we must accept this fact with sobriety and serenity. Besides patient and continuous effort, we must bring to the task a little of a sense of mission—and I emphasize little. A consuming Messianism will surely lead us to false hopes and frustration, while action without purpose is action without meaning or hope. But a little of a sense of mission can guide us—unencumbered by either extravagant hopes or unwarranted despair—toward worthy and attainable objectives.

These are not easy counsels. But they are, I think, counsels of reality. We must learn, among other things, that there are limits to foreign policy and limits to the objectives which a nation can hope to realize in the world—even so powerful a nation as the United States. One of the principal lessons of the two world wars of the twentieth century is that wars, even when they end in a total victory, generate more problems than they solve. We must come to grips with the fact that there are no final and complete immediate solutions, that, while some problems can be solved, others can only

245

be alleviated or deferred while we wait for deeply rooted trends and gradually changing circumstances to reduce present tensions and to foster the conditions for solutions and accommodations that cannot now be foreseen.

Our national purpose is a process to be advanced, rather than a victory to be won. That process is the defense and expansion of our democratic values, the furtherance of which rests ultimately on the wisdom, the maturity of judgment, and the moral fiber of a society of free individuals. The cultivation of these qualities and the advancement of the democratic process, both in our own internal affairs and in international relations, are the responsibility of every individual in a free society. If we are to meet the challenges of our time, we must reject the false and simple solutions of irresponsible extremists who cannot, or will not, accept the world as it is. We must instead dedicate ourselves to the national purpose with fortitude and discipline. These are the imperatives of military responsibility, as, indeed, they are imperatives for all Americans.

ADDRESS BEFORE THE NATIONAL
WAR COLLEGE AND INDUSTRIAL
COLLEGE OF THE ARMED FORCES,
WASHINGTON, D.C.,
AUGUST 21, 1961

Chapter Nine

CREDO OF A LEGISLATOR

─────────── ⌇⌇ ───────────

39. *Freedom's Indispensable Guardian*

A book about Fulbright could have no more fitting grace note than this thoughtful statement on the role of the legislator. It was written in 1947, early in the Senator's career, and provides the gauge-line by which his subsequent deeds may be fairly measured. In a century that exalts the executive, and in a country that habitually scorns its Congress, Fulbright's is a minority opinion that touches chords of memory deep in our republican past. His essay reminds us that the legislature remains the shield of freedom and a forum of creative endeavor.

Fulbright's title is, simply, "The Legislator."

The legislator is an indispensable guardian of our freedom. It is true that great executives have played a powerful role in the development of civilization, but such leaders appear sporadically, by chance. They do not always appear when they are most needed. The great executives have given inspiration and push to the advancement of human society, but it is the legislator who has given stability and continuity to that slow and painful progress.

The legislator may not often give us the inspired leadership which is necessary in the crises of human affairs, but he does institutionalize, in the form of law, those measures which mark the slow lifting of mankind up from the rule of tooth and claw. Like the stop on a jack, the legislator may not elevate our civilization, but he does prevent our slipping back into the tyranny of rule by brute force. Many Americans are impatient at the lack of vision and initiative of the Congress, but they should not forget that it is the Congress that stands between their liberties and the voracious instinct for power of the executive bureaucracy....

An important responsibility of the legislature is to provide a check upon the tendency of the executive power of the state to become arbitrary and oppressive. It is not a mere coincidence that Hitler and Mussolini had the greatest contempt for legislatures and politicians. I am not sure that Stalin has a profound respect for his legislature. The legislature elected by the people is an indispensable adjunct of any system of self-government in which the freedom and integrity of the individual are of paramount concern. A state may become powerful under a dictatorship, but the people are oppressed. A properly functioning legislative body restrains the arbitrary power of the state. It permits the development of a climate in which the genius of individual human beings can flourish. For short periods in history, benevolent monarchs have fostered the arts and the humanities in small areas of the world, but invariably the power of the state falls into incompetent or tyrannical hands, and civilization disintegrates. With an effective legislature, there is a continuity of policy, which may not always be as enlightened as we might wish it to be, but it is never so oppressive as the naked executive power usually becomes.

In considering how to approach my subject, it occurred to me that, since there are available many excellent books on the technical aspects of the Congress and the government, and, since the reader is quite as able to read and understand them as I am, the most fruitful thing for me to do is to relate some of my own impressions of politics and the legislator. I hope that, in so doing, I may to some degree arouse the reader's interest in participating actively in politics. It is especially important for the future of the republic that men of wide knowledge and trained minds enter the political field. I need not point out the complexity and difficulty of the problems which confront our nation today and are certain to confront it in the future.

If we are to maintain our system of self-government, it is essential that the best brains, the finest talent we have, be induced to enter the service of the government. Americans complain of the ineptness of their government, but at the same time they are supercilious, if not contemptuous, toward those who devote their energies to its service. Substantial improvement in the quality of the government is unlikely until this attitude of the people is changed. To illustrate the attitude, let me mention the result of a recent poll taken in Minnesota—which is one of the more literate states of the union. The poll included the question: "Would you like your son to go into politics?" Seventy per cent of the people interviewed answered, "No!" At the same time, only fifty per cent of the adult citizens interviewed could name both of their senators. Now I do not mean to imply that knowing one's senators is the final judgment of one's general educational level. Yet it is a very serious thing that, in the greatest democratic system of self-government left, so many people do not even know their senators' names and that the substantial majority of people do not want their sons to enter politics.

If we are to maintain our system of self-government, it is essential that we obtain for the national Congress the best talent that we possess in this nation.

The first thing that every legislator has to do, obviously, is to get himself elected to office. The process of being elected to the Congress, in a predominately rural community in the South, is an experience that is not easy to describe in a few words. Until the summer of 1941, when I left the presidency of the University of Arkansas, I had never participated directly or indirectly, other than as a voter, in any political campaign. My activities had been confined to the academic world, except for a limited experience in a family business. The process of introducing oneself and talking to the people informally, in their business places and their homes, was the most interesting and satisfying experience of the campaign. With only a few exceptions, they were interested and friendly, although rarely did they indicate how they would vote. Generally speaking,

249

they were more interested in me as a person than in my views about the broad principles of government.

After the months of personal visits, with particular attention to those persons known to be interested and influential in political matters, the speaking campaign began. This phase of the campaign is very strenuous and downright hard work. Never having made a political speech, the first few efforts were excruciatingly painful. I have seldom experienced a feeling of more abject despair and humiliation than the first time I spoke on the street corner of a small village, with about a dozen curious listeners, who apparently were not listening. However, it is amazing how soon one becomes accustomed to the sound of one's voice, when forced to repeat a speech five or six times a day. As election day approaches, the size of the crowds grows; they are more responsive and more interested; and one derives a certain exhilaration from that which, only a few weeks before, was intensely painful. This is one possible explanation of unlimited debate in the Senate.

While the candidate himself is carrying on the speaking campaign, a few close friends run what is known as "the headquarters." This office prepares the advertisements for the papers and arranges for the distribution of the campaign literature. In Arkansas, and other Southern states, the Democratic primary is, as a practical matter, the real election. Since all the candidates must be Democrats, the party organization, as such, plays no part in the campaign. The organization of the campaign is on a personal basis or centers around groups of citizens with a common interest. In short, the candidate is on his own as to the strategy of the campaign.

I think that it is worthwhile to relate these seemingly trivial events, because it should prove to anyone who may have a desire to become a legislator that, given a free electorate, not dominated by an organization, anyone with energy and some understanding of human nature has a good chance of success. It is a very human experience and, even though one might be defeated, I believe that it is not without its compensations.

Furthermore, it would be exceedingly difficult to serve effectively, or get re-elected, without the intimate knowledge of one's constituents obtained in an active campaign. The necessity of reconciling the differences among people is of the essence of the legislative function, and one becomes acutely aware of these differences in the midst of a heated political campaign.

Upon assuming one's place in the Congress, the first impression is not unlike that of initiation into a college fraternity. The older Members are gracious and helpful in a variety of ways, but you are not allowed to forget that you are, after all, a freshman. Seniority is a custom one does not question lightly in the Congress, but it is one of the few rules one can rely on. Seniority determines very largely one's committee assignments and promotions within the committee. It follows from this practice that those Members with the longest service in the Congress attain the positions of influence. It is wise, therefore, for a constituency to keep its representatives in continuous service. While there may be some criticism of that practice from the national point of view, it works to the advantage of those constituencies which are stable in their political habits of thought.

The first year in office is intensely interesting. Having heard all my life, as you have, rather sharp criticism of Congress, I was pleasantly surprised to find the majority of the Members conscientious, hard-working, normal individuals. There is infinite variety among them, but on the whole they reflect quite well the virtues and faults of the American people. The effectiveness of a Member depends, to a considerable extent, upon his ability to gain the respect of his colleagues. In open debate and in committee, it is not easy to deceive them, and, to a considerable extent, except with the most fanatical, they tend to temper the more extreme prejudices of one another.

The legislator's relationship with his constituency is, ordinarily, the dominant influence in his political life. It is only natural that his constituents look upon him as their personal representative at the seat of government. It requires a high degree of political maturity, and intellectual objectivity, for them to regard the man they elected as an officer of the national government. Many of them are personal friends, but all of them who voted for the successful candidate in the heat of the campaign, when votes were earnestly and fervently solicited, naturally feel that they deserve some special consideration from the object of their favor. There is nothing reprehensible or unworthy in this attitude, but the fact is that the multitude of requests for minor services comes close to destroying the effectiveness of a great many capable representatives. The legislator finds himself in a dilemma. If he refuses to see the constant stream of visitors or to give personal attention to their requests, they may become offended and withdraw their support. In addition, it is personally gratifying to be able to be of help to one's friends. On the other hand, if he does give his attention to these matters, he literally has no time left for the thoughtful and intelligent study and reflection that sound legislation requires.

One often hears the suggestion that secretaries could attend to the personal business of constituents. It is true that the secretaries do attend to much of it, but, in the first place, secretarial assistance is limited, and, in the second place, many of the constituents will not accept the services of the secretary. They feel that they elected the senator and that they are, therefore, entitled to his personal attention. I can see no solution to this dilemma until the constituents learn that, in demanding the personal attention of their representatives in the Congress, they are in a very real sense injuring their own larger interests. They must realize that the popularly elected legislature is the real bulwark of the people against the arbitrary power of the state, and, if they hamper its effectiveness, eventually it will be destroyed by the executive bureaucracy. The struggle for power that constantly goes on between the legislature and the executive bureaucracy is an unequal struggle so long as the legislator must give most of his time to the personal affairs of his constituents.

I think that it is safe to say that already the great majority of the bills enacted by the Congress are drafted in the bureaus. For the most part the legislator simply reviews, criticizes, and amends the bills presented for his consideration by the departments. Even for this task, he has too little time to do the job effectively and adequately. The Congress is conscious of this shift of power to the bureaus. The almost continual carping about the bureaucrats is but the outward evidence of the realization that the power of initiating legislation and of determining policy is passing to the departments. These departments, staffed by employees, protected by civil service statutes, are not noticeably responsive to congressional suggestions.

That there is no time to spare for extra legislative duties if legislative duties are to be properly discharged is indicated by the enormous volume of measures introduced and acted upon by the two houses of Congress. During the first session of the Seventy-ninth Congress, 6,841 bills were introduced (1,730 in the Senate, 5,111 in the House), 425 joint resolutions, 168 concurrent resolutions, and 679 resolutions. The committees of the two houses reported on 2,358 measures; 1,017 bills were passed; and more than 300 of the various resolutions were adopted. It took nearly thirteen thousand pages of the *Congressional Record* to record the debate on the floor of the two houses, exclusive of the appendix. That is a lot of talk. To consider carefully, or to understand, such a huge volume of material is entirely beyond the capacity of any man. A legislator necessarily is forced to concentrate his attention within a restricted field of legislation if he is to avoid being wholly ineffective in every field. The constituents, however, naturally believe that their particular interest or problem is of fundamental importance and cannot understand why their representative is not thoroughly familiar with it. In trying to meet the demands of his constituents, to be all things to all men, the legislator often becomes superficial and unable to do constructive thinking on any subject.

If the power and initiative of the Congress is to be maintained, it is indispensable that some means be found to give the individual legislators adequate time to think as they legislate. The La Follette-Monroney Committee report contains many valuable suggestions to improve the efficiency of the machinery of Congress, but there can be no real solution without the understanding and co-operation of the constituents.

In describing the functions of a member of the Congress, it is easy to oversimplify. It is simple, in arriving at final decisions on particular bills, for example, to say that a Member voted in accordance with the wishes of his constituents, of his party, or of some pressure group. As a matter of fact, all these considerations enter into decisions on matters of major importance. The extent to which they influence a particular Member's decision varies with each Member and with each measure. Some Members believe that it is their duty to follow closely what they think is the majority opinion of their constituents. This policy may be more pronounced immediately before an election than subsequent thereto. Other Members feel that they should make their decisions without regard to their constituents' wishes in the first instance, and then undertake to educate and convert the constituents. In other words, they seek to lead rather than follow their constituents. Some Members are strong party men and follow blindly the program of the party leaders. The so-called "pressure groups," except when they are very powerful in the home constituency, are more of a nuisance than a real influence on the average Member. There is a misapprehension on the part of many citizens that a good dinner and a few drinks will get a bill passed. A mistake that many businessmen make is to think it necessary to employ a high-powered representative to contact legislators. If they have a good case, and are well prepared and able to present it, they can do just as well, if not better, by appearing before the committee themselves. In any large group of human beings there are always a few unorthodox individuals, but in the Congress there are certainly very few to whom illegitimate or dishonest inducements have appeal. It is my belief that the American people hold a lower opinion of the integrity of their Congress than they are justified in having. There may be justification for criticism because of provincialism, lack of vision, or pettiness, but not because of dishonesty.

If there is one characteristic of Members of the Congress that stands out above others, it is sincerity. With few exceptions, they are deeply concerned over reaching the correct conclusions on every controversial issue. They go through agonies of mental torture in their effort to reconcile the interests of their constituents with the demands of fellow Members and their conception of the national welfare. It is so easy for the citizen back home to have a positive and complete answer for every question. This average citizen sees the issue from the viewpoint of his own business, his own community, and his own private prejudices. He has not heard the other side. The chances are that he knows very little about conditions in the forty-seven other states, not to mention the other nations of the world.

He simply cannot understand why his representative hesitates and compromises with his colleagues. He usually concludes that he is just a political trimmer after all. The legislator, however, finds himself caught between the heavy pressure of the advice from home pushing him in one direction and the pressure from his colleagues pushing him in the opposite direction. The result, necessarily, is a compromise in which the facts and the judgment of the legislator play a large part.

The average legislator, early in his career, discovers that there are certain interests, or convictions, of his constituents which are dangerous to trifle with. Some of these convictions may not be of fundamental importance to the welfare of the nation, in which case he is justified in humoring them, even though he may disapprove. The difficult case is where the particular conviction concerns fundamental policy affecting the national welfare. A sound sense of values, the ability to discriminate between that which is of fundamental importance and that which is only superficial, is an indispensable qualification of a good legislator. As an example of what I mean, let us take the poll-tax issue and isolationism. Regardless of how persuasive my colleagues or the national press may be about the evils of the poll tax, I do not see its fundamental importance, and I shall follow the views of the people of my state. On the other hand, regardless of how strongly opposed my constituents may prove to be to the creation of, and participation in, an ever stronger United Nations Organization, I could not follow such a policy in that field, unless, and until it becomes clearly hopeless. This process of evaluating the significance of an issue is one of the most difficult tasks of the legislator. In many instances, the greatest amount of heat is generated by the people and the press over some trifling matter of temporary interest, while at the same time the really significant policies are practically ignored. While I have not computed it, I venture to guess that ten times as much space in the press, and effort in the Senate, has been devoted to the Pearl Harbor inquiry as has been devoted to the organization and development of the United Nations.

I have already mentioned the growing power of the executive branch of the government as compared to the legislative branch. It is, I repeat, of first importance that the Congress be strengthened if we are to avoid arbitrary government and the destruction of the freedom of the individual. There are certain organizational reforms that can be helpful, in addition to freeing the legislator from the necessity of running errands. Probably the most important among these is the creation of a more effective method of communication between the Congress and the executive. One way to approach this would be to set up a legislative-executive cabinet, consisting of the President's Cabinet and of leaders of the Congress. This group should consider and advise upon the over-all policy of the Administration, so as to avoid stalemates such as we have recently had in the Senate. Another difficulty that may confront us again, as it did in the last two years of the Wilson and the Hoover Administrations, is to have the Congress controlled by the party opposed to the President. This situation virtually destroys the effectiveness of the government and is exceedingly dangerous in a period such as the present, just as it was in 1918 and 1930. Some means of avoiding such a disaster, by special elections, should be worked out, although it would call for constitutional changes. Thomas K. Finletter, in his book *Can Representative Government Do the Job?,* has some interesting suggestions on this subject. Indeed, there are many other recommendations in that book for the improvement of the Congress that are worthy of our attention. Among others, I might mention the Kefauver Resolution, which provides for a question period in the Congress, in which the heads of the executive departments are given an opportunity on the floor of the legislative bodies to defend their programs and to answer the questions of the Members. This would be an excellent way to reduce the friction between these two branches of the government. This parliamentary procedure has been employed for many years in the House of Commons.

In the beginning, I said that I thought the Members of the Congress reflect quite well the virtues and faults of the American people. By this I do not mean that the Congress is literally a mirror of the nation, nor do I think that it should be. As a representative republic, and not a pure democracy, it is proper that we should strive to send to the Congress the wisest and the most able men and women we have. That we may have a substantial number of illiterates or simpletons in our population is scarcely a good reason for sending them to Congress. A recent pamphlet by the American Political Science Association had this to say about congressmen:

The ideal Member of Congress should have a large fund of information about public affairs and understanding of social psychology. He should have a sense of history, a sense of values, and a critical habit of thought. He should know enough about public problems to vote independently and intelligently, instead of blindly following the lead of committee chairmen and the party whip. Without being an expert on all questions, he should be able to see their interrelations and ramifications and anticipate how proposed measures will work out in practice. He must be able to take an over-all view of a problem and to weigh the long-run benefits of a proposal against its short-run drawbacks. He must be intimately acquainted with his constituents, their needs and aspirations, and with economic and social conditions in his district or state. But where conflicts of interest arise between his district or state, his party, and the country as a whole, he must remember that his primary obligation is to the general welfare. He should be a man of intelligence, courage, and zeal, with exceptional qualities of mind and spirit, skilled in the rare art of mediating between the public services and the people, able to exercise foresight and balanced judgment.

To measure up to this standard, a legislator would have to be a paragon of virtue and wisdom such as one seldom sees in any walk of life. Assuming, however, that such men do exist, it is unlikely that many of them would choose, or be chosen for, a political career. Until such time as the esteem with which the office is regarded is more commensurate with the responsibilities involved, ideal legislators will be scarce. Improvement in the quality of our legislative bodies is primarily the function of the voter, not the legislator.

The role of the legislator is seldom glorious. The conscientious, competent, and useful Members of the Congress rarely receive the approval of the press or of the public at large. The technique of a good legislator does not attract the attention of the press—but let him act a fool, and it is in every paper in the country. For example, it is generally conceded by most of the Members that Senator Carl Hayden is an excellent technician and an exceedingly useful legislator, but I venture to guess that very few of this audience know anything about Mr. Hayden or his contribution to the public welfare. To obtain agreement upon any measure of importance requires infinite patience and persistence, in addition to a thorough knowledge of the subject matter, but such qualities are not newsworthy.

The very fact that the press and the public respond so readily to the extravagant and ridiculous in their public figures is in itself a strong temptation to a man with a forum like the Senate floor. This is especially true if he begins to feel neglected or abused. A legislator, like other people, has an ego that requires expression and recognition if it is to avoid becoming warped and eccentric. Like other human beings, he desires the approval of his fellow men, and, if this is denied him, he tends to become cynical and disillusioned. It is truly unfortunate that the people do not understand more clearly the character and the function of the legislator.

In conclusion, I wish to call your attention to the recent resignation of two of the outstanding Members of the House of Representatives, Mr. Woodrum of Virginia and Mr. Ramspeck of Georgia, in order to accept positions in industry. These two men are in the prime of life, with long experience as legislators, and were undoubtedly among the wisest and best men in the Congress. It is a serious indictment of our system, and of the American people, that such men should quit the public service, for which they were so well qualified. It was not merely a question of remuneration that caused these men to leave the government, although the meagerness of their salary certainly influenced the decision; but of even greater importance, I believe, was the common attitude of the people of this

258

country toward their legislators. As Senator George wrote in an article not long ago:

Castigating Congress seems to have developed, of late, into a pernicious national pastime. To my mind, the thoughtless disparagement of Congress is part of the whole pattern of cynicism that many people have adopted toward the legislature. The tendency is alarming. In this totalitarian era, only two major nations—Britain and the United States—still function with legislatures that perform vital roles. Now is the time for Americans to value, rather than to abuse, their democratic heritage.

Honorable men in public life can take the abuse that is heaped upon them by the public only so long, and then they succumb to a sense of futility and frustration. It is true that some of the frustration that afflicts the Members of Congress is due to the antique and obsolete organization of the Congress itself, and it should be remedied. But of far greater influence upon the decision of good men to enter, or to remain in, politics is the attitude of those whom they seek to serve.

This attitude will change, and the character and quality of the Congress will improve, only when the people understand and appreciate the function of the legislator in the preservation of their freedom and welfare.

"THE LEGISLATOR," REPRINTED
FROM *The Works of the Mind*
(UNIVERSITY OF CHICAGO PRESS, 1947)

40. *Threnody for a Subway*

There are established rituals on Capitol Hill for all things, including humor. By bicameral convention, the leg-pulling legislator must employ heavy parody, deadpan delivery and hope that the Record will show [laughter]. As befits a native of Mark Twain's state, Fulbright has made his own contribution to legislative levity. This sample sally was prompted by the passing of the old wood-and-

259

wicker subways that used to shuttle between the Capitol and the Senate Office Building. In 1961, the archaic cars were supplanted by sleek, plastic-looking creations as part of a multimillion dollar "improvement" campaign that also saw a space-age terminal installed to link the Capitol with a new Senate Office Building. A horrified traditionalist in these things, Fulbright sought to stay unholy innovation. His effort was vain; the old cars are now deposited along with other relics in the Smithsonian Institution.

Mr. President, on Thursday the majority leader made a short announcement on the Senate floor which should have been received with sadness by every Member of this body. It was a simple statement that attracted no attention in the press and probably very little here on Capitol Hill. I quote his statement in its entirety:

Mr. President, for the information of the Senate, I announce that one of the old trolleys in the old tunnel will continue in operation until at least the end of the present session.

This announcement signals the end of the line for one of the most stable, reliable, and popular institutions on Capitol Hill. These remarkable old cars have seen a lot of history made in the Congress. They have performed their function well, and I, for one, am saddened and depressed to see them replaced.

I shall long remember with pleasure the swift, silent manner in which they conveyed me to and from the old office building. There was a minimum of friction and noise as they responded to the operator's gentle manipulation of the lever. There was an intimate camaraderie among the Members as they piled into or out of the open seats unhindered by doors or other obstacles arbitrarily barring the way. In short, these old cars were soothing to the jangled nerves and put the Members of this body in a friendly and amicable frame of mind when they arrived to do battle over the nation's business.

Mr. President, I considered for some time introducing a resolution which would have insured continuation of the old system and disposition of the new one. I even went so far as to draw up a resolution which I thought was appropriate to the situation. However, since I

260

am a realist and have participated in the legislative processes of the Senate for some time, I was forced to admit that my resolution had little or no chance of passage and that it would have been a waste of scarce tax money to introduce it and have it printed in proper form.

In order to make my views known on the demise of our old subway system, I ask unanimous consent to have the resolution I prepared printed in the body of the *Congressional Record* following my remarks....

Whereas the Senate is a unique institution among legislative bodies of the world and possesses a unique transportation system in keeping with the character of the Senate; and

Whereas in this era of rapid destruction of established traditions and values, it behooves us to preserve those institutions which have proven themselves with the passage of time; and

Whereas the members of the United States Senate, their staffs and visitors to the U.S. Capitol have been transported swiftly and comfortably by an efficient subway car system for forty-five years; and

Whereas these ancient subway cars have become an institution of the Senate and have been trusted servants of the Congress and the general public; and

Whereas a new system of inferior conveyances is being foisted upon the Senate and the public as a substitute for these remarkable vehicles; and

Whereas these creations are ungainly, uncomfortable, unpopular and unpredictable; and

Whereas it is suspected that the irritable, testy, acrimonious atmosphere prevailing in the Senate this session is in part induced by the jolting, jarring, nerve-racking ride to the Senatorial Chamber provided by the new subway cars; and

Whereas the new subway system cost the American taxpayers several millions of dollars; and

Whereas the new subway cars have created an additional expense burden on Senators for frequent repairs to their wives' coiffures; and

Whereas all Senators need more exercise to keep their minds and bodies in proper condition for arduous night sessions, early breakfasts with constituents, and making difficult voting decisions, and use of the old subway system would require more exercise on the part of the Senators with suites in the New Senate Office Building; and

Whereas the United States Senate should frankly admit that it has made a monstrous mistake and return to the tried and true old subway system: Now, therefore, be it

Resolved by the Senate, That (a) there is hereby created a select committee of the Senate to be known as the Save Our Subway Committee to be composed of five Senators appointed by the Vice-President.

(b) This committee shall take immediate steps to insure continued operation of the traditional subway cars between the Old Senate Office Building and the Capitol.

(c) The committee will also take such steps as are necessary to discontinue the new subway system and dispose of the subway cars and related equipment as expeditiously as possible. In disposing of such cars and equipment the committee may enter into negotiations with:

(1) Disneyland;

(2) Coney Island;

(3) Any other public or privately owned amusement park;

(4) Moscow (U.S.S.R.) Subway Authority.

The committee will make every effort to recoup as much of the taxpayers' money from such sale as possible.

(d) The committee will study ways for efficient utilization of the space in the abandoned subway tunnels. Among uses to be studied it shall consider, but not be limited to, the following possibilities:

(A) Rental of office space to Members of the House of Representatives;

(B) Partitioning of the space for use as senatorial refuge from job seekers;

(C) Additional parking space for congressional employees.

262

(e) The committee shall report its findings and recommendations to the Senate by January 31, 1962.

SENATE ADDRESS,
MAY 29, 1961

41. *The Senate and Foreign Affairs*

This is a topic on which no one can speak with more authority than the chairman of the Senate Foreign Relations Committee. The following address, delivered in April, 1961, only a few days after the Cuban debacle, contains Fulbright's considered thoughts on an uneasy relationship and is an attempt to define the unmarked boundary between the Senate and the executive in the area of foreign affairs. But is is also an appeal for a way of thinking that, in Tocqueville's words, shows a "kind of instinctive regard for the regular connection of ideas"—a phrase which also sums up the quality of Fulbright's eloquence.

The central theme is that the Senate is equipped to play a supporting but not an initiating role in foreign affairs. In an address at Cornell University on May 5, 1961 (reprinted in the fall, 1961, Cornell Law Quarterly), Fulbright went even further, remarking: "My question ... is whether we have any choice but to modify and perhaps overhaul the eighteenth century procedures that govern the formulation and conduct of American foreign policy ... I wonder whether the time has not arrived, or indeed already passed, when we must give the executive a measure of power in the conduct of our foreign affairs that we have hitherto jealously withheld." Thus this volume concludes, perhaps appropriately, on a note of critical speculation.

It was suggested that I discuss with you this evening the role of the Senate in foreign affairs. In view of the difficulties which confront us in this area of interest, it is a timely subject . . .

The only reference in the entire Constitution to the specific powers of the Senate and of the President with respect to foreign policy occurs in the same paragraph of Section 2, Article II.

Here, the Constitution provides that the President

> ... shall have Power, by and with the advice and consent of the Senate, to make treaties, provided two-thirds of the Senators present concur; and he shall nominate, and by and with the advice and consent of the Senate shall appoint Ambassadors ...

It is not my purpose, here, to render a constitutional disquisition on these powers. But the Senate's powers of advice and consent, and the coupling of them with the only specific reference to the President's own powers in foreign policy, indicate that the founding fathers intended a close relationship between the President and the Senate. The Senate, apparently, was to be a council of elders. Madison said that the unique value of the Senate was that it would proceed "with more coolness, with more system, and with more wisdom than the popular branch." No doubt the power of advice and consent was also reserved to the Senate as a part of the concept of Federalism, which had such great influence upon the entire structure of the Constitution. That is, the powers in foreign affairs, which the States were assigning to the Congress were to be exercised in that branch, the Senate, where the states, as states, were uniquely represented, tending, in a degree, to detach these powers from the people, as represented by the House.

By subjecting the powers of the President to the system of checks and balances which runs throughout the Constitution, the Constitution built into the conduct of foreign relations a potentiality for conflict and discord rather than unity. This was not long in making itself felt. Washington stalked out of a meeting with the Senate, after attempting "consultation" on an early treaty with the Indians, vowing never to return.

Secretary of State Jefferson wrote that Washington "had no confidence in the secrecy of the Senate."

The subsequent development of political parties enhanced the potentiality for conflict, and it has made itself felt, particularly in those periods when the executive and legislative powers were in the hands of different parties, and when strong-willed senators contested with weak Presidents.

In the first sixteen years of the republic, only thirteen treaties, as such, were submitted to the Senate, and during the next ten not a single one was submitted.

There were periods of relative quiet in foreign matters while the nation was preoccupied with the great issues of internal development and slavery. But up to the year 1901 the Senate had so altered between eighty and ninety treaties placed before it, that almost one-third of them failed entirely or were virtually abandoned. In the following twenty-five years, fifty-eight proposed treaties were changed by the Senate and, of this number almost forty per cent were abandoned or discarded because of these changes.

John Hay, when Secretary of State, wrote that "a treaty entering the Senate is like a bull going into the arena. No one can say just how or when the final blow will fall. But one thing is certain—it will never leave the arena alive."

The conflicts between the Senate and the President were not limited to the treaty process.

The War Hawks of the House took the leading role in agitating the War of 1812, and President Polk's determination to round out the continental boundaries led to the Mexican War. But it was in the Senate, beginning soon after Cleveland lost control of it, that American imperialism under the pseudonym of "manifest destiny" reached its peak of agitation and, finally, when McKinley succeeded Cleveland, led to the Spanish-American War. Having liberated Cuba, we found then—and perhaps it is a lesson for us today— that the responsibilities which accompanied direct intervention in that revolution were exasperating in the extreme. It was not until 1934 that the Platt amendment, under which we retained control of Cuba's foreign policy, following its liberation, could be repealed. The several subsequent interventions in Cuba under this power, and elsewhere in that area, with the accompanying American economic domination, brought resentment throughout Latin America and contributed, eventually, to the situation we face there today. This experience we should ponder well, before we take any rash action.

Another unhappy contest between the Senate and the President, with which we are all familiar, was that of the Senate's "irreconcilables" against Woodrow Wilson in the defeat of the Treaty of Versailles and the League of Nations.

Another long and frustrating contest has taken place over U.S. participation in the old World Court under the League of Nations, and, later, in the successor Court under the U.N.

Continuously between 1923 and 1935, United States adherence to the old World Court was advocated by Presidents Harding, Coolidge, Hoover, and Franklin Roosevelt. For these twelve years, the Senate Foreign Relations Committee, under the influence of such Senators as Lodge, Borah, Hiram Johnson, and Walsh, kept the Senate from reaching a conclusive decision on this matter, without crippling reservations. When the matter finally came to a vote in 1935, the resolution of adherence was defeated. All the while we were asserting our desire to establish the rule of law among nations.

While the United States subsequently adhered to the successor Court, in 1946, it did so with a reservation (the Connally amendment) which reserved the right to determine the Court's jurisdiction, and neither Presidents Truman and Eisenhower, nor, for that matter, Kennedy so far, have been able to provide for full United States participation in this Court. The Connally amendment in effect nullifies the effectiveness of the Court.

In spite of the basic commitment of every President since Wilson, to full U.S. participation in a World Court, the Senate, or, at least, a sufficient number to block action, remains unconvinced.

In 1932, a *New York Times* editorial said of the Foreign Relations Committee's treatment of this issue: "Year after year, session after session of Congress, it goes on weaving a tangled web about the subject." We are still entangled in that web.

Perhaps one of the most dangerous and reckless senatorial excursions into foreign policy occurred under the name of McCarthyism early in the last Administration.

This phenomenon, which I am not at all sure lies wholly in the realm of the past, fundamentally affected our ability to lead the free

266

nations of the world. Our friends abroad heard accusations that our churches and schools were infiltrated by Communists, as was our army, foreign service, and information agency. They heard a political party, in charge of a government which for twenty years had maintained the friendliest relations with them, accused of treason. They heard the author of the Truman Doctrine, which drew the line against Communist aggression, similarly accused, and they heard the same of the author of the Marshall Plan, which saved them from economic ruin. Some of them saw us in a hysteria, a madness of fear and frustration, whose only logical end was war. This led many of them to doubt our ability to govern ourselves in a sane and tolerable way, much less to lead the democratic world and to guide the new and uncommitted nations. This remarkable period of our most recent history obscured and frustrated rational approaches to foreign policy questions and virtually paralyzed our ability to deal with the hard competition of international communism, ironically, because intelligent discussion was paralyzed by fear of domestic communism.

There have, of course, been many instances of presidential-senatorial co-operation in constructive endeavors. They are largely obscured, because, by their nature, they constituted quiet negotiation and consultation. They do not attract the attenion of historians or the press, perhaps because, as in the case of other current events, it is conflict rather than co-operation which attains notoriety.

But in recent years there have been examples of such co-operation, at such fortuitous times and under such compelling circumstances, that one must marvel at them. Senator Vandenberg's dramatic change in viewpoint in 1945 and his later co-operation with the Truman Administration, helped to lay the groundwork for the United Nations, the Marshall Plan, and NATO. The negotiation of the Japanese Peace Treaty was another example of executive-senatorial consultation.

Very recently, the Majority Leader of the Senate, Lyndon Johnson, came under criticism from his own party because of his support of President Eisenhower's foreign policy. This was a difficult road because there were many differences between senators and the executive, and attack would have been easy. While this policy of abstaining from attack may have been wrong with respect to particular issues and events, it was basically right as a proper long-term procedure because failure to support the President, particularly a weak one, and particularly at a time of divided government, easily could have led to political warfare between the parties over foreign policy.

It seems clear to me that in foreign affairs, a Senate cannot initiate or force large events, or substitute its judgment of them for that of the President, without seriously jeopardizing the ability of the nation to act consistently, and also without confusing the image and purpose of this country in the eyes of others.

This does not mean that the role of the Senate is confined to one of blind obeisance. When Vandenberg was co-operating with Truman and Acheson, neither he, nor his committee, nor the Senate, were without influence upon the course of events. He and his colleagues, by persuasion and by their example, exercised great influence upon the other members of the Senate as well as the executive. They were making judgments, essentially political, as to the "art of the possible"—what could be done and how it could be done—but, always, I believe, from the standpoint of what had to be done. The determination of this last they left, pretty much, in the hands of the executive. Vandenberg and his colleagues found ways to do what had to be done.

Of men and government, Woodrow Wilson wrote:

"Government is not a body of blind forces; it is a body of men, with highly differentiated functions, no doubt, . . . but with a common task and purpose. Their co-operation is indispensable, their warfare fatal. There can be no successful government without leadership or without the intimate, almost instinctive, co-ordination of the organs of life and action. This is not theory, but fact, and displays its force as fact, whatever theories may be thrown across its track."

The role of the Senate is also influenced by the nature of foreign policy as it exists at any given time. That its nature has changed drastically can be indicated by recalling what Washington described in his day as "our detached and distant situation" which, he said, would enable us to "defy material injury from external annoyance." Washington was a very great man, but as a prophet he was something less than infallible, judging from the morning paper.

Yet, even though Washington maintained peace in a world at war, it is useful to recall that he did not do this easily. At the time of the French Revolution. Washington's Administration was declared, by its opposition, to be "an aristocratic and corrupt faction, ...a paper nobility" which "induced a tame submission to injuries and insults, which the interest and honor of the nation required them to resist." The people, in short, wanted war with England, but they had to wait until 1812 to have their way.

The attitude of the Senate continued to reflect our detachment from foreign affairs for many years to come. Even in 1889, Henry Cabot Lodge could write with much truth: "Our relations with foreign nations today fill but a slight place in American politics, and excite generally only a languid interest."

Today—or at any rate tomorrow—the moon may be said to be closer to us than was Russia in the time of Washington, or even of Lodge.

The concept of the founding fathers, that the external interests of the nation were given to the President and the Senate because, in a degree, this would detach foreign policy from control of the people, is no longer realistic.

The idea of the President and the Senate, in council on foreign affairs, often in secrecy and always with coolness and deliberation, no longer applies.

Today, the ability of the government to conduct its external affairs depends to a great extent upon its success in developing a consensus among the people regarding our purposes and responsibilities in the foreign field. While only the President can act, only the people can arm him to do so.

The powers formerly held, or at least intended to be held, by the President and the Senate have been diffused by certain other developments during the course of our history. Foreign affairs, like so many other governmental activities, depend upon appropriations, taxes, tariff policies, and upon education. Consequently, the House of Representatives now plays a greater role than it formerly did. But this role, as is the House itself, is merely a partial reflection of the dependence upon the will and the approval of the people. The decisions of the people, themselves, in their myriad numbers and varieties, determine the power of the nation. The fruits of science and industry and agriculture, education, and research, in spite of the centralization of government, are still largely determined by thousands upon thousands of individual decisions, made in limited contexts, but from which emerge the totality of national power.

This developing dependence upon the people as the source of power in foreign affairs has its pronounced handicaps.

Even in the 1830's, de Tocqueville saw fit to say that, "Foreign politics demand scarcely any of those qualities which a democracy possesses; and they require, on the contrary, the perfect use of almost all those faculties in which it is deficient...a democracy is unable to regulate the details of an important undertaking, to persevere in a design, and to work out its execution in the presence of serious obstacles. It cannot combine its measures with secrecy, and it will not await their consequences with patience. These are qualities which more especially belong to an individual or to an aristocracy."

He also wrote of "the propensity which democracies have to obey the impulse of passion rather than the suggestions of prudence, and to abandon a mature design for the gratification of a momentary caprice."

Despite what the founding fathers may have intended, the development of communications and the evolution of our political institutions have made us a democratic government. And since the ability of our nation to focus its powers is dependent upon the people, it probably would be as unwise as it is idle to speculate upon it, to turn back to that concept of the foreign-policy mechanism which envisioned the President and the Senate, as his council of elders, deciding upon the fate of the nation.

But as the fate of the nation depends upon the people, it is obviously dependent upon their understanding of the reasons for their burdens and their tolerance to bear them. It is in this role that I see the primary obligations of the Senate. That is, constantly to explain and rationalize the burden which the people bear, to help them to that degree of understanding which will compel their agreement.

Wilson wrote of this, too, and said:

Indeed, the Senate is, par excellence, the chamber of debate and of individual privilege. Its discussions are often enough unprofitable, are too often marred by personal feeling and by exhibitions of private interest which taint its reputation and render the country uneasy and suspicious, but they are at least the only means the country has of clarifying public business for public comprehension.

We cannot afford a foreign policy which represents the lowest common denominator of national agreement because too many people lack basic understandings of the world in which we live and what is required for our survival.

I have been distressed to read so much in the public press of late of the rise of a "new wave of conservatism," particularly on college campuses. This is not because I am opposed to conservatism, depending upon the definition. On the contrary, I look upon conservatism as the philosophy which guides the struggle we are waging. We seek to "conserve" the values of our Western civilization and to help others to enjoy their blessings. What I do object to is the appropriation of that word by those who, as Emerson said, "have difficulty in bringing their reason to act and on all occasions use their memory first."

There appear to be two significant elements of this new conservatism, judging by the attention they are receiving in the public press. One of these is represented by a Western Republican colleague of mine who sees no inconsistency in calling for a return to those simple routines of his grandfather, while he is traveling in a jet airplane at Mach I or II over the same Western desert which his grandfather traversed in a covered wagon. He insists that federal aid to education is unconstitutional, because the Constitution does not specifically authorize it. The Constitution does not specifically authorize an air force, for that matter, providing only for army, navy, and militia to protect the common defense. But I would doubt that this Brigadier General in the Air Force Reserve would carry his doctrine of constitutional interpretation quite that far ...

We need spokesmen for rational conservatism if, by debate and education, the people are to arrive at that consensus of viewpoint on foreign affairs which is necessary to our survival. We need conservative spokesmen who have those qualities of which de Tocqueville wrote, when, in speaking of lawyers in America, he said: "Men who have ... devoted themselves to legal pursuits derive from those occupations certain habits of order, a taste for formalities, and a kind of instinctive regard for the regular connection of ideas, which naturally render them very hostile to the revolutionary spirit and the unreflecting passions of the multitude."

I agree with this observation of de Tocqueville. These are the kind of spokesmen for conservatism we need. I also agree with his conclusion, which was: "... without this admixture of lawyer-like sobriety with the democratic principle, I question whether democratic institutions could long be maintained ..."

I would hope that the Senate, with the support of lawyers, in the type of debate about which Wilson wrote, and with the lawyer-like sobriety and regard for the regular connection of ideas, of which de Tocqueville wrote, can contribute to the establishment of a national consensus which will give true and consistent direction to our foreign policy, arising, as it must in a democracy, from the understanding of the people.

But, again, in the field of national understanding of foreign policy as in its direction, it is the President who has the greatest power. While the Senate can, as Wilson said, clarify public issues by debate, the President's voice, as Wilson also said, "is the only national voice in affairs. Let him once win the admiration and confidence of the country, and no other single force can withstand him, no combination of forces will easily overpower him. His position takes the imagination of the country. He is the representative of no constituency, but of the whole people. When he speaks in his true character, he speaks for no special interest. If he rightly interpret the national thought and boldly insist upon it, he is irresistible; and the country never feels the zest of action so much as when its President is of such insight and calibre ... He is the only person about whom definite national opinion is formed, and, therefore, the one person who can form opinion by his own direct influence and act upon the whole country at once."

I believe we now have the kind of President about whom Wilson wrote, and I hope that by his speaking more frequently and in greater depth on foreign policy issues, and directly to the people, they may acquire that "zest of action" so greatly needed if we are to win the contest of will which engages us today.

DOHERTY LECTURE, UNIVERSITY
OF VIRGINIA, CHARLOTTESVILLE,
APRIL 21, 1961.

BIBLIOGRAPHIC NOTE AND
ACKNOWLEDGMENT

Since this is the first published book about Senator J. William
Fulbright, the editor feels an extra obligation to make the path a bit
easier for those that follow. Articles concerning Fulbright are few,
but I found these especially useful and drew upon all of them:
Charles B. Seib and Alan L. Otten, "Fulbright: Arkansas Paradox,"
Harper's, June, 1956; Beverly Smith, Jr., "Egghead from the
Ozarks," *Saturday Evening Post,* May 2, 1959; E. W. Kenworthy,
"Fulbright Becomes a National Issue," *New York Times Magazine,*
October 1, 1961; and Sidney Hyman, "Fulbright: The Wedding of
Arkansas and the World," *New Republic,* May 14, 1962.

In winnowing through the Senator's mound of speeches and
articles, some of the substance and interest had to be omitted, and
those passed over might properly, and regretfully, be noted here.

Concerning the Fulbright Resolution, see the Senator's article,
"Power Adequate to Enforce the Peace," *New York Times Maga-
zine,* October 17, 1943. His reflections on sovereignty and the United
Nations were also adapted for a *Times Magazine* article, "The Word
That Blocks Lasting Peace," January 6, 1946. He has discussed the
progress of the Fulbright scholarship program in "Open Doors, Not
Iron Curtains," *New York Times Magazine,* August 5, 1951; "The
First Fifteen Years of the Fulbright Program," *The Annals* of the
American Academy of Political and Social Science, May, 1961; and
"Fulbright Urges a Larger Program," *New York Times Magazine,*
August 13, 1961.

Indeed, education has been a dominant theme neglected in this

275

book; I refer the interested reader to such major speeches in support of federal aid to education that are found in the *Congressional Record* for January 23, 1958, and May 17, 1961.

Fulbright's additional comments on European and Western unity include: "A United States of Europe?" *The Annals,* May 1948; and "A Common Purpose for the Free World," American Bar Association *Journal,* November, 1960. As a moral critic, the Senator contributed a major speech, "The Character of Present Day American Life," in the *Record* for August 21, 1958; the theme was adapted in "Challenge to Our Complacency," *New York Times Magazine,* September 14, 1958. A related indictment, "Where Do We Stand?" appears in the *Record* for March 4, 1960. His critical discussion of "The Ugly American" is also worth perusing in the *Record* for May 19, 1959, and September 7, 1959. The *Arkansas Alumnus* for October, 1961, contains a forceful statement by the university's former president, "Our National Goal: The Individual." Also, there is the formidable essay, "American Foreign Policy in the 20th Century Under an 18th Century Constitution," *Cornell Law Quarterly,* Fall, 1961, which complements the University of Virginia lecture included in this book.

In conclusion, the editor would like to note his deep gratitude to those on the Senate Foreign Relation's Committee staff and in Senator Fulbright's office who did so much to assist in compiling this volume: Carl Marcy, Jack Yingling, Seth Tillman, John Newhouse, Jan Graham, Kitty Johnson, Lee Williams, and Norval Jones.

KARL E. MEYER

WASHINGTON, D.C.
DECEMBER, 1962

INDEX

277

Santos, Eduardo, 203-204
Senate, U.S., and foreign relations, xxvii-xxix, 263-273; and 'McCarthyism', 73-85
Soviet Union, 15, and wartime alliance, 20-22; postwar expansion, 48-52; and John Foster Dulles, 94-123; and Berlin, 136-140; and U-2, 140-148; and Europe, 158-159, 166, 170-172, 189-190; and Cuba, 200-201, 206-208; and radical right, 242-243
Stalin, Joseph, 242, 248
Stone, Julius, 176
Sugar Act, 217-220
Swift, Jonathan, 72

Taft, Robert A., 62
Thomas, Elbert, 155
Thomas, Norman, 203
Thurmond, Strom, xix, 221-222
Tocqueville, Alexis de, xxxiii, 70, 226, 270

Truman, Harry S., xviii-xix, 52-55, 61-62, 66-67, 157-158, 266-268
Tunisia, 108-109
Twining, Nathan, 114-115

U-2 flight, 140-148
United Nations, xxxiii, and ratification, 23-33; and the atomic bomb, 34-35, 40-43, 46, 51, 155; criticisms of, 169-171, 175-186; 255-256

Vandenberg, Arthur, 267-268

Walker, Edwin A., 221, 229
Washington, George, 264, 269
Wilson, Woodrow, 18, 174-175, 244-245, 266, 268, 271-273

Young, G. M., 134
Yugoslavia, xxix

Zwicker, Ralph, 77, 81